Birding on Borrowed Time

By Phoebe Snetsinger

PRATT
2003

Birding on Borrowed Time

By Phoebe Snetsinger

Illustrations by H. Douglas Pratt

American**Birding**
ASSOCIATION

2003

Library of Congress Control Number: 2003105614

ISBN Number: 1-878788-41-8

First Edition
1   2   3   4   5   6   7   8   9
Printed in the United States of America

Phoebe Snetsinger (1931-1999)

Editors:
Allan Burns, Cindy Lippincott, and Thomas Snetsinger

Layout:
Ed Rother

Illustrations:
H. Douglas Pratt

Map
Virginia Maynard

Cover painting:
A male Blackburnian Warbler among early spring leaves
of northern red oak, by H. Douglas Pratt

Distributed by:
American Birding Association Sales
P.O. Box 6599, Colorado Springs, Colorado 80934-6599 USA
phone: (800) 634-7736 or (719) 578-0607
fax: (800) 590-2473 or (719) 578-9705
email: abasales@abasales.com
website: www.americanbirding.org

Acknowledgements

T he flood of touching letters, cards, and phone calls that we received after Phoebe's death make clear the huge number of people whose lives Phoebe touched.

That her friendship, reputation, or story influenced so many people emphasizes the point that while most of her adult life revolved around the obsessive pursuit of birds, the sharing of that passion with others was where she found her most joyful moments. It is clear that her life and its reflection in this book would have lacked color and vibrancy without those connections. Even posthumously her influence on the lives of many continues, and we are pleased that the publication of this book will allow her to communicate her passion to a potentially wider audience.

There are a number of individuals who contributed in a very substantial way to the preparation of this book and deserve both recognition and our heartfelt appreciation for their assistance with this project. The American Birding Association has been steadfast in its support for this project, and we have felt extraordinarily fortunate to work with their new Director of Publications, Allan Burns. Allan worked closely with us in sensitively editing Phoebe's original manuscript. He also artfully orchestrated the collaborative efforts of the many individuals necessary to bring this book to its final form.

In addition to offering early constructive comments on the manuscript and being an enthusiastic supporter for the project, Doug Pratt created a wonderful series of original artwork that beautifully captured the diverse spectacle of the world's avifauna that ensnared Phoebe's imagination.

While we were generally removed from the friends and colleagues with whom Phoebe shared her passion, and thus often only heard passing remarks about acquaintances, Peter Kaestner clearly stood out as a respected friend. He was someone who shared Phoebe's approach to birding and pursued this passion with the same drive, intensity, and integrity. So, we were thrilled that he agreed to write the Foreword to this book.

Virginia Maynard worked closely with us in preparing a map that effectively displayed the breadth and scope of Phoebe's travels. We appreciated her openness to our comments and her dedication to the project.

In addition to the positive ways they each touched Phoebe's life, in the days and weeks following her death, Field Guides' leaders Terry Stevenson, John Coons, and Bret Whitney provided us with all of the support and assistance we could ever have hoped for in dealing with her death, overseas, in remote Madagascar. We are grateful to Bret for taking the time to read Phoebe's original manuscript and to offer us his thoughts on it. We are also grateful to John for providing written notes about the trip prior to Phoebe's death. These, along with Phoebe's own notes, provided the basis for the description of the tour in the Epilogue.

We deeply appreciate the generosity of many of Phoebe's friends in sharing their photos and stories from trips on which they accompanied her or memorial trips they took in her remembrance. We particularly thank the following individuals for granting permission to reproduce their photos in this book: Michel Kleinbaum, Bob and Myra Braden, Kathy and Steve Martin, and Aileen Lotz.

David Snetsinger
Thomas Snetsinger
Carol Snetsinger
Penny Snetsinger
Susan Snetsinger

NOTE: *Bracketed bird names in the text provide the standard English species names from James F. Clements' Birds of the World: A Checklist, 5th edition in cases where Phoebe used an alternate or an older name. For example, Phoebe reports seeing a Gibberbird in Australia; the Clements name, Desert Chat, appears in brackets after Phoebe's preferred older name. Phoebe also anticipated impending splits of field-identifiable subspecies, e.g., her Tibetan Eared-Pheasant is a subspecies of White Eared-Pheasant, not (yet) recognized as a full species by Clements. Phoebe's close attention to subspecies and impending splits served her well.*

One can't force poetry or spring,
Love or friendship—these are never sure.
Intensity by definition can't endure
And futile my attempt to make it cling.
I live too much for peaks in alpenglow,
And tend to venture forth too soon
To seek the unexpected bird or bloom,
The season's first *Hepatica* in snow.

—from an untitled poem by
Phoebe Snetsinger, 12/3/78

Contents

List of Illustrations

Black & White Illustrations:

Color Plates:

Foreword

By Peter Kaestner

P ublic tragedies unite us in history,
because we all know where we were
when they happened. Familiarity allows
us to refer to these events with a kind of

shorthand that instantly conjures up unforgettable scenes of shock and devastation: JFK, *Challenger*, 9/11. There are also private tragedies that affect us with equal intensity, even though relatively few people share our sorrow and sense of loss. Word of Phoebe Snetsinger's sudden death on Thanksgiving of 1999 affected me so profoundly that the moment has been etched on my psyche ever since. For some time afterward, I would be walking along and suddenly be overcome with a wave of sadness at the loss, as if she were a favorite aunt.

Phoebe was, in some ways, my soul mate—we shared so much: a love for birds, a passion for birding, and an obsession to get the bird and to get it well. But, amazingly, for being so close, we met only twice. The connection was made largely by long distance and through that most precious birding commodity, reputation. Since I do not usually bird on organized tours, I had not had the pleasure that so many had had to travel and bird with her. Nevertheless, I had heard the legend of Phoebe Snetsinger from everyone I bumped into who had met her. A cancer death sentence, a brutal assault in Papua New Guinea, a shipwreck in Indonesia—how could it all be true? How could someone keep going on? Not only did she "go on", but she succeeded beyond what anyone before had achieved. Her intense preparation and capability to understand the birds was mythical. She was highly competitive, yet everyone had effusive praise for her. How could she be so focused, so driven, and yet so nice and generous, all at the same time? By sharing her memoirs, Phoebe gives everyone a chance to know this remarkable person and to learn that the legend is true—and then some.

I finally put Phoebe on my life list of birders in 1991 while I was living in Malaysia. I was birding at the Pasoh Forest Reserve in August of that year when I heard that the she was in country on a tour. That very day she would be birding at The Gap at Fraser's Hill, only about a four-hour drive from Pasoh. Drawn as if there were a life bird there, I immediately drove up to The Gap on the off chance that I would finally meet up with this living legend. After driving all morning, I arrived at the crest of the hill and immediately saw the tour group. They were standing on the lawn behind the rest house, enjoying the subtropical birds that inhabit this montane forest—and a marvelous view down the valley. Nervous at my first encounter with this modern-day goddess of birding, I gathered up my courage, walked up, and introduced myself. Her trademark smile—warm, sincere, and welcoming—immediately put me at ease. Old enough to be my mother, she greeted me like a long-lost nephew. Since we had no history, we immediately started talking about birds—what she was seeing and what she was looking for. Her knowledge of Malayan birds was impressive; she knew everything about what we were looking at and what we were missing. She had been on a clean-up trip, so characteristic of her later days when she was just looking to add a few choice species to her immense list. We felt an immediate easiness that usually comes from years of familiarity.

A slender brown bird zipped by, just a flash flying down the hill in front of us. The leader called out, "Little Cuckoo-Dove", and most of the tour clients dutifully wrote down the new species in their notebooks. Some of the birders were especially delighted as the species was a lifer for them. Phoebe was much too polite to shake her head, but the look in her eyes said it all: she was wondering if the people who had just put that bird on their lists had actually learned to identify a fast-flying Little Cuckoo-Dove for themselves. Her personal integrity and birding skill were absolutely beyond reproach, but, more importantly, she had a wealth of patience for people who may have been lacking in both. Her talent for accepting people as they were was one of the many reasons that no one ever had an unpleasant thing to say about her. Our attention was quickly diverted as other birds flew by. Meanwhile, Phoebe was working almost as hard as the leader to keep the other participants on the new species, sharing her wealth of knowledge and experience freely. As the tour leader started to gather his flock to move on, Phoebe and I agreed to a rendezvous in Kuala Lumpur after her trip was finished.

One of the secrets of Phoebe's success was the hard work that she put into each bird. She devised a file-card system that allowed her to review and revise her sightings as taxonomy changed. Phoebe's card system was legendary: she kept all the critical information about the bird sightings on file cards. She recorded each sighting, including information on subspecies, plumage variation, and habits. Her cards were color-coded so that she could easily know in which faunal area a bird had been seen.

After having reached the milestone of 8,000, she stopped submitting numbers to the American Birding Association (ABA) for publication starting in the 1996 list year. She was "officially" out of numerical competition.[1] When I saw her the second time in Namibia, I queried her about her retirement and urged her to keep listing. She told me that she was out of the listing game for several reasons, including the fact that she wanted to give me a chance to be number one. She added that she didn't keep her list according to the ABA standard, Clements' *Birds of the World: A Checklist.* She had no quarrel with Clements or the ABA; she just had a different way of counting species. Her decision to stop submitting her list to the ABA was typical of Phoebe in that it was

---

[1] The Snetsinger family decided to submit Phoebe's posthumous totals to the ABA's List Report in 1999–2001 as a way of honoring her memory. *Ed. note.*

principled and uncompromising, full of generosity. She added that she was looking forward to just birding for fun and to snorkeling more. In a world where champions too often tenaciously hang on to their faded glory, Phoebe's retirement was just right; she went out in her prime.

Like many world birders, Phoebe had an abiding interest in bird taxonomy, especially as it affected the number of species that you could add to your list. In her later years, Phoebe developed her own list of the birds of the world, based on Monroe and Sibley's *A World Checklist of Birds*. In order to compare different lists, she proposed to the ABA a reporting method that uses a percentage of the total, rather than a raw number. The birding world has not yet accepted Phoebe's idea of reporting percentages, but some day it just might.

Phoebe's memoirs also serve as a personal recollection of a Golden Age of birding, of which she was such an integral part. This Golden Age has been the result of a variety of factors developing simultaneously. Advances in knowledge, technology, and the popularity of birding have combined to fundamentally alter the birding equation. In 1980, the ABA was a fledgling organization, looking for stability and respect. The top world list was 5,420, and Louis Agassiz Fuertes' posthumous life list of 2,000 was still being published. As we kick off the twenty-first century, the ABA is a vibrant and growing organization, and at least two birders have cracked 8,000.

Politically, the world has mostly opened up over the past 25 years, though some areas, such as the Middle East and the Moluccas, have become less accessible. With the demise of the Cold War and the warming of relations with Communist China in the mid-70s, birders have had many more opportunities for international travel. Birders visit Mongolia, Kazakhstan, and other central Asian countries that our fathers had never even heard of.

During the past twenty years, the amount of information available to the increasing number of world birders has grown exponentially. People like Ted Parker in South America and Ian Sinclair in Africa have significantly augmented the body of birding knowledge single-handedly. Parker, especially, made an inestimable contribution to ornithology through his prodigious work documenting neotropical bird sounds. Internet list-servers and email bring the world's birders into immediate contact with their colleagues across the globe. Whereas twenty years ago one largely had to develop contacts through personal acquaintances and a lot of luck, everyone is now only a computer terminal away from the world of birding. Trip reports for just about everywhere help in planning exotic adventures.

The bird-book business is a perfect reflection of the explosion of information. The proliferation and evolution of bird lists starting in the 1970s is just one part of this phenomenon. In 1981, when I went to India, there was the ten-volume, *Handbook of the Birds of India and Pakistan*, but it was not something that could be put into one's pocket (or even backpack). Other smaller books were either incomplete or inaccurate. Trying to identify *Phylloscopus* warblers in the field then was an impossible undertaking. Nowadays, many of the leaf-warblers encountered in India can be confidently identified because of the vast literature on the subject. A couple of excellent field guides are now available, and there is even a birdfinding guide to the subcontinent. When I visited South Africa in 1978, there was no really adequate guide. Now there are several excellent ones, including the Sasol *Birds of Southern Africa*, which ranks up with the best field guides in the world.

Just before Phoebe started her world birding, there was only a handful of bird tour companies, mostly visiting relatively easy-to-get-to places like East Africa, Costa Rica, and Australia. Now there are scores of tour companies about, taking their clients to see such rarities as the Marvelous Spatuletail, Mt. Kupe Bushshrike, Cerulean Paradise-Flycatcher, and Orange-throated Tanager. I have just returned from a boat trip to Marion Island—a place I had not even heard of not too long ago—where I saw the Kerguelen Tern and Lesser Sheathbill [Black-faced Sheathbill], two species that I never dreamed of seeing. In addition to international experts such as Robert Ridgely, Kevin Zimmer, Don Turner, Paul Coopmans, and Mark Van Beirs, local birders are becoming more and more proficient. Indeed, I recently met an excellent local guide in Addis Ababa, Ethiopia, who commands a daily fee that is almost three times the yearly per capita income of his compatriots! The use of local guides is beneficial in that it transfers resources directly to the communities that are entrusted with the care of the habitat, thereby increasing the value of conserving the species to the people in the best position to make a difference.

Scores of new species have been described in the past twenty years, not only increasing the number of birds to be ticked but also opening whole new areas for birders to investigate. Bob Ridgely's Jocotoco Antpitta from southern Ecuador and the weird Pink-legged Graveteiro from Eastern Brazil are whetting birders' appetites. The extraordinary run of ornithological discovery in the Neotropics started over forty years ago by Louisiana State University in the wilds of Peru continues, as new forms are still being found and described. Recently a whole group of species restricted to white-sand forests in eastern Peru has been described.

Amazingly, some of the new species discovered recently have turned out to be reasonably common, to wit the Cryptic Warbler, a widespread species discovered in the forests of eastern Madagascar only in 1995. Others, like the Talaud Rail, will not make it on to many birders' lists. (The rail inhabits an isolated island south of the Philippines.)

In addition to the new species, many birds known only from historical records are being rediscovered. The most exciting was the diminutive Kinglet Calyptura, a beautiful species that remained unrecorded just outside of Rio de Janeiro for over 100 years before it was dramatically rediscovered in 1996. (It promptly returned to hiding and has not been seen since.) Some species, unknown in life until very recently, are also proving to be easy to see once their particular habitat requirements and/or calls are known. A good example is the critically endangered Honduran Emerald, which can be found with little effort in its restricted arid scrub habitat in north-central Honduras. The Black-hooded Antwren, another Rio de Janeiro bird that had gone undetected for almost a century, was rediscovered at Angra dos Reis and is now easily seen in its tiny coastal range. With greater numbers of birders in the field, more and more rare birds are being found and staked out.

The surge in professional and amateur fieldwork worldwide has resulted in a much better understanding of the birds in the field and their systematics. Taxonomic revisions over the past two decades have been based on our better understanding of the birds and on huge advances in biochemical analysis that have permitted researchers to peer into the genetic past of species. For example, Peter Ryan in Cape Town discovered that the Long-billed Lark, a South African endemic, actually comprised five separate species. Bret Whitney and Mort and Phyllis Isler's pioneering work on antbirds has resulted in many new taxa being recognized—with the promise of more to come.

In addition to the vast improvements in information, technological advances during the latter part of the twentieth century have affected birding as well. New optics, with dazzling images, and spotting scopes that pull in the farthest species have given us a much better view of the birds we are finding. Tape recorders allow skulkers to be seen easily, and pre-recorded tapes and CDs give most everyone access to the calls of the birds. The digital revolution has also had an impact on birding, from Global Positioning Satellite (GPS) systems to digital audio. GPS allows people to pinpoint the location of a place with perfect precision, permitting others to go to the exact spot where a rare bird was seen. Used in place of a compass, a GPS can help keep a birder from getting lost. In late 2002, I heard an unusual bird call in the Brazilian state of Rondônia. I was able to record it, download it onto my computer, convert it to an MP3 file, and email it to Bret Whitney in the United States. Bret confirmed the identification as a Thrush-like Antpitta within 24 hours.

Finally, improvements in transport and roads cut into previously inaccessible areas have allowed birders to reach the most remote spots in the world. The Divisor Mountains, which separate Brazil and Peru, were once so hard to get to that a book was written about an expedition there in 1987 (*A Parrot Without a Name, The Search for the Last Unknown Birds on Earth* by Don Stap). Now, a road from the town of Cruzeiro do Sul, in Brazil's Acre state makes the mountains accessible to anyone with a 4x4 and a bit of adventure. I just read in a Brazilian travel magazine that an ecotourism company is offering week-long hikes up to the top of Mount Roraima, one of the remote endemic centers of South America.

It is hard to say how much longer the Golden Age of birding will last. Since 1980, several species have become extinct in the wild, including most of the endemic avifauna of Guam Island, the California Condor, and Spix's Macaw. Ironically, none of these examples is related to what is likely to be the greatest threat to birds: habitat destruction. In many instances, the loss of habitat has been precipitated by road construction, most clearly demonstrated in Amazonian Brazil. Vast areas of rainforest are being cut each year, potentially endangering scores of species. The question is just whether enough critical habitats can be preserved before the species start disappearing. Birders (as evidenced by the evolution of the ABA) are more conservation conscious and are helping to preserve our wild heritage through organizations such as Partners in Flight, Birders' Exchange, and, of course, through traditional conservation NGOs. On the other hand, advances in information and technology continue apace. I believe, however, that the magic of the last quarter of the twentieth century, with its marvelous discoveries and incredible growth in knowledge and accessibility, may never happen again.

The incomplete but vivid image of Phoebe that emerges in this memoir is remarkable. She was an extraordinary person who lived an extraordinary life during extraordinary times. As she describes the hours after she was brutally gang-raped and left to die in Papua New Guinea, she says of the people who came to her aid that, "I had my faith in the basic goodness of most people restored over and over again that memorable night." She recuperated for a few months and then set out again for more birds, this time to a safer country (Chile) and as she puts it, "With a few stories to tell!"

Death and how Phoebe faces it are essential elements of this story. Her death sentence at 49 years really started her quest. A fear that stopping might give the cancer a chance to take over was one of the reasons for her supreme dedication. At several points in her memoirs, Phoebe discusses her mortality. While she never discusses an automobile accident as a way to go, she was clearly concerned that she not suffer a long illness or slowly become dependent on others as her own mother had done. In 1990, when she discovered a fourth malignant melanoma, she abandoned her dying mother, her family, and her own medical reality—and went birding to Australia and Papua New Guinea! She rationalized it by thinking that it just might be her last trip, and she wanted to "go down binoculars in hand"! Her passing, while sudden—and therefore a blessing for her—robbed the birding world of one of its most respected and productive members. I am sure that when she died on that lonely road in Southwest Madagascar, she had her binoculars in hand.

Phoebe finished with her 1991 Malaysia tour, having picked up almost ten lifers, and was back in Kuala Lumpur. With a free day ahead, we spoke about possibilities, but there were precious few birds that I could find for her. The best possibility was the handsome Ferruginous Partridge, a shy foothill species that I had recently seen less than a mile from The Gap where I had initially met Phoebe. In addition, the elusive Long-billed Partridge was a possibility at Fraser's Hill, another half-hour past The Gap in the mountains of the Malay Peninsula. We got an early start and quickly made the trip in time for some good morning birds. We briefly looked for Pin-tailed Parrotfinches in the bamboo at The Gap before starting to hike up to the point on the road where the trail descended into the lush forest. Arriving at the spot where I had seen the partridge a month before, Phoebe and I sat down in the forest and started playing a tape of the bird's distinctive call. After about five minutes, a single bird started responding and eventually walked right up in front of us. I was thrilled that I had been able to find my hero a new bird so quickly, especially such a handsome animal strutting his stuff. Phoebe's gratitude and excitement were palpable. A new genus, the partridge was not only a rarity, but it counted toward Phoebe's goal of seeing as many genera as possible. Flushed with optimism, we climbed the 800 meters back to the road and walked back down to the gate and my car.

Getting a good look at the wood partridge was important for Phoebe, who did not count heard birds. We both had argued with the ABA to reverse its rule of allowing heard birds, to no avail. (We believe that there is just too much room for misidentification of sounds in the forest and for people to count species pointed out to them, when they had no idea what the call of the species was. After all, we are bird watchers, not bird listeners!)

We continued up to Fraser's Hill, a former British hill station that allowed colonials a respite from the oppressive heat and humidity of lowland Malaya. Since the Long-billed Partridge calls in the early evening as it flies up to its perch, we spent the day doing some light birding. We tried for the Rusty-naped Pitta (I still had not seen it here, having dipped over a dozen times) and fortuitously bumped into a couple of Large Scimictar-Babblers—a lifer for me! Now this day was really working out. We both had lifers, and we still had a chance for another new one for Phoebe. Coincidentally, our life lists were almost the same in 1991: at 6,780, I was only approximately 100 birds behind her.

As the afternoon wore on, we got some fabulous birds characteristic of the Malayan highlands, such as the Cutia, Blue Nuthatch, and Fire-tufted Barbet. The weather was beautiful, and the quality of the birding and bird talk made the day perfect. The more I learned of her and her commitment to birding, the more I was impressed.

In the late afternoon, we positioned ourselves for the partridge, inside a piece of fine cloud forest on the highest part of the mountain. The usual dense afternoon fog had rolled in, and the gloom of the evening soon enveloped us. Then, all of a sudden, there was a piercing call in the ravine just to the left. We hurried along the path, realizing that the Long-billed Partridge would not call for long after it had found its perch. Another call rang out just below where we were now standing. By now it was almost completely dark, as the evening fog had permeated the forest. I pulled a flashlight out of my daypack and started weighing the options.

Phoebe did not hesitate for a second as she plunged off the trail and down into the thick undergrowth that filled the steep ravine. I hustled after her, and we swiftly picked our way into the darkness and unknown. In the end, the bird did not call again, and the fog was too thick, so the partridge eluded Phoebe that night. Regardless, I will never forget the wonderful time we shared. The sight of her disappearing down the ravine after the Long-billed Partridge sums up Phoebe for me—committed, fearless, and never looking back.

~1~
Beginnings

W hy is it such a rarity for little
girls to become intrigued with birds
at an early age as compared to little boys?

The question has been asked many times, and I have no good answer. By all reasonable criteria, I *should* have become hooked on birds early on. I was an independent type and a tomboy who found that boys did more interesting and enjoyable things than girls. I had two much older brothers, and I spent many long and happy hours with Joe, the younger of the two, who (quite astonishingly, as I look back on it) tolerated my tagging along on many adventures. We scoured the nearby woods, fields, and marshes for frogs, snakes, toads, turtles, and any other creatures we could find to bring home as pets.

The regular Midwestern U.S. birds were certainly all around me during these outings, but I scarcely noticed them. No one in the family had binoculars or was interested in *identifying* natural things when I was a child. We certainly had an abundance of books, but I don't believe I ever encountered any kind of field guide either at home or school until I was much older. I do recall being a member of a Junior Audubon Society in my second-grade class and wearing a pin with a Scarlet Tanager on it—but I never saw this bird until I was grown. Endless opportunities existed in my childhood that could have stimulated my awareness and curiosity about the natural world—but nothing took hold, and I can't quite explain why.

My parents moved from suburban Chicago to a farm in Lake County in northern Illinois when I was 12, and I lived there until I left for college. Again there was constant exposure to the outside world, and I loved tramping the woods and fields and just being outside. Likewise, when I went east to a college near Philadelphia, I remember taking long spring and fall walks in a beautiful wooded area adjacent to the campus. It must surely have been a truly wonderful spot during warbler migration, but I was oblivious to it all. Were there no birders at Swarthmore in the early fifties? I certainly never met any and don't even remember seeing anyone wearing binoculars. But I was heavily into intellectual pursuits back then, and the natural world simply hadn't yet come into focus for me.

After college, I taught science and math to a broad spectrum of age groups in a private girls' school outside Philadelphia. I clearly remember actually teaching a unit on "BIRDS" to my fourth-grade science class. Here was a gift-wrapped golden opportunity for catching my attention and interest, if there ever was one. But did it work? In retrospect, I can't believe I never even took those kids outside to *see* anything they were learning about. I cringe at such memories now.

So when *did* it finally happen, this awakening that has ultimately let me get the real world in focus and that has given me my bearings for navigating through the best years of my life? Probably when I saw my first Blackburnian Warbler in 1965.

It was May, the best of months nearly everywhere and certainly in Minnesota, where I lived with my husband David and four small children. I was 34, busy with family and household chores, and I enjoyed my opportunities to get outside to explore our property, which consisted of a few acres of big trees and open fields adjoining an oak woods and bordering a small lake. I don't think I knew it at the time, but my mind was probably starving for some kind of outlet that didn't revolve around raising a family.

My neighbor, Elisabeth Selden, was a birder, the first one I had ever encountered, and she, too, liked exploring the woods that lay between us, the fields and lake edge—but she came with binoculars and a Peterson field guide. This highly intelligent woman had a purpose in her meanderings. Finally, I was ready to see what had lain before my eyes for all those years. Elisabeth showed me some plates in the field guide, told me about warblers and spring migration, pointed out some flitting motion in the newly-emerging oak leaves and dangling blossoms above us, and handed me her binoculars to try. What an incredible gift! The first bird I really saw through those binoculars was a fiery-orange male Blackburnian Warbler that nearly knocked me over with astonishment—and quite simply hooked me forever.

The triggers for turning points in one's life are mysterious things. A whole spectrum of different factors with complex physical, intellectual, and emotional overtones is involved, and all of them have to merge in the same place and time to form the blinding white light that urges one along a new path. Sheer chance plays an enormous role, unless one is programmed to believe (as I do not) that it was all meant to be. All the crucial factors came together for me in brilliant clarity that spring over thirty years ago, in the mind-bending sight of that one Blackburnian Warbler— reinforced daily after that by the Magnolia, the Black-throated Green, the Golden-winged, the Cape May, and all the other warblers streaming through our backyard on their way north. It was a season of true magic, perhaps all the more powerful because of its belated entry into my life.

Minnesota is blessed with an abundance of wetlands, and it was easy to branch out from woodland birds to those of other habitats. Shortly after seeing the Blackburnian Warbler, I accompanied Elisabeth Selden, my new-found mentor and companion, to a Great Blue Heron nesting colony. Once again, I was totally staggered by the sight. "What an unpromising setting for success in raising your offspring," was one of the thoughts that went through my mind as I observed those flimsy and seemingly precarious stick nests in the tops of dead trees, attended by the gangly adults. "How can they ever get food into those fuzzy chicks without stabbing them to death with their bills?" Watching those creatures do what they had been doing successfully for millions of years, without any help from us, finally let me learn not to judge everything by human standards.

One evening, we had driven to a nearby marsh, where we were privileged to witness an event that I have never seen since. We spotted an American Bittern stalking along the edge of the cattails, which was exciting because it was a "lifer" for me. (I now had acquired a whole new lexicon.) As we watched, the bird stopped hunting, froze, pointed its bill to the sky, and began the most amazing neck and breast contortions as it repeatedly uttered its deep, booming *oongk-ka-choongk* calls.

It was a season of euphoria. I acquired my own binoculars and field guide and could hardly wait for my next adventure in the field. There were daily consultations with my friend over what I thought were the finer points of identification (little did I know!) and always surprises and new sights in every bush and tree. We found a Great Horned Owl nest in our woods early the next year and were able to watch almost daily as the young grew and fledged. I figured the waterfowl out pretty quickly that next winter and well remember my feeling of triumph when I identified a lone duck as a female Bufflehead. No sooner had I said the words than a male popped up beside her.

One winter's day my son Tom (age five) came back at dusk, exclaiming about a huge white owl he had seen while hiking with a friend around some snowy fields on the backside of our woods. There was not much doubt in my mind that they had seen a Snowy Owl—and, of course, I wanted to see it as well. But it was not to be, at least not then. (I didn't catch up to this species until many years later.) This disappointment was my first experience of what my British birding friends term a "dip" or being "gripped off". I didn't know those terms at the time, but I knew I didn't much like the situation.

Still, the excitement of birding far outweighed the disappointments. Almost every birder has a first magical season of wonder, whether it happens at age five or fifty, during which some of one's most cherished and indelible birding memories take shape. I look back with a bit of envy now at the childlike innocence and openmouthed astonishment with which I entered the world of birding.

~2~

Learning

───────── ❦ ─────────

O nly about two years after my in-
troduction to this new world of
wonders in Minnesota, my husband
changed his employment, and we moved
to Webster Groves, a pleasant suburb of St. Louis, Missouri. I knew
about birders now and knew that there must be some in St. Louis
as well. The Audubon Society was a logical starting point, and they
quickly pointed me toward the Webster Groves Nature Study Society. The really active, knowledgeable local birders and botanists be-
longed to this organization, which ran (and still runs) local field
trips every Thursday and Saturday throughout the year. This group
turned out to be the answer to my prayers. With a young family to
care for, it was nearly impossible for me to go birding on Satur-
days—but Thursdays, well, I could manage that somehow.

I found a good babysitter to cover the home ground. With two
kids in school all day now and one in kindergarten, I could manage a day's outing. Thursdays became the highlight of my week.
A few of the Thursday regulars were highly skilled and very
knowledgeable birders (even by today's standards), totally familiar with all aspects of birding in the St. Louis area. Some others
were women of my age, many with families and the same kinds
of conflicts I faced. As a novice, I couldn't have been in better
hands. Thanks to all the help, advice, and instruction of all those
people on countless Thursdays, I learned how to be a good birder

───────── ❦ ─────────

during my early St. Louis years. Without the inspiration, fun, excitement, and learning on those many memorable Thursdays, I certainly never could have, or would have, achieved what I have.

I am forever grateful for this early, solid grounding on my home turf. In my later travels, I became aware of the "listing trap" that is so easy to fall into on well-run bird tours. If you haven't learned properly how to deal with identifying shorebirds, fall warblers, and look-alike sparrows in your home area, you're much less able, or less likely to care about working out the identity of a neotropical flycatcher or Asian babbler—especially when there's a leader there to identify everything for you so you can list it. My St. Louis birding taught me that identification is fun. Yes, it's a challenge and often hard work, but infinitely rewarding and satisfying in a way that goes far beyond simple list keeping. Learning how to identify birds wherever I am, as well as enjoying them and listing them is a large part of what keeps me going in this endlessly fascinating game.

Occasionally on these early St. Louis Thursdays, a woman named Bertha Massie would come along for the day. She was probably in her sixties then and had traveled worldwide and seen a staggering number of birds—*over 3,000!* She was at that time the leading woman lister in the world, and she was fascinating to listen to as she recounted bits of her recent travels and adventures. I hung on her every word. What a simply *wonderful* way to live! Would it ever be possible for me to take a foreign birding trip and see some of these exotic creatures for myself?

As my competence and experience increased, I began to take St. Louis birding very seriously and became fanatic enough about it to set the local area year-list record (275 species) in 1978. (This record was broken by one species by a good friend in 1986, and that record stood for ten years, until 1996, when a total of six people broke that number, and the new record setter saw an amazing 290 species, nearly repeating the feat a year later with 287). I was pursuing both Missouri and Illinois state lists during this period, and as our children were growing and becoming more independent, it became easier for me to take occasional excursions farther afield in North America.

Our annual family vacations were an important factor in broadening my birding experience during the decade after we moved to St. Louis. We covered a good bit of the U.S. during this time, driving and camping, hiking, climbing mountains, and seeing beautiful natural areas. Maybe some of these excursions were birding trips disguised as family vacations, but at least they introduced the kids to new parts of the country. Certainly, they provided me with a lot of great birding. My horizons were expanding.

One of my quest species of this era was White-tailed Ptarmigan, and coincidentally (?) we were headed for Rocky Mountain National Park that July. Daughter Carol (who had adopted the nickname "Marmot" during early childhood because of her instantaneous love affair with the alpine environment) was the only one to accompany me on the recommended path off Trail Ridge Road. I'd carefully explained that the birds were said to resemble lichen-covered rocks, until they moved. I recall this information being viewed with some skepticism. As we walked slowly along, I scrutinized all the rocks, while Carol, I think, was concentrating more on the backdrop of snowy peaks, already anticipating her future years of serious mountain-climbing. Nonetheless, she suddenly came to a dead stop, and with saucer-sized eyes announced, "Mom, there really *is* one!" Actually, there were several. The "rocks" suddenly began to get up and walk, one after another.

The event was clearly remembered years later when Carol was taking a NOLS (National Outdoor Leadership School) leaders' training course. She spotted a White-tailed Ptarmigan near their remote camp, showed it to her friends, and explained that it is rare and that she had found her mom's "lifer" for her. Not long thereafter, it became clearly evident to all that the birds were very common around camp. It was duly reported to me that there were remarks made like, "Rare bird, huh! Your mom must be some lousy birdwatcher to have missed this one!"

White-tailed Ptarmigan

~3~
Early Traveling

By the late 1970s, I had become a competent and respected St. Louis birder, and had traveled enough in the U.S., both with family and on occasional organized birding trips (Maine, Arizona, Texas, Florida), to have seen over 500 North American species. I had also accompanied my husband on a couple of business trips to Europe and Mexico, where I spent my time, mostly on foot, scouring whatever nearby natural habitats I could find for birds.

Europe at least had a field guide, thanks to Roger Tory Peterson, but his Mexican field guide wasn't yet in print when I first went there on a short trip with my husband in 1970. Bertha Massie had told me about the Desierto de los Leones west of Mexico City, and I enthusiastically decided it would be a good plan to rent a car for the day and drive there. I'd done things like that in this country, so why not in Mexico? (By the end of that day I had accumulated a substantial list of the pros and cons of such solo foreign adventures!)

I set out bravely (and naively) in my rental car from the downtown hotel with a map, a vague idea of where I was going, very little gas, and even less knowledge of Spanish. Somehow I got to a main highway and promptly made the wrong choice when faced with the options of occidental vs. oriental (neither term was then part of my very limited vocabulary). Trial and error, accompanied by a few minor mishaps and moments of utter panic in a part of the city I'd never really intended to go to at all, finally led me to the Desierto.

The reason for the name of this place eludes me to this day. It is certainly *not* a desert, and as far as I could tell, is totally devoid of lions. I had rarely been in a more impressive forest—predominately enormously tall conifers with a varied deciduous understory. I'd arrived about nine in the morning, when mist and cold were shrouding the treetops, but gradually, as the sun broke through, the trees burst into a frenzy of avian activity accompanied by a beautiful array of vocalizations. Red, Crescent-chested, and Golden-browed Warblers, Mexican Chickadees, Mexican Juncos [Yellow-eyed Juncos], White-eared Hummingbirds, plus many others—all of them momentous "firsts"—as well as an assortment of unidentified glimpses, kept me totally engrossed all morning. I had an excellent study of a mysterious, ground-scratching bird with a striped head, black face band, white throat, and olive back and wings, which the limited resources I had gave me no clue about. It wasn't until the Peterson guide was available years later that I knew I'd seen a Green-striped Brush-Finch.

My absorption was ultimately broken many hours later by the realization that I was being followed by a man I hadn't seen until now and that I definitely wished to have no contact with—so I walked quickly on, he disappeared, and I returned promptly to my car unmolested—but considerably dismayed to see an armed man standing by it. We had no common language, but it seemed (I think) that he had been guarding my car for me—from what, I wasn't entirely sure. Lions, perhaps? His gesturing seemed to convey some agitation, and I realized only after I'd driven off that of course he'd been asking for a tip. Naive, yes, and very lucky to get away with it!

Under the intoxicating spell of the day and the adrenalin-surge of my "escape" at the end, I drove back into Mexico City with the confidence and daring of a native. It did cross my mind at the time, however, that there might be more certain and somewhat less risky ways to see foreign birds.

Yes, there are indeed surer, easier, and less risky ways to see the birds of the world. Sometime in the mid-1970s the availability of organized foreign bird trips impinged seriously on my consciousness. My son had become rather interested in birds as an early teenager, and we were giving each of our children, as part of their (and our) growing independence, the opportunity to take a trip, foreign or domestic, that particularly interested them. Tom was fascinated by the Galápagos at that stage and wanted to travel there—and he was still young enough to accept his mother as a companion.

So we did the Galápagos in the summer of '76, with an appetite-whetting excursion to mainland Ecuador afterward. I returned home content with the reasonably complete (for that time period) Galápagos experience, which also included my first exposure to the wonders of snorkeling. The mainland birding, however, left a lot to be desired, which was glaringly evident even to someone as inexperienced as I. It was the briefest sampling of a seemingly inexhaustible treasure-chest of birds—and I knew I badly wanted to go back. (I've experienced this feeling time and time again in countless spots around the world.)

One aspect of this kind of travel that became very apparent and significant to me was the admitted luxury of being able to put the logistics and organization of a foreign trip entirely into the experienced hands of professionals. What a perfect set-up: they arrange the meals, lodging, and transportation to great spots, where I can simply look for birds and try to work out what they are without having to worry about all the other headaches.

The reality is that the professional leaders, who these days have become incredibly talented, experienced, and competent, usually have a bird sighted and identified before we mortals can find it or get it as far as the right genus. But the knowledge and ability to work out the proper identification in the end does pay off. One knows immediately what to look for on a given species—what field marks should or shouldn't be there, and one can either concur with or (rarely) question the identification, thus learning something from the process in either case. And gratifyingly, from time to time one can even manage a significant find and identification ahead of the pros. Of course, there's also the rewarding feeling of knowing what you're looking at when you're alone.

Back when Bertha Massie was doing most of her world travels in the 1950s and 1960s, there wasn't a lot of choice in tour companies, but that picture had changed significantly by the time I started to travel. By the mid-to-late 1970s, there were at least three or four American companies advertising trips essentially year round, including both foreign and domestic destinations. What temptation—more than enough to fill several lifetimes at my early rate of one or two foreign trips a year.

The Galápagos/Ecuador experience had been exciting and wonderful in many respects, but I could also see that I craved a more specifically bird-oriented type of trip and one with a lot fewer people. The next year David and I went to Kenya with the late Burt Monroe, Jr. and just three others. David had signed up for only the first two astounding weeks, which covered the major game parks but also produced a whole zoo-full of birds for me as well as animals for him. And was Burt *ever* into birds; here was the kind of obsessed and knowledgeable leader I'd been dreaming of. The last two weeks consisted solely of intensive birding, and I simply didn't want to return home. We'd seen nearly 600 species (a great success for those days), which had about doubled my life list, and I'd learned a tremendous amount. It was all incredibly stimulating and satisfying. I was truly addicted.

The thought occurred to me that I might even go back to Kenya one day to reinforce it all and to fill in some of the gaps. In mulling the trip over in my mind on the flight home, a great insight struck me about how best to keep my records, which up until now had consisted mainly of check marks and dates in various books and a handful of checklists from my few assorted trips. Bertha kept her list in the first edition of James F. Clements' *Birds of the World: A Checklist*, but there was really only space in it for the date and place of one's initial sighting. It was fine for counting your list, but what if you also wanted to record what you'd learned or precisely what features and behaviors you'd seen? What if I saw some of these Kenya birds again some day, under different circumstances? Wouldn't I want a record of both events, so that I could eventually accumulate my whole experience with a species, add comments about interesting behavior, new field marks, things I had learned and seen that weren't in the books, interesting vocalizations, etc.? Thus was born my card file system—and now I could hardly wait to get home to get it started.

My family tells me I might as well have been still in Africa during the intensely concentrated period I spent at home recording my bird sightings on 3x5 cards. The project seemed such a success to me that I also made out cards for my roughly 600 species seen to date in North America, Mexico, Ecuador/Galápagos, and Europe. Color-coding the cards in the upper right-hand corner with felt-tip pens according to world region added a nice splash of color and also made it immediately apparent in which part(s) of the world I'd seen the species. When the second edition of Clements' *Checklist* was published in 1978, it established the obvious taxonomic order in which I would arrange my cards.

Essentially, my record-keeping system did not change over twenty years, despite the advent of computers. Some cards became a rainbow of color, indicating worldwide sightings of species such as Ruddy Turnstone or Osprey. Many cards were stapled together, if they represented many repeated sightings that called for extensive comments (e.g., Olivaceous Woodcreeper). Clear-cut examples of distinctive subspecies that may one day be split (e.g., Seebohm's Wheatear [Northern Wheatear]) have gotten a separate card, stapled together (until split) with the "original" form. Species "heard only" have been assigned a penciled card and are thus in the record but *not* counted, despite recent listing rule changes made by the ABA.

Taxonomic order can be changed by simple rearrangement. I changed from Clements' order to that established by Sibley and Monroe's *Distribution and Taxonomy of Birds of the World*, because the latter seemed to me to represent a clearer and more complete picture of the world's avian forms with better distributional information and a superior index. My original two small file boxes expanded to over twenty larger ones. One of my daughters, who recently saw me working with my card file, commented that it was obvious to her why I didn't want my records on computer—such mechanization would destroy the personal, intimate relationship I have with each card.

My two foreign birding trips in 1976 and 1977 were intoxicating, and I knew I'd entered a very exciting world. Early 1978 brought the opportunity for a trip with some local friends to Trinidad and Tobago. Here was a view of South America in microcosm, and it's clearly where I should have started, rather than plunging in over my head with the birds of Ecuador. Some of my very favorite early memories of tropical birding stem from this trip: watching an Ornate Hawk-Eagle from the veranda at Asa Wright, waiting for first light and the arrival of hummingbirds, especially the male Tufted Coquette, at the flowering vervain in the garden, the eerie experience of the Oilbird cave, the Scarlet Ibis festooning the trees of the Caroni Swamp, and the potoo on the stub on the boat ride back. I remember Tobago as much for the incredible snorkeling just off the hotel beach as for the specialty birds. All in all, it was a truly magical time in my life.

But in these last three years I'd been neglecting my own country. When I went to Trinidad, my North American list was at about 450 species. That winter there was a major owl invasion in Duluth, and I had friends who were seeing Great Gray, Boreal, and Northern Hawk Owls, while I was watching Scarlet Ibises. Long, hard winters in northern climes have a way of enduring, however, so when I returned from Trinidad in February there was, fortunately, still time for Duluth and all those wonderful owls.

Southeast Arizona was calling me, and I took one of my few organized domestic birding trips there in late July. It was simply spectacular, and wildly successful, with the expected (and some unexpected) Mexican post-breeding rarities, as well as the Arizona regulars. I learned not only a lot about species-level identification, but also about ages, stages of molt, and racial subtleties.

There was a lot more to this identification game than I'd ever realized, and I was learning about it from the pros. I ate it up, and
I loved Arizona. The Chiricahuas and Huachucas remain one of
my all-time favorite birding areas in North America.

Trips that fall took me to Monterey and introduced me to Pacific
pelagic birds, as well as to Yosemite. After Christmas, an excursion
to southern Texas with my husband brought me yet more lifers, so
that at the start of 1979 my North American list stood at 560, a gain
of over 100 species during the previous year. Looking back on that
year of 1978, I remember it as a wonderful and exciting but relaxed
one. When I realize that it was also the year that I broke the St.
Louis area year-list record with 275—well, maybe it wasn't quite so
relaxed after all!

My gains put me within striking distance of a respectable 600
for North America (south of Alaska), but to reach that mark soon
I'd need to concentrate on the goal for a year and postpone any
foreign birding. I was still under fifty and in good health, so there
would be plenty of time ahead for international travel. I had no
major goals in foreign birding, and it could certainly wait. I
birded Texas and Florida (including the Dry Tortugas) in the
spring, Maine in the summer, and connected with a surprising
number of lifers in my home area of Missouri and Illinois, getting
both state lists over 300 in the process. By the end of 1979, I'd
found a Ross's Goose among the thousands of Snows and Blues
[Snow Goose] in northwest Missouri, and my North American
list stood at 599. Getting to 600 clearly wasn't going to be a major
problem, so I could start thinking internationally again for 1980.

Ecuador had been nagging at me to return for four years; I just
had to do a better job of it than I'd done in 1976. So I signed up
for a February trip with Bob Ridgely, a leading authority on South

American birds—and we did it properly for that era, which was a bit prior to the advent of serious tape-recording. In any case, we saw a *lot* of those birds I'd hoped to see in 1976 and hadn't, so I felt I'd taken enormous strides forward. On the way to Quito, my traveling companion and I stopped in Florida for a few days, and I found a Short-tailed Hawk—my 600th North American bird—so I was over *that* hurdle!

My second trip that year (aside from Big Bend and a few more North American species) was to Central Brazil in October, where I saw Hyacinth Macaws, various guans, Bare-faced Curassows, extraordinary Cock-tailed Tyrants, and my first Agami Heron. This heron was standing in a classic location, in shadow along a blackwater pool. I spotted it first, and it etched itself so indelibly into my memory that I'll never see the species again without remembering that first one.

What an amazingly wonderful life this was! My children were nearly grown (three in college, the youngest 17 and about to fledge) and all doing well, and my husband was busy, happy, and successful in his professional position with Ralston Purina. Birds and travel were becoming the focus of my life, and the prospects seemed very rosy. I had some independent funds and could easily take two or three birding trips a year for many years and learn a great deal about what fascinated me beyond all rational comprehension. I'd learned how to be a good birder on my home grounds, so I had plenty to keep me occupied in St. Louis when I was home, which was eightypercent of the year. But by now I'd also had a taste of other worlds and was ready for broader horizons. I would be 50 in another year, had no health problems, and my mother was still thriving at age 87. My longevity genes were evidently good, and the prospect of a long and interesting life sprinkled with occasional birding trips seemed to stretch many years into the future. Hubris? Overconfidence? Little did I suspect that life would soon go staggeringly, shockingly, blindingly from rosy to black.

PRATT
-2002-

Short-tailed Hawks

~4~

Preparing, Recording, and Listing

B efore our 1977 Kenya trip, I'd spent about six months studying mainly the early Williams' guides to the birds and the national parks of East Africa. I had a

checklist from a previous trip that Burt Monroe had led, and I concentrated largely on the over 500 species that they had seen on more or less the same route at the same season—which was plenty for my inexperienced mind to deal with.

The previous year I had tried to do similar advance preparation for the Ecuador/Galápagos trip, though the mainland birds seemed extremely hard to come to grips with. I was using the early Harris's guide to the Galápagos and Meyer de Schauensee's *Birds of South America*. With the latter, I found that I had *really* jumped off the deep end. The mainland possibilities seemed absolutely endless, with many identifications tricky if not impossible. There was also an early distributional checklist of the mainland of Ecuador compiled by Thomas Y. Butler, which I found helpful. But in reality, we birders had hardly even begun to scratch the surface of Ecuador's vast and overwhelmingly diverse avifauna.

I discovered early on that I liked the security of knowing a good deal about the birds we might see ahead of time. Associating names with mental images came quite easily to me, and I derived a great deal of pleasure from building up a mental edifice of detailed knowledge about the avifauna that we would encounter. Studying, like identification, was challenging and fun. The payoff has always been simply enormous. Foreign birding, especially in the tropics, which I enjoy most, often happens way too thick and fast to absorb even a small percentage of it on the spot. A neotropical specialist such as Ted Parker could rattle off with machine-gun speed the names of birds he saw and heard in a large, fast-moving flock—which then disappeared forever in the blink of an eye. If you don't know ahead of time what at least *some* of those creatures look like, how can you ever possibly link name and bird securely enough in your mind to call it a "lifer" —or to name it yourself if you should see one again an hour or a day or a week later? There's certainly no time to write the information down and learn it then and there, or even to repeat it into a recorder, because in the time you do that, your leader has probably located another half-dozen species (that you *now* wish you knew something about!). Such are the problems of the neophyte in the tropics everywhere around the world, but most especially in South America.

Of course, there are slower times, when for example, you're seeing bits and pieces of a mystery species in the undergrowth. At least you're concentrating on one bird at a time now! Maybe it's an antbird, but you certainly have to know what features to look for to identify it, to separate it from other possibly very similar species that it might be. Your leader may name it, and sure, you've seen a skulking black bird—but it's infinitely more satisfying to know in your own mind that because this skulking black bird has certain features which *you* have seen and recognized the importance of, its specific identity is therefore known to you.

If you have a lot of this sort of basic identification knowledge in your mental bank to start with, it's so much easier to learn more about the birds on the spot, and the whole birding experience becomes just that much more meaningful. One of the great rewards of struggling through the initial mastery of the important features of most of the potential birds on a list is the residual effect. If you've learned it well the first time, and especially if you've then seen many of those birds in the field, it'll all come back surprisingly quickly with just a short "refresher course" prior to the next time you plan to be in the same area. And the next time around, you can build just that much more onto your previous experience.

Yes, such an approach *is* time-consuming, but I have never regretted beginning my birding career at a slow and comfortable enough pace to do this kind of important advance preparation. It became my style from the beginning and has given me the great advantage of feeling that I'm working from a stable platform.

The fun of a proposed trip starts for me right from the time I first gather the necessary materials. Obviously, a field guide to the birds of the area and a checklist are indispensable. If it's an organized tour, a copy of the daily checklist to be used on the tour, with English and scientific names, is usually the most useful tool. Most tour companies send these lists out well ahead of time. Additionally, trip lists from previously-run trips can give you an idea of how likely you are to see a given species. Your checklist can be marked up in any number of ways, by indicating lifers, or new birds for the region, or short identification notes. The more you work with any list in various ways, the more familiar the names become, and if you use a good field guide in close conjunction, the appearance of a bird begins to fall right into place in your mind along with its name. If it's a do-it-yourself tour, you can often locate a complete checklist for the country involved, or you can make one from the Bird Base/Bird Area computer program.

One of my quite early trips was to the Himalayas in early 1982 with Ben King, a leading expert on Asian birds. At the time, any useful portrayal of the birds in this region was scattered among a number of different sources. No readily available, comprehensive guide to the Indian subcontinent even existed, and there were very few family monographs. Learning these birds ahead of time was going to be a real challenge; even the English names seemed incomprehensible—minlas, yuhinas, fulvettas, etc. How was I going to put this all together in my mind? The solution for me seemed to lie in compiling a notebook, starting at the beginning of the very long checklist, methodically going down the list species by species, and writing a paragraph or two of description in my own words, based on whatever information I could find anywhere, with the emphasis on the most important features of every species with which I was not already familiar—and that was 99 percent of the whole list! It took months. Writing something down has always been the most effective way for me to learn it, and once written down, the information was there for review, or for double-checking during the trip. In the left margin, I included abbreviated references to where I'd found the information, or where the relevant plate (if one existed) was located.

So I learned Ben's chosen English names for these Asian birds and was able to associate most of them with an appropriate image—but the one thing I'd seriously neglected was the scientific nomenclature. Dale Zimmerman, an authority on birds of Africa and Asia, was on that trip, and there were countless times when he and Ben would discuss a species by referring to the genus or the species in Latin. I could usually look it up, sometimes even while the conversation was going on, or I could interrupt to ask what bird they were talking about, but I was dismayed at my ignorance and swore never again to be in such an uninformed position. Compiling that notebook had paid off, however. There was at least one particularly gratifying moment I recall, when I made some remark about the presence or absence of rufous in the primaries of an owl we were looking at. Ben simply looked at me and said, "When did you start to study for this trip?"

My Himalayan experience taught me two very valuable things. First, the notebook idea was an excellent one. I continued the method faithfully for every trip after this one, learning and reinforcing a tremendous amount of information in the process. Later, I wrote comments on a much shorter list of species prior to trips (mostly potential lifers). There are so many excellent field guides, handbooks, and family monographs available now that reviewing the plates for each species has become easy and fun. Usually, I simply squeeze a few penciled words into any available space after the species name in my daily checklist, just to refresh my memory on salient points where needed. I generally find that I'm well prepared for a trip if, when I read through the proposed itinerary (which usually mentions a great variety of species in no particular order), the appropriate bird images and field marks leap immediately to mind with every species mentioned.

The second thing I learned is that scientific names, particularly genus names, are *important*. This fact became even more evident in Peru—my next trip—than it was in the Himalayas. The legendary Ted Parker led this one and daily reinforced my growing awareness that many species in the enormous families of parrots, antbirds, ovenbirds, flycatchers, etc. fall into distinctive groups, or genera, which have similar appearances or behavior patterns and thus can give the informed observer meaningful clues about at least where to start with the identification process. I recall in the first days of the trip finding a woodcreeper and saying, "Here's a *Lepidocolaptes*." Ted whirled around and said, "I'm impressed. Participants don't usually say things like that. Yes, it's a Spot-crowned [Montane Woodcreeper], the higher elevation species, not Streak-headed. They're the two possible *Lepidocolaptes* here, and the genus is where you should always start." Time and time again someone would tell him about a bird they'd seen on their own, and his answer was nearly always: "Put it in a genus; I can't begin to identify your description without that." I recall seeing some early British checklists for countries in South America that had, for instance, a full page listing of "foliage-gleaners"—without any Latin names. No wonder their clients felt overwhelmed in South America. They hadn't yet figured out that the genus names *Philydor, Automolus, Syndactyla,* etc. actually convey useful information about a bird and help give novices (as well as experts) a meaningful way to categorize what would otherwise be a huge, meaningless jumble of birds, all with essentially the same English name: "foliage-gleaner". (Fortunately, that situation has now been rectified, and British birders toss generic names around as freely as we Americans.)

I find that doing the checklist faithfully at the end of each day is essential for me, even if it isn't done as a group. On a fast-paced trip I find it's amazingly difficult to recall exactly what I saw where after even only one or two days have passed, whereas on the same day it's quite easy. Another "chore" I'm very faithful about every day is legibly transcribing into my permanent trip notebook the field notes I've scribbled in my pocket notebook during that day on locations, elevations, details of any lifers or interesting sightings, etc. All this information will eventually go into my card file when I'm home again, and in the notebook it gives me a permanent running commentary on what we've done and seen day by day. All this re-writing may sound tedious, but it's very reinforcing. By the time I've scribbled the original notes, copied them into my notebook, and then once again onto my species card, I'm much more likely to remember the information.

Another time-consuming project, but to my mind one that is absolutely necessary and really enjoyable, is the record keeping done after the trip is over. I faithfully maintain the discipline of recording each species seen on a trip (not just the new ones) on the proper card in my card file. Sometimes it's just a quick annotation of month, year, and country, but often I'll include a line or two of comment about something new I learned, saw, or heard this time around—maybe a distinctive race, or color morph I'd not seen before, or an interesting behavior or vocalization. If I've written some notes about a particular species in my trip notebook, they go onto the appropriate card. Obviously, the lifers get new cards, but usually I make those out during the trip or on the flight home, which saves some time. No wonder

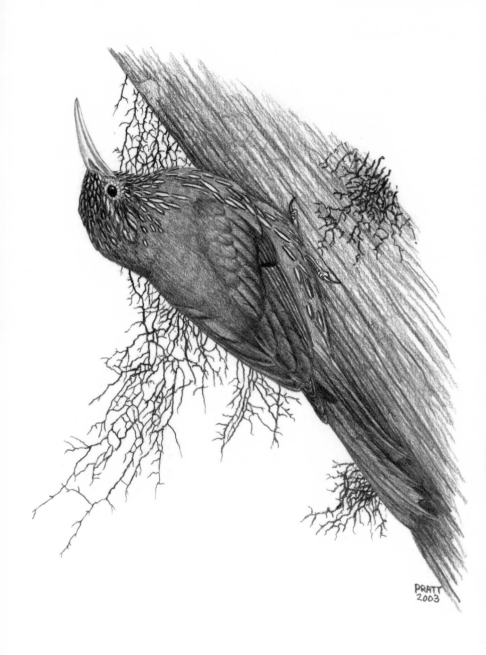

Spot-crowned Woodcreeper
[split since Phoebe saw it: now known as Montane Woodcreeper]

it's fun; this record keeping is essentially re-living the trip.

By the late eighties, I had been doing all this for about ten years and had a really extensive card file, with repeated sightings and annotations on many species, often running to two or three cards stapled together. There were times when I wondered why I was bothering to make yet another entry on Slaty Antshrike, for example, or Sirystes, or Great Gray Shrike—but I just kept doing it for the sake of completing my records and noting plumage or vocal differences where relevant.

My reward came when Sibley and Monroe's *Distribution and Taxonomy of Birds of the World* appeared at the end of 1990. Overnight there was taxonomic upheaval, and something like 500 newly-created "split" species appeared on the "official" world lists. The vast majority of these splits could be geographically defined, so that if one had seen Slaty Antshrike west of the Andes, for example, it was *Western* as opposed to *Eastern* Slaty-Antshrike. My card file listing the locations of all my records for each species (often with significant plumage or voice annotations) gave me an easy answer in nearly every case as to whether I'd already seen one of the new splits. I knew other world listers who simply gave up on the numbers at this point, having kept track of only their initial sighting of a species. Many listers simply had no way of re-constructing how many forms they'd seen of what had previously been called a single species. The Sibley and Monroe list also brought to our attention a large number of "groups" under various given species that might one day be accorded specific status—so my detailed file cards on Great Gray Shrike, for example, or Olive Thrush, let me know immediately which of these groups I'd seen. *Now* I knew why I'd been entering all those repeated observations and realized that with taxonomy in such flux it was very important to continue doing it. Such are the tangible (or at least countable) rewards of detailed record keeping.

I was delighted with Monroe and Sibley's compact and informative *A World Checklist of Birds* when it was published in 1993. My card file is presently in that taxonomic order, and the book is filled in with date and location of all my lifer sightings. I usually have the book along with me on a trip, not only to enter the new lifer information, but also as a convenient reference source for all sorts of questions that typically arise. I've now added a number of write-ins (based on Clements' annual updates to his checklist), because unfortunately there hasn't been any official updating of this valuable list since Burt Monroe's untimely death from cancer in 1994. (He was my age.) And what if I lost it, or it got stolen along with my luggage? I could, of course, reconstruct it from my card file, but I also have another back-up system at home.

This back-up system developed as a result of my submitting regional/area lists (Asia, Africa, South America, etc.) yearly to the ABA, along with the combined factors of current taxonomic revision and the ABA's re-definition of regional boundaries, particularly the border between Asia and Australasia (revised yet again in 1996). Clearly, I needed some way to come up with accurate numbers for my regional lists that would reflect the new ABA official world taxonomy—Clements' 4th edition, which aside from taxonomic order differed through 1993 in only very minor ways, and virtually not at all numerically, from the Monroe and Sibley 1993 checklist—as well as the newly defined world regions and areas.

The idea occurred to me while traveling, and again I could

hardly wait for a span of time at home to start it. I would photocopy each page of the Monroe and Sibley 1993 checklist and attach it to a pre-prepared "grid" format, with vertical columns for each world region or area where I keep a list and with horizontal lines following along the lines for lifer information that accompanies each species in the checklist. 11x17-inch sheets proved to be a perfect size. I attached each photocopied checklist page on the left, which allowed space on the right for my desired 16 regional/area columns, plus additional room at the extreme right on the horizontal lines for comments about any taxonomic changes. There was also space at the bottom to add new species. Thus, each species had a "box" in each regional column for a potential checkmark (in my card-file color code, of course) if I'd seen the species in a given region or area. The result turned out to be very visual and very attractively gaudy on pages like those concerned with shorebirds, where I'd repeatedly seen a lot of widespread species. It was also great fun to do, but again *very* time-consuming. Of course it took months to finish, but at last I had an easy way to count down each column for accurate regional totals and could see at a glance the various places where I'd observed any given species. The index in the Monroe checklist can get me immediately to the proper page number on my sheets, so finding what I'm looking for is easy; if I want more detail, I go to my card file.

In theory, all my grid sheets could be photocopied from one master copy. Alas, in practice this turned out to be impossible. It worked fine for the 16 vertical columns I wanted on every page for the various regions/areas. However, it turned out—to my considerable dismay—that the horizontal spacing of the species on every page of Monroe's printed book is slightly dif-

ferent. Thus I was going to have to draw in *every* horizontal line
on each of the 336 sheets with a ruler. So I did, which is one reason the project took so long—but it was fun to do and worthwhile in the end. I keep it faithfully up to date and enjoy making the colored check marks when, for instance, I see a bird in
a new region.

Within the last couple of years (somehow, it got to be 1998
when I wasn't looking!), another aspect of this endlessly fascinating avocation has now become impossible to ignore: the taxonomic explosion. At the end of 1996, Sibley produced a computer disc (only) version of *Birds of the World* (2.0), containing
9,946 species. It has been increasingly evident from my reading
of many publications and journals worldwide that new species
and splits, resulting from new research or from changing species
concepts or both, are now appearing in print at an unprecedented rate.

Quite obviously, there are a lot of legitimate taxonomic
choices these days. Reading some of the European birding literature (e.g., *Dutch Birding*, *Birding World*, and the various excellent regional bird club publications published in the U.K.)
makes one's mind boggle at the incredible pace of taxonomic
changes. All indications are that the situation will only get
worse—or better, depending on which side of the taxonomic
fence you're on. We all recognize that many decisions ornithologists make about what is or is not a "species" are arbitrary and
that species concepts vary radically from one expert to another,
or from one time to another. Even ultra-conservative listers find
it difficult to adhere to any taxonomic "bible" these days, with
so much in flux.

Changing taxonomy has been a growing dilemma for me

over recent years, but during nearly all of my active birding career, when I was avidly playing the competitive listing game, *numerically* I adhered strictly to ABA rules and the official Clements list. Not until "retirement" after 1995 had I achieved enough background knowledge, awareness, and confidence to branch out into another system, to be discussed later.

For the sake of a more complete picture of my record keeping and listing methodology, I've jumped way ahead chronologically. Now it's time to return to a very significant time of my life—1981.

In her study at home in Webster Groves, Missouri, Phoebe prepared and filed index cards on each of her sightings from a recent trip, c. 1988

~5~

Turning Point

A t the beginning of 1981 I was feeling very happy with my present life and future prospects. I was comfortable with my birding pace and style as well as

with the general preparation and record-keeping methods I'd developed (which were to evolve further in the coming years, as I've already described). Our youngest child was 17 and would be through high school in another year, and our oldest was due to graduate from college in June. I'd made a place for myself in St. Louis birding and had now seen over 600 species in North America south of Alaska, which I planned to visit soon. I signed up early for an extensive summer Alaska trip with Rich Stallcup and Jon Dunn of WINGS, which would include Gambell and the Pribilofs. I was very excited by the manifold birding possibilities, as well as by the lure of seeing Alaska at last.

This year was to start with a trip to Panama in February with Mary Wiese, a good friend from home, and with two leaders I hadn't met, but about whom I had heard very good reports: John and Rose Ann Rowlett. I now had about 1,900 species on my world list, so a successful trip to Panama should certainly put me over 2,000. It did—and then some. With a stunning view of Black-breasted Puffbird, I reached the 2,000 milestone. (I'd seen my 1,000th species somewhere on that 1977 Kenya trip, but I wasn't keeping close numerical track back then, so who knows

PRATT
2002

Black-breasted Puffbird

what it was—probably some cisticola.)

The Panama trip was memorable and wonderful for countless reasons, but one aspect that literally blew me away was the field use of tape recorders, which both John and Rose Ann handled with absolute virtuosity. I had never yet experienced anything like it, and it opened vast new horizons. The tapes brought responses from Black-and-white, Spectacled, and Crested Owls almost as though the birds were on a string. My Black-breasted Puffbird had appeared in tape response, and we saw any number of skulking undergrowth species with this impressive new (to me) technique. Additionally, both John and Rose Ann could recognize a vast number of bird voices, so they often knew that something interesting was present and could be recorded on the spot and "worked on" for all to see. I've seldom had a better, more exciting time on a birding trip.

There was one seemingly minor problem marring my euphoric mood at this period of my life. Toward the end of the previous year, I'd noticed a small swelling (lump?) under my right armpit. My gynecologist had looked at it and pronounced it something insignificant, like a swollen gland. During the Panama trip, however, I became increasingly conscious of it, though it was completely painless. Upon return home and further medical consultation, the conclusion was unmistakable: it was certainly a lump, not just a swelling—and it had most definitely grown.

A bit of past history becomes significant here. During one of our family vacations in 1972, our oldest daughter Penny had called attention to a large mole on my back (which I'd had since childhood). Sometime since I'd last been conscious of it, however, it had grown quite black and was lumpy and bleeding on one edge. Trouble for sure. It was indeed diagnosed as malignant melanoma, and I went in for a traumatic day of outpatient surgery. The mole and a large chunk of tissue surrounding it were removed under *local* anesthesia—a huge mistake, I realized during the course of the painful operation! Anyhow, it was successfully accomplished, and for five years of annual check-ups there was no evidence of any further problem. Apparently the excision had done the job, the threat was over, and with all the birding and interesting things happening in my life during that time, it was easy to relax and essentially forget about it. But now, over eight years later, that excised mole loomed large in my mind.

I was quickly referred to a surgeon who had removed many cancers from his patients. He took one look at my situation, including my history of melanoma, and wanted to remove the lump immediately and have it biopsied. I went into the hospital feeling that life was suddenly becoming unreal and quite terrifying. Shortly after recovering from the operation, I was given the biopsy result that I dreaded: metastatic malignant melanoma.

The medical world entered my life as in a nightmare. There were brain, liver, and bone scans to be done, to look for any further spread. The only good news of the whole agonizing time was that all the scans proved to be clean. But the melanoma had been in the lymph nodes; it was a metastasis from the original, superficial one on my back. Consultations with three independent oncologists gave me the same shattering prognosis: three months of good health, then inevitable, rapid decline with further metastasis, and death within a year. I could hardly believe this was really happening. "I'm healthy, and I'm not even fifty!", my mind kept protesting. I went through all the stages you read about—denial, anger, bargaining—I think I even reached acceptance. At least I *did* truly come to believe that it would happen as all these knowledgeable, experienced professionals told me it would. I definitely did *not* feel defiant in the sense of "I'm going to beat this cancer". Mostly, I just felt totally shattered and defeated.

The sudden turn-around from health and happiness to facing imminent death is as traumatic an emotional time as I have ever gone through. We all live our lives with the *intellectual* awareness that we will die one day. I was now facing an *emotional* confrontation with my own fairly imminent death, which was an experience totally apart from any I'd ever encountered. I dreaded waking from sleep in the mornings, because reality would strike me with an intense physical blow whenever I did. There simply wasn't much I could do to avoid dwelling on the horror of it all and pondering over how I was going to deal with it.

At the time, there was no proven effective treatment for melanoma; neither radiation nor chemotherapy had been shown to have any significant beneficial effect. Therefore I wasn't under pressure to take *any* standard follow-up treatment, simply because there wasn't any. There were some experimental possibilities, but at least one of these was a lengthy, totally debilitating, even life-threatening process—which was easy for me to turn down. Any potential experimental treatment would have essentially meant medical incarceration and giving up total control of my life, which I was unwilling to do.

I desperately wanted to continue running my own life, because I was healthy and, physically, felt just fine. I'd accepted the fact that my life wasn't going to last long, but I very quickly came to the conclusion that I preferred a short span of quality living under my control, followed by a quick death, to a longer life protracted by various all-consuming medical treatments and their effects, probably followed by a lingering death. So given the options, I decided to do nothing, except take regular high doses of vitamin C, which at least wasn't going to do me any harm, and just possibly might do some good.

While I was recuperating from the surgery for the removal of the melanoma and regaining full arm motion, I frequently went out by myself or with a friend, just to be alone and to try to come to grips with my situation. Birding was certainly not foremost in my mind these days, but as much from habit as anything I'd take along my binoculars, or even my scope, and before I knew it, I'd start concentrating on something beautiful or interesting, or get involved in an identification puzzle—and my overwhelming personal problems somehow, albeit briefly, would fall aside because I'd temporarily become so involved in what I was seeing during those magic moments of total absorption. Then, of course, my problems and fears would descend on me again with the same gut-wrenching physical impact that happened on waking every morning—but meanwhile I'd had a glorious respite.

It was early spring now, and before this time of recovery and life-assessment was over, shorebirds and landbirds were much in evidence. I chased hotlines for a local Ruff and Western Kingbird and found a King Rail, new for my Missouri list. Always, in the heat of the chase and the fun of the find, thoughts of impending illness and death seemed less overwhelming. I was still managing to do some of the things I loved to do; bit by bit the magic grew, and the terror and hopelessness lessened their grip.

When I was given my death sentence by the doctors, one of my immediate reactions that I clearly remember was "Oh no— there are all those things I haven't yet done, and now will never have a chance to do." Here's where my biggest regrets lay, so I certainly wasn't going to let these predicted three months of good health go unused!

By this time, I was planning with my husband to attend our daughter Penny's college graduation in June, and I had also decided to continue with plans to go on the Alaska trip that I'd signed up for so eagerly before I had any inkling of serious illness. Looking forward to these things, and doing the preparation for Alaska, gave me a lot to focus on other than dying. My husband and children seemed very accepting of my decision not to undergo experimental medical treatment, but to continue my plans for traveling and birding. My feeling about Alaska was that if I still had a period of good health remaining to me (and June was within that predicted three-month period—barely), there was really nothing I would rather do. I wasn't just going to stay home and wait to get ill; if I got sick in Alaska, then I'd come home. *Carpe diem.* It was the right decision.

~6~
Birding for My Life

B y June of 1981 I had clearly entered upon a new phase in my life and in my birding. With the decision to go to Alaska, without really knowing it I was setting my new style. Seeing and learning about birds became a now-or-never situation, but it also became mental and emotional salvation. The preparation and primarily the birding itself, plus the record keeping afterwards, all enabled me essentially to forget the threat to my life (or at least to push it aside) and to immerse myself totally in what I was learning, doing, and seeing. If I had seemed focused and compulsive before, I was now rapidly on my way to becoming obsessive.

Alaska proved to be absolutely brilliant. Eleanor Marcus, a birding friend from home, went with me, and I was very fond of the primary leader, Rich Stallcup, so I didn't feel as totally alone as I otherwise might have, considering the trauma I'd been through and what seemed like the very real possibility of serious illness during the trip.

We began at Gambell, spending many hours sitting on The Point with scopes and absorbing the non-stop flight of alcids and other seabirds, which surpassed anything I had ever seen or even imagined. Land birding was strenuous, with long walks over difficult terrain, incessant wind, and hard work finding the good birds. By the sixth day, we'd seen most of the expected specialties, including a Bluethroat. We'd had our fill of unceasing northeastern wind (western or southwestern could have brought unheard-of Asiatic marvels), and everyone wanted to be on the first shuttle flight out of there. Early the next morning, however, we successfully followed up a report of a Red-necked Stint, and on the way back found three or four beautiful Eurasian Dotterels, a Gray-tailed Tattler, and a flock of Spectacled Eiders offshore—and now no one wanted to leave! But the wind remained steady from the northeast, and the bird flurry was over, so we left as planned for Nome and the mainland.

After a couple of days of immersion in new species like Rock and Willow Ptarmigan, nesting Long-tailed Jaegers, Aleutian Terns, and Arctic Warblers, many lovely breeding-plumaged shorebirds, spectacular scenery and glorious wildflowers, I celebrated my fiftieth birthday one evening at the local saloon in Nome—and a very fine birthday it was, considering that I wasn't supposed to have any more.

From there, it was on to the Pribilofs and more excitement: dramatic seabird nesting cliffs (with close-up views of many of the alcids we'd seen at Gambell), Red-faced Cormorants and Red-legged Kittiwakes, finally a fine Yellow-billed Loon, and the biggest surprise of all—at the culmination of a day-long effort, a totally mind-blowing experience with a Bristle-thighed Curlew.

Denali (Mt. McKinley back then) yielded the important big mammals, as well as a close pair of Gyrfalcons, plus a Northern Goshawk female attending a nest. The Homer-Seward ferry trip (to Kodiak Island, and around the tip of the Kenai Peninsula) with its amazing pelagic spectacle was the wind-up of an absolute dream of an Alaskan experience. I came home happy—

and still healthy.

Time had run out on my "three months of good health" with no indication of any problem whatsoever. My decision to go to Alaska had been an unqualified success—so what now? Well, there was an interesting-sounding Australia trip coming up in the fall, and my friend Mary Wiese wanted to go. Australia was far away, certainly, and the trip was a month long, but it was also a civilized kind of place from which I could fly home relatively easily if a health problem developed. It was also a few months in the future, which would give me time for some serious preparation (this was a totally new part of the world to me), as well as for a summer excursion I was planning with another friend, Barbara Spencer. The die was cast.

Ross's Gulls had recently been found breeding at Churchill. I hadn't been into chasing North American birds when a Ross's Gull had shown up at Newburyport, Massachusetts in 1973, and it was the one bird I'd been hoping for on the Alaska trip that we had missed. But now that "wraith of the Arctic" was retrievable, and if we drove to Winnipeg and flew from there to Churchill, we could also pick up some upper midwestern species that Barbara and I both needed.

All in all, it was a resoundingly successful do-it-yourself trip. Stunning views of Ross's Gulls were the highlight (despite the unforgettable clouds of voracious mosquitoes that hot 4th of July weekend), but we also scooped up Baird's Sparrow, Sprague's Pipit, and Chestnut-collared Longspur. With a bit of a detour to Yellowstone and the Tetons on the way home, we pulled out Sage [Greater Sage-Grouse] and Blue Grouse, Black Rosy-Finch, and several more. By the end of that summer, my North American list (now including Alaska) stood at 650.

I knew we'd be covering a lot of driving miles, so I'd taken along my newly-acquired Australian field guide by Graham Pizzey, trip checklist, and itinerary. I set myself the task of learning something like ten to fifteen new Australian birds per day while we drove all those miles, so by the time we'd returned to St. Louis, I was well into my preparation for what was sounding like an incredibly interesting and exciting part of the world.

And it certainly was. We did a complete standard circuit of Australia, including the southwest, so my world list leapt forward by nearly 400 species. Again, the preparation had paid off. I found my own Broad-billed Sandpiper and Great Knot on the Cairns mudflat, could successfully come to grips with the myriads of honeyeaters (paying some attention to genera of course), and even knew how to deal with the fairy-wrens and gerygones. I'd never even heard of a gerygone, let alone knew how to pronounce its name (Je-RIG-o-nee), just a few months before.

My good health continued, and we were now into October. Somehow this approach of living from short-term goal to short-term goal was working, and it certainly was keeping despair at bay. I'd even gained enough long-range confidence to start thinking seriously about 1982. I signed up for a February trip to Suriname with Tom Davis and a spring trip to the Himalayas (a grand east-to-west sweep) with Ben King. This was the year when my preparation methods took a great leap forward with my organized notebook compilation for every trip.

Tom Davis was very serious about tape recording, so the Suriname trip, with its incredible diversity of antbirds, was another valuable exposure to this technique. By now I knew what could be done with tapes, so it was terrific fun to have the benefit of Tom's depth of experience with recording and with Suriname in

PRATT
2002

Ross's Gull

Ibisbill

general. But the highlight and biggest surprise of the trip was the cooperative Zigzag Heron, a lifer for all including Tom, that Barbara Spencer and I stumbled upon during a siesta-time walk in a dry forest—most unlikely-looking habitat for that species.

Ben's Himalayan trip was, as I've already indicated, an education in itself. There were some quite unbelievably awful living conditions (welcome to remote Asia!), as well as very high altitudes (up to 12,000 feet), and Ben was then the most indefatigable birder and tour leader I'd yet run into. He simply didn't give up. If he heard the target species way over the next major hill when light was waning, we'd go for it. And he was serious about seeing night birds and seeing them well. So all in all, it was strenuous and, at times, exhausting. Nonetheless, if you had the stamina and the drive to stick with Ben through it all, there was nearly always a payoff. We went from Sikkim and West Bengal through Nepal to Kashmir and Ladakh and saw a simply incredible array of Himalayan birds. It was the last time Ben ran that full trip, and it included some areas impossible to get to now.

By the end of that trip in Kashmir and Ladakh, our party had dwindled to just three—Ben, a Canadian woman named Jo Wright, and me—for the post-tour extension. Our prime target in Leh, our final destination, was the Ibisbill. We had stunning views of this seldom-seen, unique bird on a gravel bar of the Indus River, and then enjoyed another day of relaxed downhill birding, since we were at about 11,000 feet in elevation here. Jo and I had both had a debilitating gut bug in Kashmir, so we were feeling pretty wiped out. The next day was to be the last day of birding before the flight to Delhi and home, so we all went to bed early.

Early the next morning, Jo didn't appear and didn't answer her phone or knocks on her door. There was obviously a serious problem, and Ben started to climb in the open bathroom window—from which the hotel manager, who protested that the police must enter first, dragged him back out. When they did arrive (amazingly quickly), they found Jo dead in bed, as though peacefully asleep. She had evidently died very suddenly, without discomfort or struggle. This unexpected event was, of course, mega-trauma for Ben, not to mention me. Jo and I had become good friends, she had seemed to be a very healthy woman in her sixties, and of course it was my death that had been predicted by doctors for about this time—just over a year since my melanoma surgery.

Birding was obviously over. There were endless problems and arrangements for Ben to deal with, and in addition we were weathered in so that our flight back to Delhi couldn't land in Leh for two more days. Eventually we had Jo's body cremated, because there was simply no choice; fortunately, that turned out to be what her wishes had been. A representative from the Canadian High Commission met us in Delhi and took over from there, so it was finally finished, and I was on my way home. After having death almost constantly on my mind for a year, Jo's end seemed to me the best that one could possibly ask for, and I think I'd have traded places with her on the spot if I could have. After all, we'd had an incredible trip through the Himalayas and seen some of the most amazing mountains on the planet, not to mention all those wonderful birds, capped by the *pièce de resistance*—the Ibisbill. To end it all with a sudden, peaceful death seemed pretty good to me at the time.

Increasing the Pace

I'd learned by now that to work in a
fairly tight schedule of several trips
in one year, my overall plans had to
be made many months in advance.

Confidence that my life and health might continue for a while was
indeed increasing, but it was the simple logistics of birding trips
that really pushed me into long-term commitments. Well before
the end of 1981 I was signed up for much of the following year:
Suriname, the Himalayas, and then Peru with Ted Parker in July. I'd
also decided to return to Southeast Arizona in the spring, mainly to
see the owls we had missed on our late summer trip four years earlier. We found the owls, and as usual there were some bonuses.

Most of my time that spring and early summer was devoted to
preparing for Peru, which was a formidable undertaking. There
was no field guide, and there was a simply immense avifauna, with
a *lot* of hard-to-identify species. Information was scattered, and
many of the birds weren't illustrated anywhere. The solution to
this dilemma proved to be studying and photographing museum
skins. My New York friend Barbara Spencer was going on the trip
too, so we spent many productive hours at the American Museum
of Natural History, photographing bird skins and taking notes.

This trip was called "Grand Peru" back in the early 1980s, and
it was indeed the ultimate avian extravaganza. Ted Parker's name
was legendary even back then, and John Rowlett, who had be-

come a good friend on the Panama trip, was his co-leader, so I knew we would be in extremely capable hands. By now I had outlasted all medical predictions from the previous year and was becoming considerably more sanguine about the immediate future. For instance, I no longer worried about having to abort a trip in mid-stream because of ill health.

By then I'd been around long enough to offer some comparative judgments on where in the world to go for the best all-around birding experiences, taking into consideration not only quality and quantity of birds encountered, but also scenery, variety, and general trip logistics. Peru came out well ahead of anything I'd done to date. We had a Diademed Sandpiper-Plover (my 3,000th life bird) for openers and ended with a Harpy and then a Crested Eagle on the last two days of the trip, with countless other wonders sandwiched in between.

The sandpiper-plover was a bonus of our own devising. Barbara, John Rowlett, and I planned to meet in Lima a day or so before the trip to go up to look for it—and I do mean *up*. Lima is at sea level, and the bird lives a mere three-hour drive away, in bogs at 15,000 feet. We had directions, plus words of caution and tales of acute illness in connection with the extreme altitude change. I'll confess to being a bit apprehensive, especially since Jo Wright's death in the Himalayas just two months before was thought to have been altitude-related. Even Ted, who had chronic altitude-sickness problems, had not yet seen this species. But the lure of a monotypic shorebird with such a splendid name was not to be resisted. In short, we went, found a suitable bog to scan, spotted the bird, and got as close as several feet away. It was truly a gem and an auspicious beginning for the trip.

That whole day was unforgettable. We may have been a little

Diademed Sandpiper-Plover

light-headed and headachy from the altitude (and intoxicated with success), but we never felt ill. The puna grassland well above timberline with the background of snow-capped peaks was staggering, and the place was hopping with ground-tyrants, cinclodes, canasteros, miners, earthcreepers, seedsnipes, and even an essentially terrestrial hummingbird (Olivaceous Thornbill). One bird we didn't know about at the time, because it hadn't yet been found at this location, was White-bellied Cinclodes, a huge and impressive relative of the commoner species, with a highly localized distribution. In 1996, I returned to Marcapomacocha to search for (and find) this high-priority species. I'd remembered this place as one of the most beautiful spots in the world and was rewarded by seeing that, unlike so many previously wonderful spots around the world, it really hadn't changed at all in the intervening 14 years.

The trip officially began with a drive down the desert coast south of Lima to the Pararcas peninsula, where the lack of bird life on the stark sand dunes contrasted with the teeming seabirds of the Humboldt Current. Here we found the area's few specialty landbirds, such as Slender-billed Finch, and had a boat trip to the guano islands offshore to give us close encounters with most of the seabirds, as well with the world's most beautiful tern (Inca), gull (Swallow-tailed), and cormorant (Red-legged).

Next we made a short flight from Lima to Tingo Maria, in the tropical zone on the bird-rich eastern slope of the Andes and from there worked our way up through the Divisoria and Carpish Mountains, thus covering an altitudinal range of many thousands of feet. Because one encounters a new avifauna with every major change in altitude, we checked off an astonishing number of species during this time. The variety ranged from common and not-so-common tanagers (all of them stunningly beautiful) to special and infrequently-seen birds such as Andean Cock-of-the-rock, Golden-headed Quetzal, Scaled Fruiteater, and Versicolored Barbet, to once-in-a-lifetime experiences, such as an Undulated Antpitta hopping up the Paty Trail ahead of us like a robin. Having birded these areas in their prime classifies me now as an old-timer. Years of being a stronghold for the Shining Path and subsequent guerrilla activity, with its accompanying human and ecological disasters have made the whole area not only extremely risky, but have also led to substantial habitat loss.

Cuzco, the ancient Inca capital at 10,000 feet in southern Peru, was our next destination. The views from the plane as we flew through and over the Andes were truly awesome and hardly surpassed by the Himalayas, with which I was mentally comparing them. We took the train ride along the dramatic, rampaging Urubamba River to the ancient ruins of Machu Picchu. Here we stayed overnight to experience the scenic majesty, power, and mystery of the ruins and their unique setting in peace, before and after the hordes of day-tourists had come and gone. I've never seen anything to compare with it anywhere on earth.

Our highest day since our pre-trip excursion was up and over Abra Malaga pass at 13,000 feet. The puna grassland of the western (dry) side of the pass contained some species similar to those we'd seen at Marcapomacocha above Lima, but now we were in southern Peru, so there were some significant differences. Here we finally had good views of magnificent Andean Condors. The eastern (humid) side of the pass contains some of the highest forest in the world, and the birds of this region are very special and little-known. Several of the birds we saw that day had been only recently discovered or were known from only a few specimens until the mid-1970s, such as Parodi's Hemispingus, White-browed Tit-Spinetail, and Unstreaked Tit-Tyrant. Such specialized birding gave us some of the thrill of being in on the frontiers of bird exploration, and Ted's excitement over it all was infectious. And if this weren't exhilarating enough, we only had to raise our eyes to the stunning backdrop of snow-capped Veronica, one of the most beautiful mountains in South America.

A flight from Cuzco between two awesomely close Andean peaks and down to the Amazon Basin took us to our last destination—or almost. We still had a ride of several hours in a motorized dugout canoe up the Tambopata River to the famed (at least in birding circles) Explorers' Inn. Here we lived for five days, with the opportunity to spend as much time as we wished walking trails in the virgin rainforest.

The birding here was difficult, often very frustrating, and yet vastly rewarding. Antbirds, ovenbirds, and flycatchers of many species were a major challenge, and we saw and heard some marvelous ones, such as the newly-described Bamboo Antshrike and White-cheeked Tody-Tyrant. There was all the difference in the world between being with Ted or John Rowlett, who knew the voices and the possibilities and could tell you what you were seeing (if you were lucky enough to see it!), and doing what Barbara and I did every spare moment we could find—namely, stumbling about by ourselves (Barbara carried an invaluable tape recorder), finding a few things, and working out the identifications on our own. This approach really makes one appreciate the difficulty of acquiring expertise like that of our leaders. For instance, we became intimately acquainted with a Flammulated Pygmy-Tyrant [Flammulated Bamboo-Tyrant] by voice and sight, but identifying it consumed the better part of one lunch hour.

Our biggest rewards were yet to come. Ted routinely scanned the limbs of huge trees, because he knew that big raptors occasionally perch in such locations, and from our canoe on the big lake he spotted one. We could hear the barely suppressed excitement in his voice: "Oh my God, there's a Harpy or a Crested Eagle perched over there!" Utter silence fell, and we paddled toward the huge bird, which became more obviously a Harpy Eagle the closer we got. It had an almost solid black chest, an enormous round gray head with a shaggy double crest, and legs as thick as tree branches. The bird watched us—and vice-versa—for a seeming eternity. Finally, it flapped and climbed along the branches until it was hidden in the foliage. I was quite overcome. Here was my number-one most-wanted bird in the entire world, one I'd never realistically expected to see even briefly, and we'd had these stupendous, heart-stopping views of it. (Later, days after the trip was over, Ted saw the bird again, flying over the lake with a howler monkey in its talons. Of course I wish I'd seen that event too. Some people are *never* satisfied.)

Later we conversed with Ted about his various sightings of Harpy and Crested Eagles (a small handful of each). He commented that he'd never seen a dark-morph Crested Eagle, which has the underparts evenly barred below the dark gray chest. During the middle of the next and last day of the trip, while everyone else was having a siesta, Barbara and I were out in the forest as usual. She was fiddling with the tape recorder, perhaps making or playing some sound, and I breathlessly watched a huge raptor fly in and perch silently on a branch barely fifty feet away to look us over. The bird had a big head, shaggy chest, dark gray chest with the rest of the underparts evenly barred, and the same dark, baleful, hollow-eyed visage we'd seen on a raptor only once before—

Harpy Eagle

the previous day! Here was the elusive dark-morph Crested Eagle that Ted had described. We could hardly believe what we were seeing. It was awesome and humbling, rather like a visit from a deity. The bird gave us plenty of time to study and absorb it, but alas, declined to stay around for the others to see.

We'd reaped the rewards of dogged perseverance, and it was time to go home. We'd seen the two biggest and best raptors in South America on two successive days, and had accounted for well over 700 other species during our three weeks in Peru. It had all been a smashing success with a record-breaking number of species on the official trip list. But there was still (and always will be) a lot to go back for someday, since that wasn't quite *half* of the birds of Peru.

The year wasn't over yet. Despite my having done three major foreign trips and some Arizona birding as well, it was still only August. Having come to like and admire Ted a great deal, it was a natural step for me to sign on for his upcoming trip to southeastern Brazil in November. Occasionally I thought about all these incredible experiences I'd have missed if my melanoma had behaved according to prediction—which of course motivated me all the more to keep moving. I think I began about this time to feel that maybe I was out-running the disease. Somehow I developed a feeling of virtual invincibility once I was on the plane and heading toward new places and birds; I was leaving the threat behind. At any rate, something was working for me, and I was thriving on my new lifestyle of accelerated travel.

Since I now had about three months to prepare for the complex avifauna of southeastern Brazil, there was plenty of time to work in another North American trip. In several almost yearly attempts of trying to take a late-summer or early-fall pelagic trip off Cape

Hatteras, I'd had singularly bad luck. I had spent more weekends than I cared to remember on the Cape, watching the horizontal wind socks fly with a vengeance, indicating a near-zero probability of our getting out to sea the next day or even the day after. All in all, I've been weathered out of far more birds by wind than I ever have been by rain or snow. But if you're unlucky, the only recourse is sheer, dogged perseverance. I went back again, in October this time, and we actually got out to sea as far as the Gulf Stream, and of course once there, found the Black-capped Petrels that had been a jinx for so long. It wasn't as fancy as the rare *Pterodromas* that have been reported from those waters in later years, but still, the petrels were a welcome prize back then.

November came, and I was on the plane to Rio at last. Southeast Brazil is one of those many areas of the world with a highly specialized and localized endemic avifauna, and with serious problems of burgeoning population and habitat destruction. The Atlantic forests, where the most interesting and endangered birds live, are but a tiny remnant of what was there early in the twentieth century, and the long-range prospects are gloomy.

Despite pessimism about the future, birding in 1982 in the remnant forests was absolutely sensational, and we were all immediately caught up in the excitement of it. Ted seemed to know the voices of the Brazilian birds as well as he did those of Peru, and we all benefited from his expertise and his superb recording and playback techniques. There was a variety of amazing parrots, some truly dramatic antbirds, and a hummingbird spectacle at the feeders of Dr. Augusto Ruschi (a world authority on hummingbirds) that was like nothing I'd ever seen. We birded at Iguaçu Falls and in the hills of Itatiaia, which remain two of my all-time favorite birding spots anywhere. We did very well with the endemic birds that were our main targets, but inevitably left some behind—so I hoped I'd come back one day.

And of course I did return, more than once. The truly astounding thing about southeast Brazil (and Brazil in general) is that since my first trip in 1982 there has been a whole series of exciting discoveries and sites found for species that were virtually unknown to birders 16 years ago, like Fork-tailed Pygmy-Tyrant [Fork-tailed Tody-Tyrant], Salvadori's Antwren, and Buff-throated Purpletuft. The re-discovery (and consequent generic re-classification) of Black-hooded Antwren a few years ago was a surprise to all, and more recently a new genus and species of antbird (*Stymphalornis acutirostris*) [Parana Antwren] was found. To the north, in southeastern Bahia, yet another amazing new genus and species (Pink-legged Graveteiro) was recently discovered along a major highway, and in the same short time span news was spread of the re-discovery of the long-lost Kinglet Calyptura, with re-discovery of Cherry-throated Tanager reported not long afterward. Amazingly, most of these events have occurred not far from Rio—one of the densest population centers in the whole country. Despite the habitat losses and the clear and present danger of extinction of many species, Brazil has, in the past few years, given us birders more and more instead of less and less.

Sadly, there are and always will be trade-offs. In early 1998, I finally had a realistic chance to see what has been for some time the rarest bird in the world. A single male Spix's Macaw, the only wild remaining member of its own monotypic genus had for years been probably the most closely-monitored and guarded bird in human history. The site was in the dry caatinga habitat of the Rio São Francisco in remote northeast Brazil—not an easy place to get to for a variety of reasons, one being the bureaucratic paperwork required to get the mandatory official permission for entry. Ironically, we got past the red tape and were cautiously optimistic about our chances, but we'd failed to reckon with the heavy hand of extinction. Just two weeks before the start of our trip, this unique individual bird, species, and genus simply disappeared— an absolutely shattering and heartbreaking event and so agonizingly close to our chance for an encounter. Speculation over the disappearance pointed to death from old age (the age of the bird was unknown—it could have been 50, 60, or older), predation by an owl, or who-knows-what other of the unpredictable events that all birds (and we as well) face in simply trying to live.

When I returned to Amazonian Brazil in August 1998, I learned the apparently reliable news that the male Spix's Macaw had returned to the original site after his absence of several months! Apparently, inevitable extinction has been postponed once more by a hair's breadth, for which we can all be temporarily grateful and relieved. I had my one chance to see this bird and was just incredibly unlucky with the timing.

~8~

Adding Experience

By the end of 1982, I was over a major psychological hurdle. I was no longer constantly (only now and then!) haunted by thoughts of illness and dying.

My focus was now almost entirely on seeing and learning about birds. I'd found I could handle about four major foreign trips plus some North American birding during the course of a year, and there were still endless destinations and opportunities to choose from. Once again, life was looking good, at least from a short-range view; I was now thinking ahead from year to year, rather than just from one trip to the next.

The next year, 1983, took me to Senegal, Costa Rica, Malaya/Borneo, and Bolivia, as well as to Texas and Southern California. Numbers were piling up. My biggest total year (ever) had been the previous one, when I'd seen nearly 1,000 new species, about the maximum I could possibly absorb and hope to retain. In 1983 the number of lifers per year slowed to a more comfortable 500 (approximately), where it more or less stayed for the next few years. By the end of 1983 my world list was a bit over 3,900, and I'd seen nearly 670 in North America—close enough at least to begin envisioning how I might break 700.

The Costa Rica trip in early spring brought me not only wonderful birds, but also my first and only encounter with a serious earthquake. This one registered 7.6 on the Richter scale, and we were located just scant miles from the epicenter. We were staying at Las Cruces, in the southwest of the country, in a wooden building on stilts—expressly designed to survive earthquakes, as we learned first-hand! My roommate and I had just gone to bed, while others were showering or chatting in the open dining area. It began with a gentle swaying, then a total blackout and much crashing and breaking of glass. Our beds were literally heaving, and once we figured out it was *not* a raucous party and tried to stand up and walk, we found the floors heaving and buckling as well. Those showering, of course, were in a somewhat more delicate situation—nude, in total darkness, with much glass breaking all around them. We realized very quickly that it was an earthquake, and I remember thinking at the time: "What a surprise— I really didn't think my life was going to end like this!" One way or another, we all crawled and staggered across the waving floor, down the steps and outside, by which time it was all over. We did a little owling to pass some time (with no results at all), and eventually a few of us ventured back inside to try again to get some sleep. No sooner had we hit our pillows than the swaying began again, but this time we were organized and ready, and out of there in a flash. Needless to say, we slept outside on the ground the rest of the night. There were a few more aftershocks, but nothing frightening, and quite miraculously, there was virtually no damage to the well-designed building.

The very end of 1983 brought unprecedented excitement to my local St. Louis birding scene, and that winter event remains one of my all-time highlight experiences. I was home after a winter excursion to Texas, and was studying hard for an upcoming trip to northern India in January with Ben King. A good friend, Bill Rudden, had called me about a mystery dark-mantled gull he'd seen along the Mississippi River. This man was a highly experienced and talented local birder, who knew well the gulls we typically record here, and he didn't know what this one was.

Loving both gulls and identification challenges, I was greatly interested in Bill's report. Another knowledgeable friend, Ron Goetz, was also intrigued, and both of us spent long hours that bitterly cold December looking for Bill's gull—without success. He seemed to be the only one capable of finding this particular gull during the ten-day period when the bird played a frustrating game of hide-and-seek along a 19-mile stretch of the Mississippi. Meanwhile, Bill filled us in with further reports. The bird was a full adult, with various interesting features that clearly seemed to eliminate Great and Lesser Black-backeds, our normal winter dark-mantled gulls.

Speculation about the identity of this gull was becoming a hobby unto itself for Ron and me. Careful research of the literature eliminated most of the serious contenders, many of them highly unlikely on geographic grounds alone. Literally the only possibilities remaining seemed to be: 1) Slaty-backed Gull, 2) a hybrid differing radically from any described, or 3) a totally aberrant form of some species we had already eliminated. All of the above seemed at best far-fetched. And Ron and I had not yet even seen this bird.

The end of 1983 was approaching fast, and soon I'd be off for India. Bill had seen the gull again on December 30th, so the next morning Ron and I and two others joined him in hopes of obtaining definitive views and resolving the mystery. We came armed with all the appropriate references and knowledge of the all-important primary patterning in various relevant species. Finally, we spotted the bird resting on the ice with Glaucous and

Herring Gulls [American Herring Gulls], but way across the river from where we were. Continuing what had been a morning of hot pursuit, we raced across the bridge to get as close as possible and found that the usually locked gate to our access point had miraculously been left open. The gods were with us so far.

The first step was accomplished: we were actually viewing the elusive creature through scopes at reasonable range in good light and were able to study all its very interesting details (except primary patterning) in comparison to the Glaucous and Herring Gulls. After more than an hour, the gull began a leisurely routine of preening and stretching. Few performances have held the rapt attention of an audience with such thoroughly frozen feet as successfully as this one. Tantalizing glimpses of an unusual wing pattern were revealed first, but finally the dramatic climax came when the bird held both wings aloft and stationary for several glorious seconds, revealing as in a textbook a full view of the spread wing from above and below. Yes, every other feature we'd been studying was right for Slaty-backed Gull, but here was the absolute clincher, the diagnostic wing pattern. Our wildest speculations had indeed been true. True to form, no sooner had the gull been definitively identified by our exuberant party, than it took off and disappeared downriver. Who was going to believe us? The identification had taken nearly two weeks, lots of effort, and some astounding good fortune on the final day. How could we hope to do it again in front of the inevitable skeptics?

But our luck held. Now that the mystery gull had a name, it seemed to behave more predictably, becoming regular and more or less cooperative for patient observers who came from far and wide to see it. It was the first Lower 48 record for this species, and the biggest bird event in St. Louis history (surpassed to date only

Slaty-backed Gull

by the Ross's Gull of 1992—another tale and a sad one for me). For those of us who'd struggled with the finding and identification of the St. Louis Slaty-backed Gull, it was one of those satisfying triumphs that only birders can fully appreciate.

My early 1984 trip to northern India with Ben King was splendid, producing my 4,000th species (Black-breasted Weaver [Bengal Weaver], unfortunately—but flanked on either side by species I'd have much preferred for this milestone: Siberian Rubythroat and Dusky Eagle-Owl). It was practically a private trip, with only one other participant, and we went to some (at the time) little-known spots, searching for (and mostly finding) little-known birds, some of them actually lifers for Ben. It was all very fulfilling, replete with sights of Houbara [Houbara Bustard] and Great Indian Bustard [Indian Bustard], Siberian Cranes at Bharatpur, and even a tiger skulking through the grass at Corbett. This was a year before David Hunt had his fatal encounter with a tigress there, and I shudder to recollect that Ben and I spent some time wandering *on foot* along the river through grass over our heads— where we observed tiger tracks—in our search for Great Thick-knee on the gravel bars. It was bad judgment, but we were lucky: we found the thick-knee, and no tiger found us.

My alternate option for this time period, when I wasn't sure whether Ben would be able to run this India trip, had been a trip to Colombia with Steve Hilty, an expert on South American birds. As luck would have it, this turned out to be the *last* organized bird trip to Colombia. Despite the success and overall fun of the India trip, I felt for years that I'd made the wrong choice. Colombia now seemed out of my reach forever, and its list of avian endemics and total species is among the highest in the world. Only years later did I get to some of the great birding spots in Colombia.

One lure I couldn't quite resist was breaking the 700 threshold in North America. With about thirty species to go at this point, even Attu wouldn't *quite* do the job, but it would get me close enough to scratch out those last few somehow, somewhere. I'd heard from countless friends about the magic of Attu, so I had to see it for myself, and 1984 was to be the year. Except for shorebirds, which were generally scarce, it was a good year on Attu. Many of the rarities I'd already seen in Asia—but they did count for my North American list, and that's why I was there. In addition, there were a few true lifers, one of which was Lanceolated Warbler, which occurred that year in an unprecedented fallout. After all fifty of us had seen this notorious Asiatic skulker, the next day we found them everywhere, singing from the tops of weed stalks. Essentially I got what I went for, about twenty North American species, though it was neither my happiest trip nor my preferred style of birding. Mostly, I found it a physically exhausting "big twitch", with long and arduous hot pursuits after rare finds located and identified by others. My favorite day was inland on foot, where we escaped not only the bicycles and the awful "roads", but also the depressing and ever-present World War II junkyard of the coast. Inland was the real and beautiful Attu at last, along with the White-tailed Eagle that lived there and symbolized the remoteness and wildness of the place.

Papua New Guinea (PNG) was my next trip, and again it was a preparation challenge, involving once again many museum visits and sorting through various older references to correlate the English names on our checklist with the appropriate scientific ones. Nomenclature in that part of the world seemed in virtual chaos, and it was a welcome step forward in many ways when the excellent field guide by Beehler et al. was finally published two years later.

The trip itself was simply magnificent. As in South America, many of the most sought-after birds, such as jewel-babblers, lurked in the deep dark undergrowth, and could be lured out with appropriate use of a tape recorder. Here was the center of evolution of some of the most extraordinarily-plumaged birds on this planet—the birds-of-paradise—and we saw full breeding males of about twenty species. It was as *different* a part of the world as I'd ever been to, and I could see that one visit, however great it was, would not be nearly enough. (I returned three times, seeing very special new species each time—but it was *still* not enough!)

As an interesting cultural sidelight on this trip, in the Mt. Hagen area we witnessed (from the vehicle) one of the full-dress battles between local tribes that occur from time to time in that culture for the purpose of settling grievances. As the colorful but deadly serious skirmish moved closer to the road, someone in our van unwisely decided to take a photo. This action clearly incited one of the nearby warriors in full feather and warpaint regalia, who shouted in anger, brandished his spear and fist, and started running toward us with a following crowd, all exhibiting similar intimidating behavior. Bret Whitney, a leading authority on birds of the New World tropics and New Guinea, was driving our van; as always, his reactions were quick, and he realized it was time to depart. We did, with an engine-roar and tire-screech worthy of any police-chase thriller—just as the spears were hurled by the Papuans. I'm not sure how the dents and scrapes in the side of the van caused by the spears were explained to the rental agency— but that's one of the advantages of being part of a tour: it wasn't our problem. In retrospect, though it was exciting enough at the time, it was not the worst experience that New Guinea can offer.

I haven't ever done much chasing of rarities in North America, especially if I've seen and learned the bird somewhere else in the world, but now I was only about ten species short of the 700 barrier, and I wanted to cross that threshold. We'd missed Little Curlew on our early fall Australian trip in 1981, and amazingly, one turned up in Santa Maria, California in September after my return from PNG. Shorebirds have always been one of my favorite families, so it was certainly worth a try. I flew to Los Angeles, rented a car, and drove to the site—lots of birders were there, including some old friends, but no Little Curlew. The property owners were most cooperative and had even been managing water levels to maintain appropriate habitat. As long as I was there, it made sense to stay overnight locally and try again in the morning. The target bird flew in on schedule to feed, and those of us who had come far and stayed had marvelous views. Since then, of course, I've finally seen Little Curlews in Australia, where they normally winter, but never again in North America.

November was the time for my first trip to Argentina, which proved to be all I'd expected and more. We covered an amazing diversity of habitat and saw an equally amazing spectrum of the bird life, from the tropics at Iguaçu Falls to the exciting subantarctic sea life in the Beagle Channel at the tip of Tierra del Fuego. That boat trip, with Black-browed Albatrosses and Southern Giant-Petrels [Hall's Giant Petrels] wheeling about us, was so exhilarating that it absolutely convinced me I had to go to Antarctica. As I recall, I cornered my favorite roommate, Doris Brann, on the spot, and said: "Promise me you'll go to Antarctica with me—but I can't do it for two years!" Psychologically, I had definitely made the leap to believing that I had a future.

I wound up 1984 in southern Texas. Several Mexican species had shown up that winter, and I was still slowly plugging away at my North American list. White-collared Seedeater (finally!), Fork-tailed Flycatcher, Clay-colored Robin, and a male Blue Bunting (this one a true lifer) brought me to 695.

The next year followed much the same pattern. I went with Ben King to Thailand, Burma, and Hong Kong, and in the spring to El Triunfo in southern Mexico. The major quest on this latter excursion was the Horned Guan, an improbable-looking creature that lives in the lovely mist-shrouded, bromeliad-laden cloud forest, reached by a rugged three-day uphill trek. At that time, our chances of success were rated at only fifty percent, but at least we'd see some other interesting birds in the process. We certainly did: Tody Motmot, Azure-rumped Tanager, Chestnut-sided Shrike-Vireo, and incredibly long-tailed Resplendent Quetzals displaying overhead. The search for the Horned Guan involved long daily hikes over difficult terrain and then a final, frantic, exhausting uphill race to the spot where the bird had been located by another party (shades of Attu!). The visual and emotional reward was simply exquisite, however, and more than compensated for the struggle. Achieving quality sightings of quality birds has always figured high in my reasons for international birding, and this sighting was one of the ultimate examples.

A June excursion to the Pacific Northwest and Alaska, including the long but beautiful ferry trip to Dutch Harbor in the Aleutians for Whiskered Auklet, brought my North American count to 699, but it would take me another whole year to get to 700. There was simply too much else to do in the meantime.

Most of the summer was consumed by a long trip to Indonesia with Ben King and another expert on Asian birds, David Bishop. We began with Halmahera and Sulawesi, then went on to Bali and Java, and ended seven weeks later in Sumatra. It was certainly the early days for many of these birding areas. Even at the time, they seemed arduous and primitive, and looking back, I really wonder how I did it. But we'd seen beautiful displays of Wallace's Standardwing parachuting from their favorite treetops, Maleo at their nesting mounds, the highly endangered Bali Myna, and many Javan and Sumatran endemics. We also had a simply exquisite experience with a Malaysian Rail-babbler, which responded to an imitation of its eerie, whistled call. It was certainly a triumph of birding success as well as of endurance, and I was happy I'd done it all.

A considerably more civilized experience lay ahead that fall—my first visit to South Africa and Namibia. It was another long trip, but in a well-organized part of the world. Physically, it was easy. There is quite an astonishing number of endemics in the areas we covered, and we didn't leave much behind, so by the end of it all my world list was nearing 4,900. I'd passed what I considered then the half-way mark in world bird species with number 4,500 (Small Blue Kingfisher) in Java that summer, and now it seemed clear that I could reach 5,000 during the coming year. Several other birders had passed this mark by now, but I could be the first woman to do it, and that idea rather appealed to me. Competition was indeed becoming a significant factor in my motivation by this time.

I was also approaching the five-year mark since my melanoma surgery in March of 1981. I certainly hadn't forgotten about it this time, but it wasn't on the surface of my mind anymore—until I noticed the lump in my right armpit shortly after returning from

South Africa in November. *Déjà vu*. It was in the same location as last time, and of course I knew immediately what it was. Here was the recurrence they told me I wouldn't have because the melanoma theoretically would have metastasized internally long before this time and killed me! Immediate surgery was obviously the first step, with a biopsy, and then all those scans to look for further spread. All plans were put on hold, but in any case my next planned trip was the Philippines with Ben, and that wouldn't be until February next year. Anything could happen between now and then. The decreasing time interval between recurrences (from eight years to four years) didn't seem to be a good sign, and I went into the hospital this time feeling very pessimistic but at least grateful for all I'd done since the last time.

It was, of course, the melanoma again, and I held my breath before receiving, one day at a time, results of the bone, liver, and brain scans. All came back negative, once again! I couldn't believe my incredible good fortune. Now, all I had to do was recover from the surgery, and then I could start birding and living (had the two become synonymous?) once more! From the previous trauma, I'd learned to deal emotionally with the threat to my life. Yes, the threat had been renewed. There was certainly a resurgence of many by now familiar thoughts and feelings, but thanks to experience, I wasn't nearly so consumed by it all this time around.

~9~

Milestones and Trauma

S hort-term goals had become important once again. Who knew how
long health and birding would last for
me? I was one bird away from 700 in North
America, and 120 away from the major milestone of 5,000 world
species. And I was headed for the Philippines, where it would be
just barely possible, with great good fortune, to see that requisite
120 new species.

Ben King and Tim Fisher, from Manila, a specialist on the
birds of the Philippines, guided us capably through a month of
complex logistics, agonizingly early morning departures, and
equally agonizing long jeepney rides over terrible roads. But the
birds fell into place. There are a *lot* of endemics in the Philippines,
and many very difficult ones, due to the nature or rarity of the
bird and to the island structure of the country, with its many logistical and political uncertainties. We arrived in Manila, in a
state of considerable uncertainty, on the eve of the elections that
ousted Marcos and brought Aquino to power. As a result, guerrilla activity was at a low level; the guerillas were simply waiting,
along with the rest of the world, to see what would happen.
Meanwhile, we were birding—and rejoicing with the rest of the
population over reports of Marcos's fleeing the country. Happily,
the situation had worked to our advantage.

Of all the wonderful birds we saw on that trip, the biggest and

best had to be the Great Philippine or Monkey-eating Eagle. We'd
had an arduous climb up to a knife-edge ridge top in southern
Mindanao. (Sometimes it seems like much of my life is spent
climbing steep ridges after young, strong, long-legged men in
quest of rare birds.) We knew that a nest had been located several
months previously and should by now (barring various possible
disasters) contain a nearly-fledged eaglet. From our ridge-top
vantage point, we looked down into a huge stick nest in the fork
of an enormous tree in the valley. The eaglet was indeed there,
and as we watched it, an adult came soaring in from afar and
cruised right past us with a monkey in its talons—an absolutely
heart-stopping sight. We were treated to a long observation
through scopes of the adult with that incredible floppy, golden
mop of a head and humongous beak tearing the monkey apart
and feeding chunks of it to its young.

The special birds of that trip came thick and fast—kingfishers,
hornbills, malkohas, racquet-tailed parrots, owls, babblers, a
bleeding-heart dove, tailorbirds, sunbirds, and an enormous
number of flowerpeckers. My 5,000th species held off until
nearly the end of the trip: Philippine Bullfinch [White-cheeked
Bullfinch], another endemic. There was a handful of men ahead
of me at this point, and I knew most of them. A couple of them
had even passed 6,000, which seemed impossibly far off to me. I
was certainly very pleased to be the first woman to 5,000, and
considering my very real health threat, I wasn't seriously thinking
much beyond that mark.

That spring I'd been invited to be on the Ladies' Team in the
Hong Kong Bird Race, which was a competitive event designed to
raise money through pledges for habitat preservation. Since I was
going to be in Southeast Asia, I also worked in a side trip to

Philippine Bullfinch
[White-cheeked Bullfinch]

Malaya and caught up with some important birds, including two species of frogmouth. I was to pass through Los Angeles on my way home and had learned through conversation somewhere that a good way to see Xantus's Murrelet (race *scrippsi*) was to take a scheduled boat trip in the spring from Ventura out to Santa Cruz Island. This was a species I'd been distinctly unlucky with on several Monterey Bay boat trips, so it made a fine candidate for number 700. I was there at prime time in late April, and there was an ideal boat trip scheduled. It all worked beautifully. I had fine views of the murrelets on the way out, in calm waters and perfect light. There were no other birders on board, so I had a private and quiet celebration of number 700 for North America.

That really took care of numerical targets for the foreseeable future. I had more trips, at least in the planning stages, of course, but I did feel the pressure was largely off and found it an enjoyable luxury. As an indication of my more relaxed mood and feeling of *que será*, my next planned trip (to the southwest Pacific) was not to be until September and then one more to Chile in December would finish the year. That year of 1986, in which I reached the two major milestones of 5,000 world birds and 700 North American birds, was to be very low in year lifers compared to those years preceding and following. I saw only 285 new birds in 1986, temporarily breaking my yearly pattern of around 500 or more.

My trip to the southwest Pacific had begun as a private arrangement with David Bishop and three companions the year before, and its focus was to be a serious search for that almost mythical wraith of the forest, the Kagu, on New Caledonia. As things turned out, all my companions fell by the wayside as planning progressed, so I was left with a last-minute decision to seize the (by now very expensive) opportunity to go alone with David

Xantus's Murrelet

or simply to abort the whole venture. It's probably not difficult to imagine what my decision was.

The preparation for this very different kind of trip had been one of those supreme challenges, with little-known, poorly-described and largely un-illustrated birds scattered over the several seldom-birded island groups we planned to visit. I was grateful to have a several-month span of time at home to cope with the complexities of this preparation. As usual, compiling a detailed species-by-species notebook ahead of time was the only way to go. I made up my own all-inclusive list of birds of the region on a daily checklist format, and this project alone was very time-consuming, but also an extremely valuable learning tool. Before the advent of computers and the recent, vastly increased ease of obtaining or compiling daily checklists for virtually all areas of the world, such listing had to be done on a typewriter, and the mechanics of it all were reasonably laborious.

So, with all this preliminary work accomplished, I met David as planned in Fiji in early September. Since it was my first visit to this part of the world, the birding here was very exciting and largely successful. Target species like Silktail, Golden Dove, and the interesting and beautiful shining-parrots were hugely rewarding. At the time, we had no knowledge of the metronome-like voice of the Orange Dove, so that one eluded us, as did the Black-faced Shrikebill [Black-throated Shrikebill]. I've now been back to Fiji twice and have seen them both, but not the Pink-billed Parrotfinch, which I suspect will be among those I shall never see.

One unsettling event occurred here near Suva, on about our first birding day. We were returning to our car parked along the roadside near a forest patch, when David whispered excitedly: "Get in the car *now*, quickly and quietly!" He'd noticed (and I hadn't) a man with a large rock in his hand, crouched and hiding in the ditch alongside the car, obviously just ready to break in. We got in and drove off unmolested, but certainly just in the nick of time. In retrospect, this occurrence seemed an ominous harbinger of events to come.

The flight schedule connecting to the various island groups (all separate countries) we planned to visit was mind-boggling and subject to constant change. One of the early changes gave us the time and opportunity to squeeze in an unplanned visit to Samoa, so we jumped at the chance. This trip yielded some unexpected endemics, the best of which was a surprise early morning long fly-by of a Tooth-billed Pigeon. We came, unexpectedly, upon a lovely site with Robert Louis Stevenson's simple gravestone inscribed with his marvelous poem, "Requiem":

> Under the wide and starry sky,
> Dig the grave and let me lie.
> Glad did I live and gladly die,
> And I laid me down with a will.
>
> This be the verse you grave for me:
> *Here he lies where he longed to be;*
> *Home is the sailor, home from sea,*
> *And the hunter home from the hill.*

I found it very moving.

Now on to the main quest—the elusive Kagu. We flew to New Caledonia and were prepared to spend hours in a makeshift blind (I'd brought along some lightweight camouflage material for that purpose). David had made contact with Yves Letocart at Rivière

Bleu, who was beginning a study of this seldom-seen species and who had recently observed a wild Kagu frequenting the area near a wire enclosure he had made to hold two captive birds. The birds are commonly heard (sharp *yap* notes like the barking of a small dog) in the forest of Rivière Bleu, and our original plan had been to set up a blind, tape the nocturnally calling birds, and try to lure them in at first light.

When attempts for difficult birds don't go according to plan, that usually means bad news, but in this case the gods were smiling. Yves volunteered to take us for a nocturnal hike in the forest near his captive Kagus to hope for an encounter with the wild birds he'd recently seen. It seemed a long shot but certainly worth a try on our first night there. We had to get up in the middle of the night to make it to the spot with plenty of darkness remaining, but that turned out to be the hardest part of it all. We hiked a short way up a rocky trail, and there was the Kagu, walking along the trail, seemingly unaware of our presence, its outrageously huge shaggy crest, large dark eye, and red bill and legs showing well in Yves' light. Preposterous! We savored the magic moments, realizing full well that this sighting had saved us a lot of time and trouble and that we now actually had time to relax and enjoy the rest of the wonderful array of New Caledonian endemics.

Heady with success, we went on to bird Vanuatu, Guadalcanal, Bougainville, and West New Britain, amassing a good total of endemics but of course inevitably leaving some behind. In any case, the trip was now a resounding success, and before leaving New Caledonia, I'd even found some Kagu postcards to send off to family and friends, as a report on our good fortune.

Our base in New Britain was Hoskins, and our birding was done mainly in the excellent forest where the "Volcano" or

Melanesian Scrubfowl (*Megapodius eremita*) has its nesting mounds, where the eggs are incubated by underground thermal activity, and where the local villagers routinely harvest some of the eggs. Our hotel manager had loaned us a truck, so we spent early and late hours driving the dirt road past several local villages to and from this forest. On our third morning in that forest, as we were returning along the trail to the road after having had great studies of the scrubfowl near their mounds, we met a long line of villagers with baskets, seemingly heading toward the mounds for their traditional egg-collecting. We exchanged what seemed like friendly greetings (David speaks the language) and continued on our way out—only to notice after a short time that the natives had turned around and were following us. Quickly they split up, with half the group moving in front of us, and before we know it, we were being "escorted" out of the forest. Conversation between David and our escorting party seemed strained, and when we came out to the road, there were another fifty men, all armed with bush-knives (i.e., machetes), surrounding our parked truck.

The situation had gone from worrying to frightening. David was clearly trying to explain what we were doing—pointing at birds, letting the men see through his binoculars, and showing them what such mysterious and suspicious items as the scope and tape recorder were used for. Conversation went back and forth, but tensions seemed to be lessening. They finally let us get into our truck but escorted us from ahead and behind with their own vehicles as far as the nearest village. We breathed a sigh of genuine relief when they let us go on from there alone, but we still had to run the gauntlet of all the other villages. Jungle drums or something similar had spread the word, and they all seemed to

be waiting for us. We sped by, ignoring the men who attempted
to slow or stop us. Rocks were thrown and fists and bush-knives
were brandished. We had clearly and suddenly become distinctly
unpopular with the locals, and our birding in the area was obviously at an end.

The hotel manager was at a loss to explain the local hostility
we'd encountered, but he helped arrange a flight out of there later
that day to PNG, where we had planned to spend a few days to
wind up the trip. The situation became clarified when the police
tracked us down at the airport. They had come to apologize for
the villagers. It seems there had been a recent murder that had
been attributed to whites, which more-or-less coincided with our
appearance on the scene and was compounded by our inexplica-
ble behavior and equipment. Village radio had irresponsibly
spread the rumor that we were somehow connected with this
murder, so all the villages along that road had been waiting to ap-
prehend "the suspicious whites" when we showed up that last
morning. We'd actually gone out in the dark to try for owls, but
after dawn, when they saw our truck on the road, they'd come
into the forest to find us. Given all this background, the scenario
could obviously have ended very badly for us, and we felt extremely fortunate to have escaped unscathed.

We arrived with relief in Port Moresby, blissfully ignorant that
we had lept "out of the frying pan and into the fire". David
phoned local contacts from the PNG Bird Society and was given
warnings about one area in particular where there had been some
car break-ins and robberies. Obviously we'd avoid *that* spot! It
was a site for Twelve-wired Bird-of-paradise, but fortunately I'd
seen that species on my first trip to PNG, so it wasn't even frustrating that we had to steer clear. Otherwise, things seemed

peaceful, he was told.

We birded the Moitaka Sewage Ponds outside of Port Moresby the first afternoon and spent the next morning in the hills at Varirata National Park, where I observed several fine birds, such as Chestnut-backed Jewel-babbler and Brown-headed Paradise-Kingfisher, that we'd missed on my first trip. Now there was only one afternoon left before our scheduled return home after six long, eventful, and bird-filled weeks.

It was my idea. Why not just go back to Moitaka, maybe stay late, and look for rails? The gods were *not* smiling on us this time. We spent the afternoon happily enough, but we'd run out of new birds, and none of the hoped-for rails appeared at dusk. So we headed out the dirt access road about 6 p.m., as light was failing, ready to declare the birding trip at an end. It most certainly was, but not quite as we'd planned.

Near the exit from the dirt track, David stopped the car abruptly. A massive log barricade had been built across the track, where there was a steep slope on one side and a deep ditch on the other—no way around either side. I looked up the slope to see a Papuan with a rock in his hand; another two jumped up from the ditch, and two more appeared behind us. These guys all had rocks and traditional long bush-knives and were clearly serious about robbing us. When they began to smash the rear car windows, we rolled the front ones down and handed them our binoculars and packs. We'd left passports and most of our money in the hotel room, so all we had of value were optics and my bird book.

At this point, the event began to assume surreal and nightmare proportions. These five burly, black, intimidating men knocked down most of their barricade, then piled into our rented car (a small station wagon), forcing us into a prone position in the very back.

One of them drove and took us on an unimaginably awful, terror-izingly rapid ride over rough dirt roads and around curves where we felt sure the driver would roll us over, all the while with clouds of dust and shards of broken glass swirling in from the smashed win-dows. I could hardly bring myself to realize that this was actually happening, that it wasn't either a nightmare or a movie.

After what seemed an interminable time, the car stopped abruptly, and the men forced us out. It was fully dark by now, but we could see we were in a grassy area near the edge of a large body of water. Two of the men forced David flat on his back on the ground and held a bush-knife at his throat. The others took me over a slight hill, held me also with a knife at my throat, and raped me, eventually all five of them.

I was afraid that David might over-react and get himself killed, and of course I was afraid that they might kill me. Somehow the actual rape seemed relatively insignificant by comparison. After-wards, they let me go back to the car, and they released David as well, and had us both sit in the front seat while they stood nearby and conversed about what to do. David could understand them, and I knew instinctively that they were talking about killing us. With bush-knives, it was going to be a bloody, terrible business—and not quick. I wished they had guns, but in retrospect, I think then they might actually have killed us, because it would have been easy. Maybe it was simply the awful prospect of butchery with those knives that put them off. David told me later that one of them suggested they cut our bodies into small pieces and throw them into the lake—in which case we'd simply have dis-appeared without a trace. Maybe even these "tough guys" could-n't handle that kind of deliberate, savage bloodshed.

It's quite amazing what self-protective devices the human psyche comes up with under severe stress. I found myself being grateful I'd sent those Kagu postcards, in case we never came back home. Somehow, a cushion of shock had enveloped both David and me, and we were both behaving appropriately and not triggering their anger. I wasn't having screaming hysterics, and he wasn't trying vainly to fight or resist. True, we might be hacked to death in the next few minutes, but right now we were reasonably okay, aside from being frightened to death. It was an altogether different kind of death-confrontation from that which the cancer had given me—certainly more immediately, heart-poundingly threatening, yet somehow an amazing inner calmness and fatalism prevailed. They were in control, and there was simply nothing we could do, aside from pleading that they let us go. At least David could plead in their own language, though one or two of them did also speak some broken English.

The conversation among our abductors became heated and confused, and soon stopped rather abruptly. The ringleader came up close, said they were leaving a guard, and would come back. Then silence...and darkness...I think we were holding our breaths. After a minute or two, it became apparent that there was no one out there, or at least no sight or sound of human presence. We knew if they returned, which could be any minute, we were doomed, so we'd nothing to lose by making a break for it. We crept silently out of the car, kept low, and ran along the dirt track away from the water, which was where we'd last seen them. We ran and walked and ran again, as fast and steadily as I physically could, leaving the track to dive into the grass and bush to hide whenever we thought we heard a sound behind us. (We'd seen a large poisonous taipan in similar habitat the day before, but it seemed a minor worry compared to what we thought was coming after us.) We'd long since lost any sense of where we were, but we could see the lights of Port Moresby in the distance, and we headed generally that direction.

After a couple of hours had passed and we were still walking, apparently unpursued but still feeling totally lost and vulnerable, it began to dawn on us that our abductors had probably just decided to leave us and disappear into the night. They knew it would be a long time before we could reach help, and that by then they'd be long gone and untraceable. Common sense had prevailed among them in the end, I think, but I still shudder to think that it might not have—and I do feel it came close.

Just as we were coming to feel a bit less threatened, we heard men's voices and dogs barking nearby. We knew the dogs had detected us and that even though it was very dark, we'd be unable to stay hidden for long. From the direction and tones of voice, however, we were quite sure it wasn't our abductors. David decided to approach them, after having me hide in the bush, and try to get help. If he didn't come back, I was to stay hidden until daylight and then head toward Port Moresby. Before long, I heard David's confident voice mingled with others, including women, and then I knew we'd come through all right.

Just at the point when David was returning to my hiding spot with the men he'd found—also armed with bush-knives—a car came up the track from behind us. Our first thought was that it was our abductors (who had kept the car keys), in pursuit at last. Our adrenalin was really flowing, because now that we had our own armed team, and a considerably larger one at that, we were ready to take them on! Feeling safe at last, I was ready to string them up and castrate each one with a rusty knife. It wasn't our abductors, of course, but instead simply another law-abiding PNG citizen who volunteered to bring the police.

We'd come upon a friendly village, with sympathetic, consoling women who put their arms around me when they heard what had happened. We were safe and unhurt, and at that point nothing else really mattered. The police came, listened carefully to our tale, and took us back to the remains of the barricade at Moitaka, from which we tried to lead them along the track of the hair-raising ride to where we'd left the car. Certainly easier said than done, but we finally got around to the far side of the lagoons, and there was the car with its smashed windows still in the same spot and even with my telescope still in the back seat. The conscientious police fingerprinted the car, but the five thugs managed to disappear forever, taking with them two good pairs of binoculars and my bird book. As far as we could learn, they never joined the PNG Bird Society.

The police were most considerate and thoughtful and took me to the hospital to be checked for injuries. The doctor was as warm and concerned as the villagers had been, and all in all, I had my faith in the basic goodness of most people restored over and over again that memorable night. It wasn't until waking the next day that I realized I'd been so traumatized that I hadn't even been able to cry.

The following two months at home were a necessary and therapeutic hiatus. I was able to unload the emotions of the awful episode in conversations with family and friends and to realize that the same thing could happen to me in St. Louis or Chicago or many of the other places I go birding alone or with a friend. Certainly we'd been unlucky, but probably also naive to set a pattern of going to the same city-outskirt site two afternoons in a row. It had taken time and deliberate planning to erect that massive barricade. We'd doubtless been watched the first afternoon, and then when they saw us drive back in the next day, they had the trap ready for us. Still, we addicts can't just stop birding because of the risks of some unsavory spots; we just have to learn to minimize them. Time and understanding gradually re-built my confidence, and anyhow my December trip would be a safe and easy one to Chile with an organized tour group. I had a few stories to tell.

Phoebe at Forest Park, St. Louis, c. 1985

Mid-Stream

———— ❧ ————

C hile had been just wonderful. I
loved the country, the mountains
and scenery, the birds, and my companions—not to mention the wine. It was just

a grand, good time, and exactly what I needed to get over the traumatic experience of PNG. Our pelagic trip into the Humboldt Current off Valparaiso was one of the best I'd yet experienced, with constant action, including three *Pterodromas*, five albatrosses, and numerous other new and exciting seabirds. There were marvelous landbirds as well, such as some great, hulking tapaculos and interesting furnariids like Crag Chilia and Des Murs's Wiretail.

But we were into 1987 now, and as she'd promised two years before on the Argentine Beagle Channel boat trip, my good friend Doris Brann was going with me to Antarctica. This February trip was on the Society Expeditions' *Explorer*, with Peter Harrison, renowned seabird authority, as naturalist and about 100 passengers, only a handful of whom were birders. We departed from southern Chile, crossed the Drake Passage to Antarctica, and returned north via the Scotia Arc, through the South Orkneys to South Georgia and the Falklands, and thence through the Straits of Magellan back to Punta Arenas. It was the world's ultimate pelagic trip, and with almost 24 hours of daylight, it was really beyond human physical endurance to stay on deck day after day as long as one's mind and soul might wish to. I gave it a good try, though, and kept many early morning hours of solitary vigil, not only watching seabirds, but just absorbing the majesty and grandeur of this starkly black-and-white part of the world.

We were surrounded by various penguins (but alas, not Emperor), petrels, albatrosses, prions, skuas, shearwaters, diving-petrels, and storm-petrels, plus some very interesting landbirds like South Georgia Pipit (the world's southernmost passerine) and the beautiful Black-throated Finch, with a constant and exuberant commentary from Peter Harrison running through it all. I absolutely loved it.

In the spring, I went to Jamaica and the Dominican Republic, my first step into the Caribbean. A comprehensive and extraordinarily successful early-summer trip to Japan with Mark Brazil, the leading expert on the country's birds, turned up virtually everything we were looking for, from Fairy Pitta to Blakiston's Fish-Owl, and even included the island specialities of the Izu Islands, Okinawa, and Amami-oshima. That July and August found me in equatorial west Africa—Ivory Coast, Gabon, and a short extension to Mt. Cameroon. Early fall took me to Amazonian Brazil, where I saw my first Crimson Fruitcrow from an amazing 150-foot tower with a view over the rainforest canopy to surpass one's wildest dreams. The year wound up with my first (of several) trips to the "different planet" of Madagascar and, finally, New Zealand. No wonder that my year total of lifers was back up into the five hundreds, and I was over halfway between five and six thousand.

The following year led me to yet more new places and new birds: Venezuela, southern and western Mexico, and Manu, that extensive and extraordinary wilderness area in southeast Peru, filled the first half of 1988, along with a return visit to Hong Kong in April. Our brief one-day visit to the Mai Po marshes, which represented the height of the glorious breeding-plumage wader spectacle, gave us excellent studies of Nordmann's Greenshank and, best of all, I found my own first Spoonbill Sandpiper. Just as well that the day had been so memorable for me, because it was not only the beginning, but also unfortunately the end of that trip. The group was to go on to mainland China for three more rugged weeks of tough and uncomfortable birding, but I had developed a more-than-inconvenient bleeding problem and had to return home from Hong Kong the next day to have an emergency hysterectomy. The problem had developed a week or so before the trip, and my gynecologist had given me medication, which he hoped would control the bleeding. It hadn't, and clearly my body was giving me no choice but to return home. The operation went smoothly, there was no malignancy, and now all I had to do was recuperate for six weeks so I could go on the Manu trip in July—which I did.

The rest of 1988 amounted to nearly total immersion in Africa. Two of our daughters were then actually living in Kenya, Carol leading wilderness trips for an American organization (NOLS), which had a base at Naro Moru near the foot of Mt. Kenya, and Sue teaching science in a school in western Kenya near the Uganda border. What an opportunity! My husband and I decided to take our two oldest children, Penny and Tom along, and organize a private safari in August for the six of us through some of the best parts of Kenya and Tanzania. Such a splendid time! David and I re-lived a number of our wonderful 1977 experiences, and the kids all got to see many new areas and creatures. For the two from the U.S., it was a whole new continent, and even for our two African "natives", there were new experiences galore, plus the fun of all of us being together as adults in an exciting part of the world.

Our U.S. contingent of Penny, Tom, my husband, and I had a return home that we'll never forget. We left Nairobi on an Alitalia plane that had experienced some problems on the ground prior to take-off, but take off we finally did. Pre-dawn in the air, we were awakened by a somewhat alarming "thud", followed by an announcement (in Italian) saying something about "problems". It turned out we were over Khartoum, Sudan (where Alitalia had no landing privileges), but the pilot evidently made it clear that this was an emergency, with an engine out, and that we were coming in to land. We landed without mishap and were relieved to be on the ground, whatever happened next.

The first hour went by, and now it was light enough to see. There were a few ponds near the runway where our plane was parked, and I was delighted to find my lifer Abdim's Stork—a fine view with binoculars from the plane window. We were not to be allowed off the plane, unfortunately. Hours passed, and by now even I was tired of the Abdim's Stork. We'd seen the movies, consumed all the food and drink, and should long since have been in Rome. We had on board with us a boys' band from Nairobi, which (un)fortunately had at least most of their instruments in the overhead bins, so once the movies were done, we were subjected to periodic bursts of live entertainment. The rare announcements (all in Italian) gave little information, but some of the first-class passengers who spoke English conversed with the captain and brought periodic updates back to us. More hours passed, and the toilets were becoming unspeakable. Fortunately, there was at least a semblance of air-conditioning, or at least air movement—but no more food or drink. There was talk of collecting our passports— for no good reason. It was becoming somewhat alarming, and we even began to think perhaps we were actually being hijacked and just hadn't been told yet. It was unclear whether the plane was being repaired, or whether there was some other plan. After 12 hours on the ground, we were given the information that they were flying another plane from Rome to pick us up, and after two more hours it actually arrived. With enormous relief, we piled out of our defunct aircraft into a bus and then onto the most welcome relief plane, which took off shortly thereafter. At last we could relax, have a drink and dinner, and leave the problems of our missed connections to Alitalia. Alas, we had not reckoned with the planning ability of the airline. They had sent the relief plane without any provisions at all. No food, no beverages. Presumably there was fuel?

Just a month later I returned to Africa, but this time farther south, to Zimbabwe and Botswana, in pursuit of special birds like Swynnerton's Robin, Pel's Fishing-Owl, and White-backed Night-Heron. The end of this trip coincided nicely with the beginning of one to Madagascar, so I planned to join that flight in Nairobi and try to pick up some of the important species we'd missed on the first Madagascar trip, like ground-rollers and, inexplicably, even Cuckoo Roller. I did see Cuckoo Rollers this time but returned to Nairobi still ground-roller-less.

Because my two daughters were still in Kenya, and because I had a time period between this Madagascar trip and a private one to Zambia in October, I'd decided to hire a car and driver and visit each of my girls on their home turf. I had simply made Nairobi my home base that fall and from there made an excursion to the NOLS base at Naro Moru, where I lived in Carol's hut and ate

ugali with her friends but unfortunately missed seeing her because she was off in the wilderness somewhere, and we hadn't
been able to coordinate times.

It was a long two-day drive from Naro Moru to Chwele in
western Kenya, but at least I knew Sue would be there at her
school. She came racing across the campus to meet me when she
saw the car drive up, and we had a splendid few days together.
Among the several things we did was visit Kitum Cave on Mt.
Elgon, where there were supposed to be forest elephants. We saw
none, and learned many years later upon reading Richard Pre-
ston's *The Hot Zone* that this site was apparently the source of in-
fection for a gruesome and fatal case of ebola. We also spent a
weekend in Kakamega Forest, where I was able to wander along
the grid of trails with my tape recorder and really enjoy the forest
birding at leisure.

I went back to Nairobi, then off to Zambia, where Bill and Harriet Davidson, friends from Michigan, were joining me for a trip
I'd arranged privately with Bob Stjernstedt. I didn't know Bob, but
the leader on our Zimbabwe trip had put me in touch and
vouched for his abilities. Bob was working with a local safari out-
fitter, who was theoretically providing our vehicle and driver, as
well as full camping facilities and support staff, who were to pre-
cede us everywhere and have our facilities set up when we arrived.

It all sounded very organized and promising, but logistics
began to fall apart on day one and never really got any better—
indeed sometimes they got considerably worse. On the positive
side, Bob Stjernstedt was an auditory genius in a class with Ted
Parker. He knew virtually every song and call from every species
in Zambia but had only cumbersome and malfunctioning taping

equipment. Fortunately, I'd brought my Sony 5000 and Sennheiser mike, so I simply turned that equipment over to him, and he managed it beautifully. For birding, we were in good hands. For camping and eating, we were on our own. The safari outfit was a disaster. They were always a full day or so *behind* us due to constant vehicle breakdowns, so they were doing us no good at all. At one point when we did encounter them, we simply took some basic survival equipment and food and carried it in our own vehicle. We slept out a lot and ate so much rice and pineapple (available from roadside stands) that it was a long time before I could face either one.

Our primary target in this whole Zambia undertaking was to get to the Bangweulu Swamp, where there was an excellent chance of seeing a Shoebill. This grotesque and ungainly creature (now thought to be allied to pelicans) has such charisma and such a reputation for living in inaccessible papyrus swamps that it has always been something of a "holy grail" for birders.

Well, we were on our way. The Bangweulu is a long way from anywhere, on poor dirt roads, but we had a Land Rover and a willing driver, and Bob knew where to go. We even had some basic food rations for the day, and there was supposed to be a rudimentary place to stay. Things were looking quite hopeful—until the front wheel came off the Land Rover and rolled along into the ditch, where the vehicle itself promptly joined it. Of necessity, we'd been going slowly, so no one was hurt—but the vehicle seemed terminal. Something major and irreparable, like an axle, had simply snapped. We'd been having constant daily problems to sort out, but this one really seemed totally insurmountable for the time being.

We were on the outskirts of a very simple village, inhabited by

sullen, unfriendly, and unhelpful natives. There was *zero* car traf-
fic on this road, and the Bangweulu Swamp was still many miles
ahead—way too far to contemplate walking the next day in the
sun and heat. It was now late afternoon, and clearly we would
just have to spend the night here on the roadside and face to-
morrow when it came. Meanwhile, we were stopped at the edge
of a large reed bed, and a bird was sitting up on a stalk—Marsh
Tchagra—a lifer! (Like the Abdim's Stork after the forced landing
at Khartoum, here at least was a slight silver lining).

Shortly afterward, a glimmer of an idea arose in all of us when
we saw a man on a bicycle ride into the village near dusk. Our
driver could speak the local dialect, so he went to talk to the villagers about the bicycle. Man and bike had simply disappeared,
and everyone absolutely denied any knowledge of any bicycle in
the whole region. They simply were not going to help. The only
thing for us to do was to try to get some sleep and be there on the
road before first light, in case the "non-existent" bicycle-rider appeared again. It was a very long and restless night. Bill Davidson
had a bad back, and Bob was suffering from recurrent malaria at-
tacks, so we let them have the two seats in the car, and Harriet,
the driver and I slept on the ground. We felt pretty vulnerable,
but at least the villagers weren't hostile, just totally indifferent.

We were all standing in the road over the bicycle tracks before
6 a.m., when the rider materialized on his bicycle, carrying a large
bunch of bananas. He was off to sell them and couldn't possibly
let us use his bicycle. Thanks to our driver's ability to communicate, we eventually just made him an offer for bike, bananas, and
all that he couldn't refuse. It was a major fortune—about $50—
and he walked off with a grin. We ate some bananas and then put
Bob on the bike with a supply of bananas and water and started

him off toward the Bangweulu for help, since he was the only one who knew how to get there, and there were a number of turnings ahead.

The rest of us spent a long and worrisome day, watching the Marsh Tchagra, eating bananas, and trying to nap and remain cheerful. It was tremendously frustrating to be this close to my most-wanted bird in the world and be unable to get there. Afternoon came, and we heard a car coming. Whomever it was, we certainly had to stop them, so we all stood in the middle of the road. It was another Land Rover, and Stjernstedt was driving it! He'd gotten to the Bangweulu and located a safari camp that was still open this late in the fishing season, and they'd actually been willing to lend him their vehicle until we could sort our situation out. It was just too good to be true. Jubilation reigned.

The rest was almost anticlimactic. We got there, I scanned the papyrus edge with the scope, and there one was: a Shoebill, just as advertised, with all those absurd characteristics that give this bird such appeal, like the tuft on the back of its head and the built-in smile on that grotesque bill. We spent hours watching several Shoebills, even taking a boat along a waterway through the papyrus. It was an evening of celebration, and we all slept happily that night—*not* on the ground!

Our Zambian adventures (and mis-adventures) were legion. We routinely got ourselves lost in the featureless miombo woodland, where the sun always seemed to be overhead and where before we knew it Stjernstedt would be off after an interesting bird sound without paying any attention to direction. He turned out to have an even worse sense of direction than mine and once admitted to having lost his green Land Rover in a forest for two days before he finally stumbled back on where he'd parked it. Our as-

Shoebill

tute driver saved us from such a possibility, however. After an hour or two had passed and we hadn't reappeared, he'd honk the horn a few times to give us a bearing.

This driver also performed a very impressive feat of tracking. Harriet's umbrella had accidentally slipped off her belt during one of our lengthy and convoluted woodland excursions, and when we got back to the car, she remarked that she'd lost it. No problem, the driver assured us—he could find it. We simply indicated where we had gone into the woods, and from there on he accurately re-traced our footsteps (totally invisible to us) over the dry ground, showed us where we had paused or sat for a while, and eventually of course came upon the lost umbrella, whereupon he turned and strode in a direct line back to the car. It was totally uncanny, and absolutely beyond the abilities of any of us!

Offsetting such major and minor problems, we found a staggering number of really special birds, such as Thick-billed Cuckoo, Boehm's Bee-eater, Pale-billed Hornbill, Blue Swallow, Bocage's and Sharpe's Akalats, Fuelleborn's Longclaw, Souza's Shrike, Anchieta's Sunbird, Bar-winged Weaver, and Locustfinch. A major highlight for me was having an African Pitta (doubtless on migration back to its breeding grounds in the Zambezi Valley) fly in and perch over my head for a splendid view one late afternoon when I was on a solo excursion along a streambed to try for a better view of an incredibly boring Gray-olive Greenbul.

From September to December of that year, Nairobi had been my base for all these varied African excursions. I knew that when Nairobi began to seem like home, it was certainly time to return to the U.S.A. Africa had really gotten into my blood, however, and I returned yet again at the end of December for a Christmas-New Year's trip with a British group to Tanzania and Rwanda, giving me my first opportunity to see gorillas. Of course, the major purpose of the trip for me was birds, with scarcely an advance thought about gorillas—so I was quite overwhelmed to find the most truly magical hour of the trip was spent in the gentle company of a family group of these totally captivating primates. The impact of a close encounter with one's forest kin was unexpectedly mind-bending, and a wonderful way to begin the year of 1989.

Phoebe in Cameroon, August 1987

~11~
Breaking 6,000

1 989 was to be a year of several repeat locations as well as some new
adventures. There had been some substantial taxonomic changes, mostly
splits, in the avifauna of Ecuador since I had last been there, and
birders were also now regularly seeing species that had been
deemed impossible when I was there nine years before. Much of
this surge in findable species was due to the vastly increased
awareness of bird vocalizations, and the growing use of tape
recorders and development of skills and techniques for using
them effectively. Clearly, it was time to do Ecuador again, and I
selected a comprehensive trip led by two of my favorite and most
skilled leaders, John and Rose Ann Rowlett.

I was not far short of 6,000 at the beginning of the trip, so
reaching that milestone was a virtual certainty. It was not a very
dramatic bird, that first Olive-chested Flycatcher, but it had the
distinction, at least, of also being a lifer for both very experienced
leaders. No one had yet broken 7,000, so I was currently in the
rather exclusive "highest thousand" club with about five others,
all men. And it was going to be a long, hard haul to the next milestone—too far even to envision at this point.

I'd done some foreign traveling with British and European
birders by now, but I'd seen almost nothing of the avifauna most
familiar to them, aside from the handful of the most obvious birds

Olive-chested Flycatcher

that I'd tracked down in early travels with my husband to Britain and Europe. It was time to take on this part of the world more seriously. The resolution lay in a comprehensive coverage of Spain with Tom Gullick, followed by a clean up run around Britain with David Fisher and a birding friend from home. By then, I was subscribing to *British Birds*, and the whole scene across the Atlantic was now beginning to take on much more meaning. More far-flung areas of the Western Palearctic would have to wait, but at least I'd now seen Audouin's and Mediterranean Gulls and could tell a Song Thrush from a Mistle Thrush.

The major adventure of the year was to be Mongolia-Siberia in June with Birdquest, a major tour agency out of Britain. As much as any place, the Gobi Desert had always symbolized remoteness in my mind. And I was actually now planning to go there, in itself exciting, besides which the bird possibilities looked pretty intriguing. Numerically, I could do much better in the tropics, but 7,000 seemed impossibly far off, and how else could I even hope to see Relict Gull, Henderson's Ground-Jay [Mongolian Ground-Jay], or Pallas's Sandgrouse?

All in all, it was quite an incredible journey. It turned out that there had been a prolonged serious drought in the Gobi (!), with the result that the "stakeout" lake for Relict Gulls had simply dried up, and the gulls had sensibly departed for other places (known only to them). The only solution seemed to lie in seeking out other lakes, the existence and possible locations of which were entirely unknown to us. Imaginative leadership took control, and we set out in our bus across the Gobi, asking the occasional tribesman along the way where there might be a body of water. Our excursion took several days, basically cross-desert, where we slept in tents and ate amazingly delicious meals served on a blanket on the ground by our competent cook.

In the end, astonishingly, we *did* come to a substantial body of water previously unknown to the birding world, and as expected, here was a thriving colony of Relict Gulls, giving lovely views for all. It sounds so simple, really—but just imagine the responsibility taken on by the leaders under the given circumstances!

The other avian targets also, by and large, fell into place. In addition to the desert excursion, we went into the Altai Mountains, took a spur of the Orient Express to Ulan-Ude (east of Lake Baikal), and then flew to Khabarovsk and went by boat up the Amur River in eastern Siberia, birding everywhere along the way, of course. This area was a totally new (and vast) section of the world for me and quite unlike anything I had ever experienced before. I only added about thirty new species to my list, but they were of exceptional quality and mostly ones I've never seen (nor expect to see) again.

The timing of the trip, with a return home on June 18th through Moscow and London, had by extraordinary good fortune narrowly averted a major family crisis. My mother had told me in the spring that the new Leo Burnett Building in Chicago, the new home of my father's eponymous advertising agency, was to be dedicated officially in June. "Gosh, Mom, I'm going to Mongolia and Siberia in June." "You *can't*. You just *have* to be there for the dedication of your father's building—but I'm not sure of the date." "Well, I'll be there if I can—but I *am* going on this Mongolia trip." Our good-byes were strained; our stands were firm. Some days later she called to say the dedication date had been set—and we both held our breaths: June 20th. Thank God. "I'll be there," I promised with profound relief. In the meantime, I'd been investigating ways of flying from Moscow direct to Chicago if necessary, but there was just no way it could be done from Mongolia or eastern Siberia.

The dedication was one of the great events of my mother's life, and my two brothers and I with assorted spouses and children were present for the ceremony and festivities. I think I won the award for having come the longest distance.

Another repeat trip was coming up. I was returning for the second time to the wilderness of Manu, Peru, a place for which not even the twentieth return would be enough. Then a new trip to the Lesser Sunda Islands of Timor, Flores, and Sumba (producing fifty new species for me) would finish the summer, leaving returns to southeast Brazil and Argentina for the fall. Much of northern Argentina was new to me, since I'd not gotten into the chaco before, and consequently, the many avian specialties of that region had eluded me. I wound up 1989 with nearly 6,300 species, so I was continuing to soar right along.

~12~

A New Decade

T he decade of the 1990s was to bring a number of significant changes to my life. As usual, it began with more exciting birds and another trip—this

time to Iquitos, Peru with Ted Parker. We flew from Miami on Faucett Airlines, ostensibly direct to Iquitos, but lost a day on either end because Faucett (which rapidly surpassed even Alitalia as my least-favorite airline) simply lied about their routing. Traditionally (I found out on the way down) the pilot waggles the wings a bit over Iquitos, announces that it's too stormy to land, and goes on to Lima—which he knew he was going to do right from the start. The return flight, which the printed schedule says will pick up passengers in Iquitos, fills with passengers in Lima, so of course they never even intend to stop in Iquitos. This kind of time loss on a short trip was very frustrating, so I suspected correctly that I might have to try this destination again in the future. Once finally in the field, however, Ted worked his usual magic, and we connected with some great Amazonian birds, including all the river island specialties and forest denizens, like Black-necked Red-Cotinga and White-chested Puffbird. We were also privileged to see the new *Tolmomyias* flycatcher ("Orange-eyed"), discovered by Ted in this area a few years before and officially described and named only in 1997.

My friends Bob and Myra Braden, whom I'd met on the

Antarctica cruise, were keen to bird in Japan, so we joined forces for a private excursion in February with Mark Brazil and saw the best of winter Japan, including my last alcid—Japanese Murrelet—from the Hokkaido Ferry, a wonderful spectacle of Steller's Sea-Eagles in the north, and all the wintering cranes in the south. From there we flew on to Taiwan, where we managed to connect with most of the endemics, with the exception of Mikado Pheasant.

After finally having come to grips with most of Britain and Western Europe, the farther outposts of the Western Palearctic were beginning to lure me. I signed on for a Sunbird trip to Israel in April, which covered the migration scene at Eilat as well as the Negev Desert and specialties in the north at the Hula Reserve and Mt. Hermon. This is often one of the first foreign trips taken by a British birdwatcher, and it was fun to share the wonder and excitement on this level once again.

May was devoted to a long-planned return attempt at mainland China, after my previous try in 1988 had to be aborted in favor of an emergency hysterectomy. This time it was to be Ben King's West China trip (Sichuan and the Tibetan Plateau), and once again we spent a few days birding in Hong Kong before flying to Chengdu. Despite having connected with a beauty in 1988 on my one day at Mai Po, Spoonbill Sandpiper hadn't exactly become a bore (could it ever?) —so it was a tremendous pleasure to renew my acquaintance with this utterly captivating little wader, as well as with Nordmann's Greenshank and all the other glorious red, orange, and black breeding-plumage waders that form such a spectacle here at this season.

China was indeed incredible. Somehow, Ben managed to produce all possible pheasants (eight of them) for all ten participants—truly his forte. It's hard to pick a favorite among Golden, Blood, Temminck's Tragopan, Chinese Monal, and the two eared-pheasants, so I won't even try. Black-necked Cranes on the Tibetan Plateau were my last of this family and left me with some unexpectedly ambivalent feelings—triumph at having finally seen them all, yet sadness that there were now no more left to look for.

Snow Pigeon, Tibetan Snowcock, Tibetan Partridge, Monal-Partridge, Wood Snipe, Tibetan Ground-Jay, Grandala, various robins, redstarts, laughing-thrushes, warblers, rosefinches, and buntings all fell marvelously well into place. It was also physically strenuous, cold—often miserably so—and with the most primitive and filthy accommodations I'd stayed in yet. To offset some of the hardship, there was plenty of very good food, as well as excellent company with which to enjoy these many splendid birds—and that, we had occasionally to remind ourselves, was really why we had come and why we were paying to do all this suffering. As (almost) always, it was well worth it in the end.

The summer of 1990 brought considerable trauma back into what had been, for a few blessed years, a smoothly ongoing series of birding adventures. My 96-year-old mother, living in a retirement home in suburban Chicago, fell and broke her hip and leg badly. She was hospitalized and had to be operated on. I drove up to be with her. Complications arose, she was in a lot of pain, and for the first time in my life I was confronting an inflexible and exasperating medical world that "knew best" how to treat her—subjecting her to useless and painful tests, refusing to give more potent pain medication "for fear of addiction", etc. I was stymied, frustrated, and miserable, and felt able to give precious little genuine comfort and assistance to my suffering and dying mother.

My father had died 18 years before at age 79 of a sudden and fatal heart attack one evening at home, after dinner and a full day at the office, and I kept wishing it could be that easy for my mother. The experience reinforced my already-formed resolve to do whatever I could to keep my own living and dying somehow under my control as far as humanly possible.

Both my brothers were traveling at this time, and ironically, Joe, who virtually never leaves Chicago, was in Asia with his sons, while I was home—a totally unforeseen role-reversal. My oldest brother Pete had by now returned from his U.S. trip, so knowing that Pete was due any time and that mother seemed temporarily stable, I told her once more I loved her and left for home, having been with her for a week—and sensing that this was a final good-bye. I'd left her so many times in her advancing years, when I thought it was likely she might die before I returned from a trip, that the pang in my heart was quite familiar. I was scheduled to leave in just two days' time for a prolonged trip to Australia and New Guinea, and my emotions were in chaos. On my drive home, I adjusted the seat belt reaching across my chest, and inadvertently rubbed a spot near my right armpit. "God almighty, there's a LUMP, and it's in the same location as my previous melanomas!" There was no doubt in my mind, not even a glimmer of hope to the contrary, that this represented another melanoma recurrence, and it hit my psyche like a bombshell.

Dilemma, trauma, emotional chaos. At least I got home without having an accident. Pete called to say it was over. He'd been with Mother for a while, and he was with her when she died. I said nothing about the lump, either to Pete or to my husband. I needed options. I was grieving, terribly afraid, and wanting above all else to flee the cloud of distressing emotions enveloping me.

The reasonable, adult course of action (which my mother would have advised), was to cancel my travel plans, go back to Chicago for her funeral, and then go immediately into the hospital for surgery and tests.

I did none of these things; I fled to Australia instead. I saw a Southern Cassowary, immersed myself totally in a wonderful birding trip across the top of the continent—and watched the lump grow. I went on to PNG, and on to Fiji after that, scooping up numerous high-priority species that I'd missed on previous trips, like Palm Cockatoo, Marbled Frogmouth, Red-breasted Paradise-Kingfisher, Painted Quail-thrush, Flame Bowerbird, four more birds-of-paradise, and finally Orange Dove on Fiji. I connected with my 6,500th species (Large Fig-Parrot) while in PNG that summer.

Through it all ran an undercurrent of serious concern. My lump had grown during these six weeks from the initial barely palpable hardness beneath the skin to an obvious swelling. Had I made a stupid choice, trading immediate lifers for years of living? My rational justification (strongly influenced by emotions and desires) for my choice of actions after my mother's death ran as follows: "Starting with the original superficial melanoma on my back, this lump represents the third recurrence. *No one* has that many recurrences, because death has usually long since intervened. Chances are, if I can feel a lump, there has already been some spread to internal organs, in which case my time of health is probably limited to a few months. *Now* may well be my final opportunity to go birding on a foreign trip, and I can't just throw that away. If it's my last trip, so be it—but I'm going to make it a good one and go down binoculars in hand!"

Upon returning home, I told my husband the whole background, and went with fear and trepidation to see my doctor. I told him about finding the lump and making the panic-stricken and probably stupid decision to travel to the other side of the world for six weeks. He took this confession all in, calmly and silently, then looked long and seriously at me and said: "I probably would have done the same thing." I could have kissed him. Whatever was to happen now, at least an informed professional had told me that he understood and accepted my decision. He had the same reaction to the new lump that he'd had back in 1981: "It has to come out immediately and be biopsied"—but I think he knew as well as I did what the test would show.

I endured surgery and scans one more time. Again, it was just short of five years since the previous recurrence; somehow, I just couldn't seem to get past that psychological five-year hurdle. And totally unbelievably, one-by-one, the reprieves came: bone scan, negative; liver scan, *negative*; brain scan, NEGATIVE! I was free to live my life—one more time!! Just in case, I'd given myself nearly two months of recuperation time, and after that had tentatively planned an ambitious undertaking of yet another Australian trip, quite a comprehensive circuit including Tasmania, followed by a return visit to New Zealand, followed by a cruise through the New Zealand subantarctic islands and Australia's Macquarie Island, and ending up back in Tasmania shortly before Christmas.

Our youngest daughter Sue was then doing a volunteer study on the Palila, one of the Hawaiian honeycreepers on the Big Island. Carol and Tom were both living on the west coast and were interested in possible Hawaiian job opportunities plus a visit to their sister, and it was easy to encourage Penny on the east coast and my husband to join forces and all meet in the Honolulu airport, where I would be arriving from Tasmania a day or so before Christmas.

It all worked. I recovered fully from the surgery in the allotted time, added something like 75 species from Australia, Tasmania, New Zealand, and the cruise, made some fine new friends, and renewed a lot of old acquaintances. It was the year of the International Ornithological Congress (IOC) meetings in New Zealand, and birders of all ilks and from literally everywhere were scattered over New Zealand or were assembled on the cruise ship that December. Such fun! I met several friends on a British tour at the base of Mt. Cook, companions from Malaysia while watching Royal Albatrosses, and numerous friends and acquaintances from the U.S., Africa, Europe, and Australia on shipboard.

My whole family had assembled in Honolulu, so we had a grand reunion at the inter-island terminal and immediately flew to Hilo on the Big Island. This area was new turf for me, my daughter was the "resident expert", and everyone joined forces to find me Iiwis, Ios [Hawaiian Hawks], Omaos, etc.—and of course Palilas. We found a lovely place for dinner on Christmas Day, did some fabulous snorkeling on the dry side of the island, watched lava flowing into the sea at night, and hiked across the lava fields of the crater floor in Volcanoes National Park. Life seemed almost too good to be true. Despite my worst fears of summer and fall, I was healthy and happy and ready to take on more birds and adventures at the end of 1990.

I had planned four major trips for the first half of 1991. I went first to southern India, which turned out to be my favorite part of that country, and on to the Andaman Islands (politically part of India, but ornithologically and geographically more closely related to Southeast Asia) where we found several of the endemics—but disappointingly missed a few others.

Next was Cuba—according to the U.S. State Deptartment officially off limits for Americans—but since the Canadians from
Long Point Bird Observatory had been running one-week birding
trips there for years and had a harmonious relationship with
Cuba's government, it was possible to join them by going through
Toronto. The birding in Cuba was really marvelous. We birded
the Bay of Pigs area, the Zapata Swamp, and the pine forests outside of Havana, finding a great many of the really special endemics, including four quail-doves (the fanciest being the unforgettable Blue-headed), Cuban Trogon with its extraordinary tail
structure, two owls (Stygian wouldn't cooperate), the famously
tiny Bee Hummingbird, endemic woodpeckers, warblers, etc.,
and the Zapata Swamp specialties, with the exception of the Zapata Rail. It was a very exciting week. I'd asked the Cubans not to
stamp my passport and so got back into the U.S. with no questions asked.

April meant a return to Thailand, this time including the
peninsula that reaches south toward Malaya and holds a chance
for some exceptional birds, such as Gurney's Pitta and Masked
Finfoot. Down here we stayed in the wooden buildings near the
forest patch where this jewel of a pitta had been re-discovered a
few years before. Attractions (other than avian ones) included a
marvelous swimming hole and some of the best and most varied
meals I've ever eaten, produced by the local village women and
all seemingly created from one black pot suspended over an
open fire.

The first afternoon, our small group heard a Gurney's Pitta
calling reasonably close, but it was early in the season, and it
seemed unresponsive to tape. Two of us decided to stalk the bird

instead of continuing on. The pitta led us on a merry chase, luring us like a will-o-the-wisp ever on through the forest and staying tantalizingly just out of sight over the next rise or past the next trees. It was getting late in the afternoon, and we were running some risk of getting lost at this point—but the bird continued to call, and I just couldn't resist it. Crawling to the top of the next rise, I lifted my head to peer down the slope—and there it was, a psychedelic blue, gold, and black male Gurney's Pitta, standing in the last shaft of sunlight of the day and throwing its head back in "song". It wasn't long before it saw me and hopped away into the undergrowth, but I'd had a simply marvelous binocular view that will stay with me as long as I live. I'd really come back to Thailand for that bird alone—but as long as I was here....

Yes, we did find some other great birds as well, and one of the most memorable was the Masked Finfoot in the mangroves at Krabi. We took two slow boats at low tide up the convoluted mangrove-lined channels for what seemed like agonizing hours, until the lead boatman finally stopped and pointed at a bush well up the muddy bank. Nothing was there. He insisted, and we all looked again, peering deep into the shade at the base. Still nothing—but what was that yellow spot? Further long scrutiny revealed that the yellow spot was part of a bill—attached to a black face—attached to a long neck and body! The boatman had been watching the muddy banks left by the falling tide for finfoot tracks leading into cover, and having found those, he was *sure* the bird was there. Once its cover was blown, so to speak, the finfoot stood up, walked slowly down the bank into the water and had a leisurely swim upstream, with two boatloads of entranced birders watching every move it made.

A significant change of pace came next, in the form of a trip to Central Asia. The numerous states in Turkestan and the Caucasus were at that time still all parts of the U.S.S.R. Logistically, we were in the hands of Intourist and Aeroflot, both decidedly no-frills operations. Despite the dreariness of ever-present cucumbers, hard bread, and bottled carbonated water, we managed to survive mealtimes and got to our many far-flung destinations safely and amazingly on time. Good birds were legion. The Caucasus gave us the stunning local versions of Black Grouse and snowcock, but the real Central Asian specialties lay beyond the Caspian—along the route of the ancient Silk Road, on the slopes of the Tien Shan range and on the steppes and lakes of Kazakhstan near Tselinograd.

The highlight of the trip for me and most others, I think, came in the form of a mystery bird that kept intruding during our pursuit of a Rufous-tailed Scrub-Robin through the bushes in the desert reserve of Repetek, near the Afghanistan border. Finally the scrub-robin simply got away, and with nothing much else to do, we began to look at this dull, gray-brown, medium-sized bird, which persisted in revealing only bits and pieces of itself. At one point it stuck its head out of a bush—and I hadn't a clue as to its identity, nor did our leader. It had a slight crest, a stubby gray bill, and a large dark eye—and not much else, even as it emerged more and more fully into the open, still persisting in being just featureless dull gray-brown. Finally the tail began to emerge—and continued to emerge—until it got to the broad black tip at the very end, at which point both the leader and I recognized it for what it was—a female Hypocolius, almost unheard-of in this region, and a lifer for all! Since the species breeds in Iraq and winters on the Arabian Peninsula (regular flocks occur in Bahrain in the winter), this most fortuitous event was going to save me a great deal of time, trouble, and expense in trying to come to grips with what is usually considered a monotypic family.

Hypocolius

~13~
The New Taxonomy

S ibley and Monroe's monumental
tome Distribution and Taxonomy of
Birds of the World *was published at the
end of 1990, in time for the New Zealand*

IOC meetings, but I didn't get my copy—or at least have a chance to peruse it—till June 1991. This book (and its companion volume, *Phylogeny and Classification of Birds* by Sibley and Ahlquist) rocked the very foundations of conventional taxonomy by approaching specific questions of what is related to what through DNA analysis in the laboratory. Not only was the conventional taxonomic order we were all used to turned somewhat topsy-turvy, but also there were hundreds of new species created as a result of splitting many forms that had previously been considered merely "races" of a given species. Thus, many previously-lumped forms that are morphologically, distributionally, and often behaviorally or vocally quite distinct were given full species status, such as the two forms of Carmine Bee-eater. Overnight, the total list of birds of the world jumped from around 9,200 to nearly 9,700. The same essential list (with only minor differences and with a more conventional taxonomic order) appears in the fourth edition of Clements' world checklist, published in 1991. Since Clements' checklist soon became the ABA "official world list", this new taxonomy turned out to be a major bonanza for listers.

I spent much of that summer going through Sibley and Monroe, species by species, and found it absolutely fascinating. I could hardly put it down; I'd even wake at night, thinking of something I wanted to look up, and get up out of bed to find the answer before I forgot the question. At this time, I realized the value of my card-file record-keeping system. Other world listers were telling me they couldn't figure out what birds they'd gained, if any, because they hadn't kept notations on possible subsequent sightings of a species once they'd recorded it as a lifer. If they'd seen a Rufous-tailed Antthrush in southeast Brazil, for example, and then ignored it in Venezuela, or didn't bother to indicate somewhere on their records that they'd seen it, then they would have no awareness that they'd seen (or maybe missed) what has now become Schwartz's (or Scalloped) Antthrush, which was formerly considered to be just the northern race of Rufous-tailed. Similar cases abound. In each case my index card for any given species told me at a glance every place in the world I had seen that bird—and so for virtually every change in Sibley and Monroe, I could determine from the range descriptions and my card whether I'd gained a new species from a split or lost one through a lump. There was just a handful of seemingly ambiguous situations, which I had to clarify by asking a regional expert, usually the leader I was with when we saw the species in question. I had a net gain of close to 150 species simply by doing all this thoroughly fascinating book work, and I found the whole exercise a most pleasurable review of all the birds I'd ever seen.

Controversy rages (and always will) over the DNA approach and the classification it seems to indicate, as well as over specifics in regard to splitting or lumping a given form, and indeed over fundamentals like the basic definition of a "species", i.e., whether a phylogenetic or biological species concept is used. There was a single supplement to the original Sibley and Monroe, and these changes are incorporated in the very convenient *A World Checklist of Birds* by Monroe and Sibley (1993), published before Monroe's untimely death in 1994. More recently, a new version by Sibley (*Birds of the World*) has become available on computer disc only. The 1996 (2.0) version discusses close to 10,000 species.

One of the major controversial issues in all attempts at achieving a standardized list is the sticky question of English names. Many English names used in the original Sibley and Monroe stirred emotions and raised hackles abroad as well as in the U.S. The arguments are endless and ongoing. As much as the taxonomy itself—and far more than the choice of scientific name—the English name questions stir regional and cultural prejudices and emotions, often precluding rational discussion or resolution. The situation is complicated by the on-going splitting, which of course requires new English names for each split form. I would certainly hope to see a single, generally-accepted and widely-used standardized world list for birders in my lifetime—but it won't be quickly, easily, or painlessly achieved, and as long as splitting remains a dominant factor, it would seem to be basically unachievable.

What to do about my own world life list had, in the meantime, become something of a vexing problem. At the end of my record-breaking year of 1995, I submitted my last official (i.e. "Clements' Checklist") raw number total of 8,040 species to the ABA and *The Guinness Book of World Records*. At that point I wanted to back off from competitive listing and devise some kind of recording and listing scheme that would be personally more satisfying to me.

Sibley's computer software program intrigued me mightily, but I knew I had to master the rudiments of basic computer literacy in order to be able even to read it. Bit by bit, thanks to my husband's willing and patient help, I managed to do it and finally to get the 1994 version of Sibley's *Birds of the World* installed and into a form where I could annotate or alter it. After many experimental attempts with the accounts of a number of species, it became clear what I wanted to do and how I would approach it, but by this time I knew that an updated version (2.0) was due out in 1996, so it made sense to wait. Once I started on this new version in late 1996, working on it became a consuming passion during my periods at home for nearly a year. I added my own annotations, comments, and opinions from other sources, and where Sibley's taxonomy seemed either outdated or inappropriate in light of other publications, I simply changed it, citing reasons and sources. I ended up about a year later, having done some of my own lumping and splitting, with 10,024 "species" (as opposed to Sibley's 9,946). And by the end of 1998, after Sibley's death, the numerous publications I've read and incorporated have led me to increase that base list to a total of 10,187 "species". Keeping current with all of these changes, adding new information or new species to my now massive base list (hard copy is well over twelve hundred pages), which happens nearly every time I read a serious birding or ornithological journal these days, is a never-ending but invariably challenging, tremendously rewarding and satisfying task, simply because I've become aware of something I didn't know before.

My feeling for a number of years has been that I learn a great deal more—and keep better track of what I'm seeing—when I use a base list that expresses more diversity and that is more broadly and explicitly inclusive of distinctive or disjunct forms, than I do when I use a list that lumps many of these forms without recognition or comment. So I'm very pleased with my present highly-detailed and constantly-changing base list, which reflects the on-going taxonomic explosion and keeps my knowledge and information current. I'm also continually adapting my card file and revising my copy of Monroe's 1993 checklist, so that they both accurately reflect what is in my computer master list. Fortunately, little has changed with the Sibley sequence of families and species, so that small 1993 volume continues to be an extraordinarily useful index.

As far as listing the birds I've actually seen, I've checked them off on the hard copy of my base list, and I keep a running tally. This 8,500+ total (as of late December 1998) is my life list or numerator, while my nearly 10,200 base list is the denominator, currently yielding a figure of 84 percent. Such a figure, expressing the percentage of "what's out there" that I *have* seen (and simultaneously the percentage I've *not* seen), seems to me a considerably more meaningful way to express one's overall birding experience than does any "raw number" figure.

Expanding on this concept, it seems apparent that anyone's total can be easily expressed as a percentage of whatever base list they choose to use, and that such *percentages* (rather than raw numbers) would form a reasonable and meaningful basis for comparison and competition. If any approach to listing levels the playing field to accommodate those many birders who deviate in some legitimate way from the "standard" Clements' list, it's this percentage method, since an individual's percentage of *any* modern list will be much the same (though raw scores of course vary widely depending on the particular base list used). As a mathematically-minded birding friend (Martin Edwards) pointed out, with a base list of around 10,000 species, percentages carried to two decimal points would express differences of as little as one species, the same degree of difference as currently in use in the ABA raw number total listing.

Taxonomy is changing so fast that it's almost impossible to keep up with, which makes percentage listing especially relevant these days. For the past many months I've found my base list (denominator) growing nearly as fast as the lifers I can add to my life list (numerator), putting me in the position of Lewis Carroll's Red Queen, running as fast as I can to stay in the same place. I'm struggling toward 85 percent, and much beyond that is clearly unrealistic for me (in my late sixties). New species for me are now simply so widely scattered across the face of this planet that I'm bumping my head against a practical ceiling in regard to increasing my percentage total. I had thought this would happen around the 8,000 point, but it didn't, and I continued to rack up significant totals in the following two years. By the end of 1998 at 84 percent, however, I've reached a definite plateau, and I strongly suspect that such a leveling out will happen to any birder who manages to struggle up to about this percentage. Hence stems my prediction that seeing 90 percent of any base list describing "what's out there" is impossible in anyone's lifetime.

Once again, for the sake of a more complete picture of taxonomic trends and how I've dealt with them, I've broken step chronologically. So back to 1991, the year in which the first, immediate effects of Sibley and Monroe impinged on competitive birding.

~14~
Toward 7,000

T he new taxonomy and all those splits had given me a significant numerical boost. That gain, combined with the major trips I'd done in the first half of 1991, brought my current total to 6,875. It was definitely possible to break 7,000, and Harvey Gilston of Switzerland, the top lister in the world since the end of 1988, did it that year—but I was closing the gap!

Late that summer I made a return trip to Malaysia, during which I was delighted finally to meet Peter Kaestner, a high world lister of impeccable reputation who was with the U.S. Embassy in Kuala Lumpur at that time. I had a Saturday free at the end of my trip, so Peter took me birding on Fraser's Hill, which resulted in a lifer for each of us (Ferruginous Partridge for me), good birding, lots of fun, and some really great conversation. He impressed me at the time not only with his obvious skills and knowledge, but also with his general birding philosophy, which includes two major tenets: "Work like hell, and be helpful to people." I'd never exactly put it into those precise words, but that certainly accurately reflected my own approach. Not only does it seem the right way to act, but it also pays off.

After the Malaysia trip, I'd arranged to meet Ben King and some others in Jakarta, where we spent a successful couple of days along the north coast of Java near Indramayu, looking for

Sunda Coucal and a few other species. But this stop was just an add-on. Our main purpose was to fly via charter plane to Christmas Island (well out in the Indian Ocean, but politically part of Australia and thus requiring a visa.).

The major attraction of our four-day sojourn was Abbott's Booby, and we spent much of our time here observing and absorbing the many fascinating aspects of this unique, primitive, and endangered sulid. The boobies streamed in toward their nesting trees in the late afternoon, coming from their feeding grounds located God-knows-where, far northwest of Christmas Island. Here at their nests, they were greeted fondly by their mates with much commotion and deep, hoarse, retching moans.

This superlative creature is without a doubt the most unusual member of its family in appearance and lifestyle. In flight, it combines aspects of some wholly unrelated birds: it is remarkably long and skinny, resembling a soaring stork with its arched body, long neck, and slightly drooped head and bill, but the wings are the long, narrow, rakish ones of an albatross. This combination of features conveys a singular impression. The first day, we all tried, unsuccessfully, to turn immature Red-footed Boobies with white bodies but blackish wings and tail into Abbott's—but once the real thing was seen, there was no mistaking it.

There were other reasons for coming all the way here, Ben's chief aim being to observe and record the endemic boobook owl [Christmas Island Hawk-Owl]. Traditionally lumped with the Moluccan boobook [Moluccan Hawk-Owl] of Halmahera because of similar barred patterning, this attractive owl called with a voice that Ben feels, after directly comparing the tapes, is qualitatively different enough from the Halmahera bird to give it species status.

Abbott's Booby

The Christmas Island birds, from the endemic imperial-pigeon [Christmas Island Imperial-Pigeon] and white-eye [Christmas Island White-eye] to the Australian Brown Goshawk, all seemed absurdly tame and easy to observe, a welcome contrast to the shy pigeons and raptors we have all encountered elsewhere. We savored the stunning beauty of the resident tropicbirds—the golden race of White-tailed, with color more intensely golden-apricot than any of us had imagined, has to be seen to be believed, and the Red-tailed, with its snowy plumage, blood-red bill, and tail wires, set off by a jet-black mask and feet, ran a close second.

Imposing and colorful crabs of several species, including a bright red one and the monstrous, multi-hued robber crabs attracted much attention, but the major non-avian event was our night spent on the beach with a three-foot-diameter green sea turtle. She emerged from the sea after midnight to haul herself up the beach above the high-tide line, laboriously dig a deep pit with her flippers, deposit 80 to 100 round, rubbery ping-pong-ball eggs, and slowly, painstakingly cover her traces with forward bulldozing and backward flipping of sand. Then, three to four hours after her initial appearance, she returned to meet the rising tide, lifted her head once toward us and her buried nest site as in farewell and disappeared in the waves. We all felt that night as though we'd given birth ourselves.

I had thought a short time beforehand that I could live happily without Christmas Island. Clearly, that was a mistaken judgment, for Christmas Island turned out to be one of the finest short excursions I've ever enjoyed.

It had been over a year since I'd added anything new in North America—so when I learned in September that there was a stake-out Eared Trogon [Eared Quetzal] in Ramsey Canyon in Southeast Arizona, I arranged a flight to Tucson. This trogon was a top priority bird and difficult to find in Mexico. It was an enjoyable hike up the beautiful canyon, and since I'd learned what the voice sounded like, finding the bird wasn't too difficult. It was a glorious male, from voice and appearance much more like a quetzal (and indeed given this name in Howell and Webb's 1995 *Field Guide to Birds of Mexico*) than a standard trogon, and I spent a long time studying and enjoying it at leisure with absolutely no one else around.

My next planned trip was to central Brazil that fall, which included some areas I'd not been to before, producing birds I hadn't yet seen, such as White-winged Nightjar, Gray-backed Tachuri, Coal-crested Finch, and some wonderful hummers, including Dot-eared Coquette and Hyacinth Visorbearer. Several maned wolves were a wonderful bonus. I went through Miami on the way down, and my timing was good. The hot line was reporting a Thick-billed Vireo on Key Biscayne, so I allowed enough time to look for that—and found it—as well as Caribbean Flamingos from the end of Snake Bight Trail for my ABA list.

In November, I joined a British tour to Mexico—which may seem a bit odd for an American, when there are so many good trips to that country run from closer to home. However, I'd done relatively little birding in Mexico, and I liked the sound of this itinerary, covering much more ground than the American tours, which are often shorter and tend to concentrate on one area. Also, on the extension to the Sierra Madre Occidental and San Blas, we would be going up the Durango Highway. This site had received so much bad press in American birding circles from some earlier robberies there, that our tours seemed to avoid it like the plague! In any case, I *very* much wanted to see Tufted Jay, as well as the many other endemics that we had a chance of finding on the main tour ranging from Chiapas to Oaxaca. I joined the tour in Mexico City, and it was all a very fine experience, including that notorious highway and its splendid Tufted Jays. That trip gave me nearly forty new species, well above my average on recent trips, and I was now fewer than 50 species short of 7,000.

The year ended with an impromptu excursion to Morocco—and probably the biggest single-species "twitch" I have ever undertaken. Anyhow, it seemed like a good idea at the time. Slender-billed Curlews, once a common wintering species in southern Europe and northern Africa, have declined to the brink of apparent extinction in the last twenty years. Little is known of the breeding area, thought to be in the Siberian taiga, which makes the species rather unusual in being an east-west migrant.

In the late 1980s, there had been winter sightings of four or five birds, then in the winter of 1990–1991 only three (one of them lame), all adults and all in one small wetland area of coastal northwest Morocco. That previous November and December, the three birds had been a virtual stakeout and quite readily findable in fields bordering the Merja Zerga wetland. But at that time I had been elsewhere, halfway around the world from Morocco, and then the Gulf War erupted. So the elusive curlews had been on my mind, and it seemed worthwhile to try to find out whether any would re-appear at the regular site this winter. It would be just possible in December to work in a quick excursion to Morocco via London to pick up a companion.

Information about the current status of birds in Morocco was not then easily obtainable, however, and as of early December my best contact in England hadn't found out any news at all. A week later he called with an enticing report: one bird was present in late October and was last seen 9 November—a month previously. But it is, after all, a wintering species and usually stays for the season. Good enough: I made plans to go. It was a bit chancy, admittedly, but not much is ever assured in this game.

Richard Schofield from Scotland hadn't seen the species either, so we made plans to meet at London Heathrow for the Royal Air Maroc flight to Tangier, where we'd arranged for a rental car. Logistics sounded good: an easy drive one hour south to a hotel, then another hour early the next morning to Merja Zerga, and two full days to search for the curlew—among several thousand other waders.

Everyone has heard of London fogs, and I've run into some, but nothing like this one. My flight from St. Louis landed in early morning fog at Gatwick with no real problem, and I made my way to Heathrow through the fog, fully expecting it to lift as the day wore on. Richard was due in from Aberdeen about 1 p.m., and our flight to Tangier wasn't until four. The wretched fog, however, thickened as time went on, and more and more "delayed" and "canceled" signs appeared on the departure board.

For some reason, Air Maroc hung in there and actually went through official check-in, but Richard had our tickets and hadn't appeared. By 6 p.m., amid ever-increasing chaos at Heathrow, Air Maroc was still talking vaguely about trying to get those passengers who had checked in as far as Paris. One couldn't check in without tickets, however, so I was helpless—and still waiting for Richard (or Godot, it seemed). At 7:30 he finally appeared, looking distraught and having spent most of the day stranded in Glasgow because of the fog at Heathrow. Just at this point, the final attempt was made by Air Maroc to round up those who had checked in to try to get them on an Air France flight *leaving* for

Paris. Now that we had tickets, we were able to squeeze into that lucky group and happily left fog-bound London behind.

We were on our way to Paris for the night and a probable flight to Tangier the next evening—24 hours behind our schedule and unable to get our rental car confirmed. By this time, the whole plan seemed less and less of a good idea. At best, even if we got a car, we'd have only one day for the search. Neither of us had ever been there, though we had a good map and information from previous years. Uncertainty reigned.

All went smoothly getting out of Paris, so we arrived in Tangier at 8:30 p.m., one day late. Richard tore out of customs and into the waiting arms of Avis, which was expecting us after all. Air Maroc, however, despite an otherwise stellar performance, had lost Richard's bag containing his wellies, tripod, and change of clothes—all unfortunately essential.

Morocco (the northwest, at least) has excellent roads, and we made our way south to Larache and a decent hotel, but since we had to leave again at 5 a.m. for Merja Zerga, it was yet another night of very little sleep, the third in a row for me. We woke to fog (the only foggy morning of the entire week, we learned later) and groped our way to Merja Zerga, where the locals were waiting. The men and boys who tend the cattle had become adept at harassing birders and generally making life miserable, extorting excessive payment to "guard the car", etc. With any luck, one Moroccan stays behind to do just that, while the rest of the horde, largely uncontrollable boys of various ages, follows along, constantly pressing in, demanding money and cigarettes (Richard had left his duty-free ones on the plane), and creating an altogether uncomfortable and highly distracting situation.

Fog persisted until 9 a.m., so we lost the prime early hours.

We covered several kilometers of good-looking habitat, trying unsuccessfully to ignore the aggressive and obnoxious locals and taking turns with our remaining scope (mine). I was wearing wellies but was still getting mucky and splashed way above my knees. Richard was slogging through the boggy fields in only his shoes and traveling pants. When the fog finally began to lift, we saw thousands of Black-tailed Godwits, some Ruffs, redshanks, Gray Plovers [Black-bellied Plovers], etc., and only the occasional ordinary Eurasian Curlew.

Noon came, but not results. We were tired, hungry (no breakfast), and psychologically exhausted from the traumas of travel and the stresses created by the following mob. It all seemed a very *bad* idea at this point—costly, unfruitful, and not even any fun. After all, our only report had been of one bird a month ago. Maybe it had gotten lonely and left, or maybe someone had even shot it. There were *thousands* of large waders (not to mention small ones) way out in the shallow lake, too far to examine. Suffice it to say that we were not sanguine about our chances of finding one bird out of the whole lot in the single afternoon we had remaining and under such stressful circumstances.

The next move (after paying off our car guardian and fleeing the mob) was lunch in the nearby town at the Cafe Milano, where a logbook is kept by visiting birders. Hope, mixed with some dismay, rose afresh. Various European birders had reported seeing one to two Slender-billed Curlews nearly every day the past week, some after lengthy searches and mostly "in the usual area" (where we had been looking). There had been a good sighting the previous morning (clear, of course), when we would have been on the spot but for the Heathrow fog.

At this point there appeared a *deus ex machina*. Hassam, the self-proclaimed local expert, who said he'd guided many birders to the Slender-billed Curlew, entered the cafe and offered to help us that afternoon. It would be "no problem", of course—except that after we had resumed our coverage, starting a few kilometers south of where we'd been in the morning, it turned out that he seldom saw the bird in the afternoon. And our return flight to London (only twice weekly) was to leave Tangier early the next morning.

Hassam was carrying my scope (he had neither optics nor boots, going barefoot instead), and shortly after setting out, he put it on a bird with much excitement and announced, "Madam, come look!" I looked and saw what was clearly an ordinary Eurasian Curlew, verified by Richard. Doubts began to surface in our minds. (Hassam certainly does know the habits and appearance of the Slender-billed Curlew and was probably in this instance, as we all have been, a victim of his own over-eagerness. In any case, he was worth any price, because he was an authority-figure in the area and knew how to keep the locals at bay. We were totally, wonderfully free and unmolested for the whole afternoon.)

We slogged on, approaching the area Richard and I had covered in the morning from the other direction. There were still thousands of godwits and only the odd single Eurasian Curlew, all now beginning in the late afternoon to move out from the marshy grass onto the mudflats in the shallow lake to roost for the night. Hope and time were fading rapidly.

Richard noticed four roosting curlews a couple of hundred yards out in the lake, heads under their wings—but one appeared rather smaller-bodied. Scope views revealed a dark-crowned bird with quite a bold eyebrow. Quick view of the bill when it took its head out briefly—*short!* Either a Whimbrel or...? Finally, we got a decent view of the entire crown for both of us—all-dark, no pale median stripe—definitely *not* a Whimbrel! And certainly not a Eurasian Curlew—it was smaller, with a short bill. The mucky-looking mud at the lake edge didn't appear very solid, but we found we actually *could* walk out. We waded out into the mud until it was over my boots tops, cutting the distance by at least half, and got close enough to see those lovely diagnostic black flank spots. The bird woke and walked around with its larger congeners, and we were able to examine all features, including the truly slender, all-black bill. *Absolutely wonderful!!* There was even a look at the contrasting wing pattern in a stretch and all too soon thereafter in flight away, to an inaccessible distance out in the lake for the night.

Then it began to rain in earnest, but no matter. We'd won the game in the end. It was a trip where virtually everything had gone wrong except for the one really important thing—so it had turned out to be a good idea after all.

Slender-billed Curlew

~15~

7,000 and Onward

F or two weeks at the very end of 1991 and into the new year I went to Darien, Panama. This excursion consisted of two one-week trips taken back-to-back,

to give me a second chance at some important species and just to make it a more thorough experience. Since it required considerable effort to go at all—a charter flight to get there, plus taking tents and camping gear—it seemed wise to extend my time in the field and maximize my opportunities. What I hadn't really envisioned was the bonus "free day" on my own when the changeover of groups was occurring.

We'd done reasonably well the first week, with fine views of nearly all of the specialties, but our half of the group had not encountered Rufous-vented Ground-Cuckoo, which was probably my main target. I wasn't really worried, however, since I still had a full week in the area. On change-over day, while the group that was leaving was packing up their tents and gear in preparation for boarding the plane that would be bringing in the next group, I was free to go off on my own, on what were by now familiar trails.

I spent a fine morning, enjoying doing my own thing and re-seeing some of the good birds that had been lifers just within that last week. I had heard the plane arrive and leave again, so I was heading back along the trail to camp, for lunch and to meet my companions for the coming week, when some sound or move-

ment up the forested slope must have caught my eye. I focused
on a hole in the vegetation and saw a large, dark eye peering back
at me, then a brown face and a flat bronzy crest, and finally a huge
greenish bill. It didn't take long to work out views of the rest of
the superb Rufous-vented Ground-Cuckoo, which was staying
quite concealed but largely ignoring me. I watched until it finally
disappeared up the slope, and then I headed back to camp on a
cloud of euphoria.

Rufus-vented Ground-Cuckoo

This exuberant mood was slightly dampened on my return to camp. The incoming leader had met a friend of mine from home on the flight to Panama City, who told him to be sure to tell me that there was at that very moment an adult Ross's Gull in St. Louis, about a half-hour drive from my home. Fortunately, I'd seen this gull very well in Churchill, but still, here was one virtually in my own backyard! I was three days too late by the time I finally got home. It was a very pink winter adult; I've seen all the photos and videos and heard all the stories. I think I was the only person from St. Louis who cared who never saw that bird.

But given the choice, I'd take the ground-cuckoo any day. That afternoon, while the new group was having an introductory walk along the airstrip, I returned to the slope where I'd found my bird. This time there was a huge, active ant swarm, with the ground-cuckoo fully in the open at very close range and too busy even to notice me. Also in attendance was the second reason I'd come to Darien—a sensational Black-crowned Antpitta, giving full views of its gorgeously scaled underparts. I pulled myself away after some wonderfully delirious moments and went to find the recent arrivals, most of whom got to share in at least some of this spectacular event.

By the end of the Darien experience, I was only eight birds short of 7,000, and I was headed for Sri Lanka with Ben King in late January. So the only question was, which endemic would be my milestone bird? Breaking 7,000 was not the only reason that Sri Lanka was an especially exciting trip for me. For years it looked as though I'd never get there. By the time I'd learned about all the great birds to be found in Sri Lanka, it was in the headlines with serious upheavals and Tamil terrorism, largely in the north of the island, while the endemic birds are largely in the south. At any rate, bird tours simply weren't going there through most of the 1980s. Needless to say, when Ben announced a 1992 Sri Lanka tour, I jumped at the chance.

We pulled off an absolute marvel of a trip, with all 23 to 24 endemics (depending on your taxonomy), including some very difficult ones and ones which at that time were almost never seen by visiting birders. Ceylon Frogmouth is one of these, and as luck would have it, it became number 7,000 for me. We had several simply splendid views of frogmouths, both at night in the light beam and then again in the daytime, with scope views of a pair (one gray, one rufous) snuggled together on a daytime roost high in a dense leafy tangle. All in all, this trip was probably the single overall most completely successful bird trip I've ever done.

Now what? I'd joined Harvey Gilston in the exclusive "7,000 Club". He was still a bit ahead of me (having reported 7,069 at the end of 1991), but I was more than likely to pass him in the coming year. John Danzenbaker, who was also on the Sri Lanka trip, was just barely behind me, and saw his 7,000th species only about a month later. There was a British couple, Sandra Fisher and Michael Lambarth—also on this Sri Lanka trip—who, once they got around to taking into account the new taxonomic splits, were not more than one or two hundred species behind.

For some years, I'd been chugging happily along, grateful for my continuing health, concentrating on doing my job well, and enjoying what I was doing. Now I was beginning to look around seriously at the competition. Both Satchel Page, the baseball pitcher, and my extraordinarily successful father had warned: "Never look back—someone might be gaining on you!" I was beginning to feel some hot breath coming up behind me, despite the innocent-sounding disclaimer from the British couple that they

Ceylon Frogmouth

"weren't competitive!" This birding game was indeed beginning to become intensely competitive for me. I think it was about now that I began to think seriously about a world record, and without carefully analyzing the situation, I felt that given about another five years, 8,000 would probably be possible for me. Would my melanoma give me those five years? Harvey and John were both older than I and beginning to slow down, but the British couple seemed very determined and were younger and, seemingly, healthier and wealthier than I. It was definitely going to be a race, albeit an undeclared one. I certainly was beginning to worry more and to keep closer track of what my competitors were doing.

The rest of 1992 was pretty well planned out. I had some productive trips scheduled, as well as some specialty excursions for priority species. In March, I did a full trip to Cameroon, which was very successful overall, except that there had been some major itinerary changes. It was an election year, with possible political unrest in a couple of places, which resulted in canceling plans to visit a site for *Picathartes* (rockfowl), an extremely difficult family to come to grips with, as well as the Bamenda highlands, a location for several endemics, including the charismatic Bannerman's Turaco.

I flew to Tokyo in late March for the express purpose of going on a boat trip to the island of Torishima, the only reliable place to see Short-tailed Albatross. My contact, falling all over himself with apologies, met me at Narita. The boat trip had been canceled that very morning due to "mechanical difficulties", but if I stayed over five days and did some birding in the meantime, they would have the boat fixed and could put me on the second trip. I accepted that plan, and—thanks to Mark Brazil, with whom I hooked up for a couple of days—managed a splendid view of a drumming Copper Pheasant, one of the few species we'd missed on our June trip to Japan a few years before. The day came to join the boat for the second planned trip to Torishima. Reports said that the repairs had been done and tested. Just as I was leaving the hotel, I received a phone call—*so sorry*, but the second trip had been canceled as well—because of continuing mechanical difficulties. It was hard to accept, in this land of technological wizardry. There was no choice but to fly home without my target albatross, truly one of my most frustrating and disappointing birding experiences ever.

Later that spring, I returned to Morocco, but this time to do the whole country properly and see specialties like Waldrapp, Thick-billed Lark, and Egyptian Nightjar. A quick excursion to Belize ultimately added Keel-billed Motmot and Ocellated Turkey, despite logistical difficulties that kept us busy improvising new plans to get to the site.

My big adventure of the spring of 1992 was a Himalayan trek to the Everest area with a British nature tour company. Since I had done a very good birding trip with Ben in 1982 through Nepal and the rest of the Himalayas, my bird targets were very few. I was really going for two major reasons. First, my daughter Carol had done some serious mountain climbing in that region and had reached the 23,000-foot summit of Mt. Pumori. Along the easier part of her route, she had encountered a number of Himalayan Monals, those iridescent, gaudy, crested pheasants of high-altitude Nepal that we had missed on Ben's trip. I was hungering to see this one and was willing to do a tough trek to find it. Second, later that year I was planning a bird trip to Irian Jaya, which was going to involve two difficult treks of a week each, and I wanted to make sure that I was in the proper shape to do it. I figured if I trekked to 18,000 feet in the Himalayas successfully, which I did, I could handle Irian Jaya. I had great looks at several of the stunning monals and a few other select high-altitude species, including Robin Accentor and Snow Partridge, while living and hiking amid some of the most majestic and impressive mountain scenery on this planet, so it was all successful, and I was deluded into a false feeling of confidence that I would also be able to cope successfully with Irian Jaya in August.

Our son Tom was at this time working for the U.S. Fish and Wildlife Service on Hawaii and had information about and access to some of the honeycreepers there and on Maui that I still needed to see. Obviously, a visit to him was in order. Tom helped me find a Hawaii Creeper, an Akepa, and an Akiapolaau on Hawaii, and then we spent a couple of days together on Maui, observing Maui Parrotbill, Crested Honeycreeper [Akohekohe], and Maui Creeper [Maui Alauahio]. Since that time, I've also birded Kauai with him, most recently (1996) trudging deep into the muddy Alakai Swamp, where he has been studying the highly endangered Puaiohi (Small Kauai Thrush), which he was able to find for me. Tom was part of a bird survey team that spent some time in the incredibly rugged and wet terrain on the wild back side of Haleakala Crater on Maui, where he was lucky enough to have good views of the most recently discovered (1973) Hawaiian bird, the Poo-uli. I've now caught up with most of the birds my far-flung children managed to see before I did, but I know this one will always be Tom's alone to cherish.

August was the time for my trip with a British company to the western or Indonesian side of the island of New Guinea: Irian Jaya. I knew it was a first, that it would be an adventure, and that it would be strenuous—but I didn't know I should have been an

Akiapolaau

Olympic athlete to undertake it! Our trek up the Snow Mountains from the Baliem Valley town of Wamena involved absolutely
the worst mud (deep and unrelenting) and "camping" conditions
(an insufficient tarp spread over the tops of sixteen bodies
stretched out like sardines in a can) I've ever dealt with—and
that's saying a good bit.

Once begun, there was no turning back. Our goal was the high
grasslands at over 10,000 feet, on the edge of which lives the fa-
bled Macgregor's Bird-of-paradise, with some other specialty
species in those grasslands bordering Lake Habbema. With our
varying speeds of travel, from the full-tilt pace of the leaders and
porters to the slow "geriatrics" like me and one valiant Australian
lady (whose flight was delayed and who had to undertake this
awful trek alone, with a guide and porter, and endeavor to catch
up), we were strung out all over those mountains. It was mostly
every man for himself, with virtually no group birding experiences. I was constantly grateful that I'd birded PNG as much as I
had, because I was familiar with most of the species and could
save my energy for the Irian Jaya specialties, most of which would
be at the top. Since every step required care and concentration in
those simply unbelievably steep, muddy, and downright dangerous conditions, I couldn't really do any birding enroute anyway.
I'd eat, fall onto our sleeping ground exhausted, often with my
muddy boots still on, and wake with the awful knowledge that we
weren't there yet—and that we still had to go *back* the same route!
Even thoughts of Macgregor's Bird-of-paradise took a back seat to
simple thoughts of endurance and survival.

In the end, we all got there, even the intrepid Australian lady,
who had to turn around and go back almost immediately (after
seeing Macgregor's Bird-of-paradise, thank heavens). The rest of

us had a comparatively easy and relaxing day at the top. The birds cooperated, including most of my target species, and what would have been a strenuous day's birding under any other circumstances (a long hike through the grasslands to Lake Habbema and back) seemed like an enjoyable day's outing by comparison to the last three—and the next three. About two years after this experience, the Indonesians built a road up the Snow Mountains, and it's now possible to get to the top where we camped by four-wheel-drive vehicle. I won't quote my reaction to this startling bit of news.

Of course, there were some more conventional, well-organized parts to this trip, such as our boat trip to the western islands of Batanta and Salawati. Here we had a perfectly comfortable and spacious thatched hut in which to spread our sleeping bags and only one morning of a tough commando exercise necessary to get to the spot for seeing the incredible Wilson's Bird-of-paradise. Birding at the old sawmill west of Jayapura was certainly reasonable, once we negotiated the tricky footing through the swamp between the vehicles and the building. I think there were even some places where we stayed in hotels of sorts, had vehicular transport to the birding areas, and took good trails through forest, so that we could actually do some birding as a group.

The second trek of this long tour was to be into the Arfak Mountains in the Vogelkop region (the "Bird's Head" of northwestern New Guinea). I knew I simply couldn't physically (or psychologically) handle another week's trek with conditions like the Snow Mountains, so I made some serious inquiries of the leaders (only one of whom had been here) as to likely conditions. It turned out that it was certainly going to be steep but probably relatively dry, so I decided to chance it rather than give up so much of what I'd come all this way to see. Amazingly, it was just as advertised: a steep, mostly rocky trail with quite good footing, so that I was able to do it all unassisted by the local tribesmen-porters. (In the Snow Mountains, the wonderful, happy, nearly-naked Dani porters had laughingly grabbed my arms at critical moments and simply manhandled me up, down, or across indescribable bits of terrain that my own legs were incapable of handling!)

With the exception of the Snow Mountain-like steep, muddy trail to our hut at Bini Bei, there was nothing particularly awful about the Arfak. The birds were quite wonderful, especially since I could actually look at them, instead of watching my feet at every step. When we finally got back down some days later, the best beer I have ever tasted in my life was waiting in the vehicles at the bottom. This trek was the alleged end of the arduous part and nearly the end of the trip as well.

Only Biak remained, which by comparison represented civilization—and a hotel. We spent a morning of pleasant, regular roadside birding, connecting with most of the endemics of this island in Geelvink Bay. The wind-up on the final afternoon of the trip was to be an hour's boat ride out to a smaller island to look for a megapode, which was lumped at the time with one I'd already seen, so it wasn't even a major quest for me. We started after lunch in an Indonesian double-outrigger with an outboard motor and a box-like rectangular cabin for storing gear, but which all 16 of us sat on top of. The allotted hour passed and then another. There was no island anywhere in sight, and inquiries revealed that the boat was having to take a long circuitous route around a huge coral reef because of low tide. By mid-afternoon, we participants all sensed that the mission should be aborted, or we'd be returning in the dark, without any lights. I should have spoken up, but didn't—to my later regret—and the "intrepid leaders" carried on. We got to the island about 5 p.m. and had about an hour to search for the megapode, in absolutely impossible tall grass and dense ground cover. I actually glimpsed one scuttling across a track, but that was about the extent of the sightings. We *did* hear them, but the excursion was not a resounding success.

Dusk came, and we started back. This time our route would be shorter and more direct, because we could cross the reef on the now-rising tide. But it *was* getting quite dark, and Indonesian outriggers just aren't provided with lights (or life-jackets either). Fortuitously, there was a small open boat just ahead of us, and we decided to follow its route across the reef, keeping quite close in order to see where it was going. We were still all sitting on top of the boxy cabin, and every so often our boat would lurch rather alarmingly as the bottom hit part of the reef. We finally got across the reef and into open water, where the boat rode more freely, and I breathed a short-lived sigh of relief.

The wind and waves now began to pick up, and the boat was doing some heavy rocking. Before long, a large wave simply engulfed and swamped the lowest outrigger, resulting in the top-heavy boat slowly turning over 180 degrees, with its keel ending up in the air. It was one of those events that you simply can't believe is really happening. The motion was slow enough that I was able to keep climbing up the rising side of the hull, and ended up sitting on top of the upturned keel—without even getting my head wet. Those on the sinking side were not so fortunate; several were thrown into the water, and one woman was hit on the head by an outrigger and actually trapped underneath until one of the strong swimmers was able to rescue her. It was totally dark, and all was chaos. Even determining that all 16 of us were present and okay was a major undertaking. We all shouted, whistled, and screamed to attract the attention of the small boat we'd been following, and they heard us and returned.

After much yelling back and forth between our boatmen and theirs, it was determined that the four or five poorest swimmers and most elderly of us would be taken in the small boat back to shore, where we would organize a rescue, while the others would simply continue to cling to the overturned but floating boat. It was a long two hours back. The local policeman had a list of all of our names and passport numbers (mandatory on making any travel plans within Irian Jaya), and his first and most important order of business was to inquire who had died—i.e., which names and numbers he should cross off his list. After explaining that we'd left everyone alive but in serious danger, we indicated the small island on his chart where we'd been and the reef we'd crossed on our way back, and hence the approximate location of the accident. It was another nail-biting hour before they got their police boat and personnel organized and sped out to sea. It took about another hour for this faster boat to get there and locate our still-floating boat and crew, which had drifted some in what was now a rising storm. The others had thus been clinging to this frail craft in total darkness and frightening weather conditions for over four hours, trying to keep their spirits and hopes up. All were rescued without further incident, but we all knew how *incredibly* fortunate we had been that the policeman hadn't had to cross anyone off his list.

Scopes, passports, and personal gear that had been in the cabin were mostly lost, binoculars were ruined, and the motor had gone to the bottom of the sea. But no one had died or was badly injured—people were only thoroughly frightened—and it was the end of the trip. I had seen over fifty lifers on that trip but had the distinct feeling, for the first time in my career, that *it wasn't worth it*! On the positive side, I'd learned something about the physical limits of my own endurance, and the trip had certainly given me a benchmark for all time: no matter how tough a future trip might be or how awful the conditions, I'd instantly feel better by realizing that it's not as bad as Irian Jaya!

Ironically, my next trip was to be on a boat. We were taking a cruise on the Red Sea from Eilat in Israel past the tip of the Sinai Peninsula down to the coast of Egypt. My major goal was to see White-eyed and Sooty Gulls and White-cheeked Tern. No problem with *this* boat trip, and we saw my target species well and repeatedly—as well as migrating Levant Sparrowhawks once we were back in Israel again. It was simply a pleasant sojourn and a real vacation compared to the last one. Maybe *this* is the kind of thing the British mean by their term "birding holidays"?

In October, I joined a small private group of friends for some excellent birding in western Mexico: Colima, Jalisco, and Oaxaca. Bit by bit, I was coming to grips with a fair number of those wonderful Mexican endemics, such as Orange-breasted Bunting and Slaty Vireo, and at long last a visible Collared Forest-Falcon. The year ended with another return to Madagascar in November, my third trip there. *Finally*—not just one ground-roller, but three, as well as some of the other intriguing endemics that I'd been unlucky with before, such as the Madagascar Crested Ibis [Madagascar Ibis].

It had been an amazing year, all told. I'd seen over 200 new birds after breaking 7,000 in February and over 250 for the year. Three or four more years at roughly this pace should get me to the next thousand—but these were now uncharted waters, and I was quite uncertain that I could continue to find my increasingly scattered lifers at this rate for much longer. At any rate, I was now number one in the listing game world wide, and my competition was beginning to face the same problems I was.

First Half of the Final Leg

O ne of my essentially untouched areas of the planet was central Africa. As fortune would have it—good fortune this time—my friend Bob Braden had arranged a private trip to Burundi and eastern Zaire, which was to take place under Terry Stevenson's leadership in early 1993. I'd accepted Bob's invitation with pleasure and joined him and the others in Brussels after spending an unsuccessful few days in Holland looking for vagrant Red-breasted and Lesser White-fronted Geese.

Once the turmoil in most of Rwanda had removed that country as a regular birding venue, Terry had been taking groups to nearby Burundi instead, and his trip lists had been impressive, both in quality and quantity of species seen. The combination of Burundi and eastern Zaire encompassed some extraordinary highlights. In the Rwegura Forest of Burundi, the thrills began with a Lagden's Bushshrike and a perched Ayres's Hawk-Eagle at the beginning, extended through the electric Purple-breasted Sunbirds, burnt-orange Kivu Ground-Thrush, Red-throated Alethe, and Equatorial Akalat, to the strange and unique Grauer's and Neumann's Warblers, to the beautifully responsive White-tailed Ant-Thrush on the way out. I've seldom had a day with such constant excitement.

Eastern Zaire holds gorillas (my second encounter with them was every bit as emotionally stirring as the first one in the Virungas of Rwanda in 1989), as well as the lowland Irangi rainforest (reached by crossing on foot a truly awesome swinging bridge made of vines and little else). A few of the local enticements are Hartlaub's Duck, Chocolate-backed Kingfisher, Bare-cheeked Trogon, Rufous-sided Broadbill, and Congo Serpent-Eagle, in addition to a host of skulking forest denizens.

En route back to Burundi, we took a one-day swing through the Nyungwe Forest of southern Rwanda, mainly to pick up the Ruwenzori Turaco, which we'd missed in the mountains of Zaire, and stumbled across one of my all-time most-wanteds—a flock of Red-collared Mountain-Babblers, as well as the turaco. We did this trip in the nick of time, while the gods were smiling. It was repeated once more the next year, and the participants got out of Burundi with some difficulty, just as war and all the ensuing human horror tales were beginning.

Another gap in my world experience was Micronesia, so I had signed up for a late-Februrary trip with Doug Pratt, a highly-respected tour leader and artist. We flew to Guam and went from the Marianas (Saipan, Rota, and Tinian) south to Palau and then east along the Caroline Island chain to Yap, Truk, and Pohnpei. These islands hold a high number of endemics, and I was fortunate enough to observe every last one.

At the end of the trip, I joined my son Tom for my first birding on Kauai, because I had a few days before a return to Japan and another try at the boat trip to Torishima. This time, I phoned my contact in Tokyo before boarding the plane in Honolulu and heard the good news that all was proceeding according to plan.

*One of Phoebe's favorite early memories of tropical birding was the exquisite **Ornate Hawk-Eagle**, which she observed from the veranda of the Asa Wright Nature Center in Trinidad.*

*A difficult 1985 trek to El Triunfo, Mexico, turned up
the rare and "improbable-looking"* **Horned Guan.**

*Regarded by some as the world's most beautiful bird, the **Resplendent Quetzal** was an added bonus on the search for the Horned Guan in southern Mexico.*

*Despite the chaos surrounding the fall of the Marcos regime, Phoebe found the **Great Philippine Eagle** on Mindanao with Ben King and Tim Fisher.*

*New Caledonia's distinctive and elusive **Kagu**, found nowhere else, was
Phoebe's main goal on a South Pacific journey with David Bishop.*

Phoebe found the rare and much-sought-after
Spoonbill Sandpiper *on a 1988 visit*
to Hong Kong's Mai Po marshes.

*The unbelievably bright **Orange Dove** is found only on two islands in Fiji.*

*Phoebe was fortunate to find **Gurney's Pitta**, the only bird
species endemic to peninsular Thailand and Burma,
and one of the world's most critically endangered.*

*Seeing **Macgregor's Bird-of-paradise** required
an arduous hike of several days in Irian Jaya,
New Guinea. The area is now more accessible.*

In 1995, Phoebe was with Steve Howell in Mexico when she "won the race" and saw her 8,000th bird, a **Rufous-necked Wood-Rail** *in the mangroves of San Blas.*

*Seeing the **Princess Parrot** [Alexandra's Parrot] required a four-day, four-wheel-drive trek on the remote Canning Stock Route in Western Australia's Great Sandy Desert.*

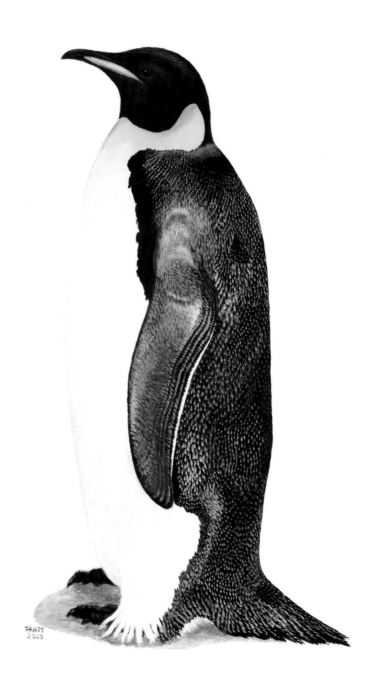

Phoebe ended 1997 on a cruise with her husband
*to see Antarctica's **Emperor Penguin** colonies.*

An exhausting hike north of Lhasa produced
*the **Tibetan Eared-Pheasant** [White Eared-Pheasant],*
completing Phoebe's sightings of Tibetan endemics.

The **Orange-throated Tanager** of northern Peru, discovered only in 1964, showed that many new species were yet to be found in the world in remote and seldom-visited places.

Koch's Pitta [Whiskered Pitta] *had been one of Phoebe's most-wanted birds on her last trip to Luzon in the Philippines, and it required a difficult, two-day horseback ride and hike, which she accomplished with an untended broken wrist.*

Phoebe's last life bird was the newly-discovered
Red-shouldered Vanga *of Madagascar.*

Short-tailed Albatross

The Japanese came through with flying colors this time, but it was a rough trip, and my English-speaking contact was so seasick that I never saw him from when we left the dock to our return three days later. Since he was the only other one on board who spoke any English, my trip amounted to total immersion in Japanese language and culture. I communicated with the Japanese birders on board by pointing at pictures in the field guide, and they would let me know when meals were served. The Short-tailed Albatrosses were magnificent, and we had wonderful views of all plumages right around the boat as we were anchored off Torishima. Single-minded persistence often does pay off, I've found.

In April, I was going back to Kenya. Terry Stevenson was doing a private trip for Bob and Myra Braden and a British friend, and I completed the party. Quite unbelievably, we came up with over fifty new species for me, a testimony to Terry's expertise and vast knowledge of the birds of this country. This trip was my first time to the coastal Sokoke Forest, as well as to several areas in the west, and there had been many new discoveries since my 1977 trip with Burt Monroe. We weren't even trying for numbers, but on counting the list at the end, we found we had seen 700 species!

Late that spring, I had another chance to return to Iquitos, Peru. By this time, Faucett Airlines had gotten its act together, and we actually *did* fly from Miami direct to Iquitos and back, without the hassle of going through Lima. Another good change was that now the incredible canopy walkway was about half completed and usable. Having already done the area with Ted Parker, it just wasn't possible to see a lot of new birds, but we did get some great ones, like Undulated Antshrike, Pearly Antshrike, and two fledgling Nocturnal Curassows.

Summer was devoted to a circuit of outback Australia, followed by yet another return to PNG, and a solo excursion to Kadavu, one of the outlying islands of Fiji and home to four endemics. Philip Maher, of Plains-wanderer fame, organized and led our Aussie outback expedition, which began in his hometown of Deniliquin with a gorgeous female Plains-wanderer (I'd seen a male with him there in 1990) and a bonus Freckled Duck. From here our circuit took us north, then west and south, through very remote country with some extraordinary species like Inland Dotterel, Bourke's Parrot, Letter-winged Kite, four grasswrens, Orange Chat, Gibberbird [Desert Chat], both rare whitefaces, Hall's Babbler, and three quail-thrushes. It was all great fun and highly productive, in some ways reminiscent of our adventurous exploration of the Gobi Desert—but in the present case Phil knew exactly where he was going and what he was looking for in those vast interior wastes. We were lucky with the weather. There had been recent incredible rains and flooding, and a week earlier many of the "roads" would have been totally impassible.

There was very little in PNG that would be new for me, but the connection from the end of the Australia trip was well-timed, and it was also going to work out well for my Fiji plans. I had a priority target list of about eight species, and knowing that I would be in that part of the world and that I'd never even have a chance to see these much-wanted endemics unless I did return, really tipped the scales. Unbelievably, I saw all of them and another couple besides.

At the top of the list was New Guinea Harpy Eagle [New Guinea Eagle]. Many people see this bird on their first trip, but I'd been unlucky on both previous full trips. This time we had marvelous, leisurely scope views of a calling pair, completing my roster of the world's large eagles. Feline Owlet-Nightjar was a close runner-up. Ever since I'd seen Brian Coates' dramatic photo of this extraordinary-looking nocturnal creature before my first trip to PNG, it had been a bird I was longing to see. We'd heard one on my previous trip but couldn't get it to come in for a view. And we certainly had to struggle for it this time! They are common by voice at night in the forests around Ambua Lodge, but seeing one is another matter entirely—and one of the most valid reasons, to my mind, for not counting heard birds. We went out pre-dawn and again after dark for seven consecutive morning and night attempts before one simply gave itself up and perched in the open for us to study at leisure in the light beam. Each time we had heard the bird call, even reasonably close, and we were all weary from burning this candle at both ends—but not one of us would be satisfied with anything less than a decent view. These two species alone made my return worthwhile, but we also had, among others, Lesser Melampitta, Southern Crowned-Pigeon, Macgregor's Bowerbird, and my last sicklebill, Buff-tailed.

I flew on to Fiji with the group and birded the first morning with them, connecting finally with Black-faced Shrikebill [Black-throated Shrikebill]. From Nadi, I took a flight to Kadavu in the southeast, where I had a couple of leisurely solo days on a "birding holiday", finding the endemics without much difficulty and winding down before returning home.

Next was a mixture of Brazil plans: Alta Floresta, Manaus, and then a private excursion to look for some birds in the Rio-São Paulo areas, which had been found in the last few years, since my last trip to southeast Brazil. The Amazonian areas were excellent, and we found all of our major targets in the southeast, including

Feline Owlet-Nightjar

simply marvelous views, at last, of the most beautiful piping-guan—the endangered Black-fronted.

Another Brazil trip of exceptional interest would just about close out 1993 for me. This trip was the first organized one to some of the little-known and seldom-birded states in the dry northeast of that vast country, an innovative trip run by Bret Whitney for Field Guides. We started with a pre-trip extension to the island of Fernando de Noronha, with its two easy endemics plus a number of interesting seabirds, then did the northeast circuit proper, ending in the state of Bahia. The finale was an extension to Carajas, a remote interior forest area south of Belém at the mouth of the Amazon, owned by a mining operation, and with access only by small aircraft. Here was an Amazonian avifauna totally different from what we'd been seeing in the northeast and with some major surprises, such as the mystery *Leucopternis* hawk, which I found and we saw so well but couldn't identify because its field marks simply didn't make sense! Perhaps a "replacement species" for Semiplumbeous Hawk from west of the Andes?

It was altogether an extraordinary experience, rich in unique birds. There are so many taxonomic puzzles still to be resolved in that part of Brazil, that we all quickly realized we were adding not only many currently accepted lifers to our experience, but probably equally as many future splits, or "bank" birds. Bret kept us well informed on the status of the many fascinating forms we encountered. We were unable to get permission to see the last Spix's Macaw but did see a number of the highly localized and endangered Lear's Macaw, as well as a vast array of flycatchers, antbirds, and furnariids, some of which had been discovered only very recently. A few of these, including *Synallaxis whitneyi*, a spinetail

[Bahia Spinetail] named for Bret, have only been officially named and described since we saw them on our trip, when we had to record them simply as "*sp. nov.*" And since our trip, an amazing new genus and species of furnariid, Pink-legged Graveteiro (*Acrobatornis fonsecai*) was discovered in southeastern Bahia, so this area continues to produce birds new to science.

Upon return home in mid-December, I was fewer than forty species short of 7,500, and I was planning a trip over Christmas and New Years to the Ivory Coast (my second visit there). The British couple, now my closest rivals in the world listing game, had also been on this northeast Brazil trip, and it became evident from their comments to me, as well as to others, that they were trying *very* hard to close the gap—fewer than 200 birds at that time. I couldn't really envision where I might find another 500 species; still I *did* feel I could beat them to the 8,000 mark, but only if I did it in the next two or three years—so I had my challenge clarified and my work cut out for me.

~17~
A New Challenge

S ince I was planning to be in West
Africa over Christmas, my husband,
David, had made plans with our four children to spend the holiday period together
in Belize, with snorkeling, sightseeing and, of course, some birding, at least for three of them. But I did not foresee what lay at the
end of these trips.

Until now, the major challenges in my life had been health-re-
lated and in no obvious way attributable to fault or neglect on my
part. This one was highly personal and emotional, with much of
the responsibility on my shoulders, and seemed in its own way
just as threatening as cancer. David had decided that it would be
best for us to separate and divorce.

When he confronted me with what he thought was the most
reasonable and fair course of action, I was totally flabbergasted
and devastated. My ally (as I had thought) had become my ad-
versary, and I was unprepared to deal with it, especially so at this
particular juncture of my life. Yes, there had in recent years been
a serious lack of communication between us, certainly some of it
(but just as certainly not all of it) my fault. He was not interested
in sharing my passion for birding, and I felt the same way about
his interests in stage magic and ventriloquism.

I deeply resented David's unwillingness to accept my point of
view: that our lives were out of synchrony in much the same way

they had been back when he was pursuing his career and I needed more adult compassion and companionship. Now he was retired, and I was pursuing *my* career, and he was feeling exactly the same lacks that I had. We'd both been guilty of a lack of consideration for the other at different times in our many years together—but was it really too late to recognize this failing and to learn from it? There was no third party involved here. I was totally and utterly opposed to a split at this time in our lives. There was *so much* to lose, for both of us, and so little to gain. I simply couldn't and wouldn't accept it. I was angry, threatened, confused, and miserably unhappy. And once again I fled—this time to the Ivory Coast.

It was a trip of mixed results and feelings for me. In general, my luck was bad, and whether this had anything to do with my inner state of turmoil is impossible to say. There was an outrageously quirky and unexpected sighting by several people of a Yellow-headed Rockfowl [White-necked Rockfowl] in a tree, but I wasn't with the group, since I was putting in a lot of time alone on the trails, with what really seemed to be a much higher chance of achieving the same result. As always, there were trade-offs: I did have a marvelous time in the Tai Forest, where I'd never been, with mind-blowing views of Lyre-tailed Honeyguide, White-breasted Guineafowl, and several other good ones. But through it all, the feeling that my life was falling apart, just as I was on the threshold of my greatest success, cast a serious pall over everything I did.

When I returned in early January, David told me that he'd talked to the children about our getting a divorce. I did resent that the kids had heard a one-sided story, and I felt I needed equal time, so obviously I had long phone conversations with each of them, to tell them how I felt about it all, namely that such a move would be wrong, *wrong,* WRONG!—for both of us.

Obviously my travel schedule required long-term commitments and flight arrangements made many months in advance. Vietnam in February was coming up, and I was still determined to do it, so there was a lot for me to deal with in January. David left to visit friends and relatives for a good part of the month; thus, I had time and space to pull myself together and think the situation through. I felt determined to fight what I felt were unfair proposals. I couldn't stop David from moving out if he wished to—but *I* wasn't going to move out and make it easy. If he had to have a different life, then it would be his move. I wrote him a long, emotional letter, trying to initiate a healing approach, and agreeing, as we had once discussed earlier, that we go to a marriage counselor together when I got back to try to resolve it all in a manner that we could both accept. I left the letter for him at home and departed for Vietnam, five birds short of 7,500.

I felt better about my situation during this trip. I'd done whatever I could do at this point to heal wounds and still be fair and honest with myself and my own needs in life. I knew what I would do, and what I wouldn't do, and initiating any action was simply up to David. I'd play a strong defensive game, and I'd work for a resolution that might just give us both what we need and want out of life. I hoped we could at least try the counseling route.

White-winged Magpie, a regional endemic, was number 7,500, early in the trip, and I had seen another thirty lifers before it was over. The company was good, with some friends I could unload my problems on, and the birding was excellent as well as fun (despite the incredibly awful leeches at Tam Dao in the north). I managed to concentrate more on the birding than on my own life this time around, so I was once again experiencing the magic healing that birding has always provided for me.

I was apprehensive enough to be almost physically ill on returning home—because I honestly didn't know what the situation would be with David. He was home, and he hugged me! And he'd moved forward and found a suitable marriage counselor. At least we were going to do something together again, and it felt right to both of us. Maybe we were on the right track, but there were a lot of problems and negative feelings to work through, and it wasn't going to be a quick fix.

A quick jaunt to see the Hawaiian Crow gave me an opportunity to visit with my son Tom as well and to meet his new girlfriend, Christina Herrmann, obviously an important relationship in his life. I was feeling so much better about life and was positively eager to begin our counseling program; I just desperately needed to *talk*.

It was a roller-coaster spring. Our counseling sessions and our own private follow-ups and emotional discussions were intermingled with on-going life and involvements for each of us— David's magic and my birding. I filled a major ornithological gap by going to Puerto Rico and the Lesser Antilles, which added over forty new birds. I also spent a couple of weeks birding Turkey that spring, another of the Western Palearctic outposts that had long been on my list of places to go.

Summer brought a return to Venezuela, an excellent private trip to Ecuador, and a short but very successful trip to the Canary Islands. We were making progress on the home front as well, and we were working out of our mutual anger and resentment toward a greater awareness of each other's needs. Life was definitely more

Hawaiian Crow

pleasant and fun at home than it had been in years. I knew that I was still well ahead of my competitors (friends kept us mutually informed) and that another year and a half would bring the race to the "last thousand" to a conclusion one way or another.

I had only two trips planned for the fall: a "clean up" in South Africa, which involved doing the whole pleasant country once again, and *finally* Ethiopia. The latter had been slipping through the cracks in my program for years. I'd put it off a few times because of something seemingly more important, and then the civil war broke out, and it was impossible to get there. As with Sri Lanka, I jumped at the next chance I got, saw most of the endemics on the regular circuit, and ended 1994 with 7,772 species on my world list.

Christmas, this year, was much happier for us all than the previous one. All four children and various significant friends came home, and it was a very welcome and warming time of family togetherness, with everyone happy that David's and my relationship seemed to be mending.

~18~
Watershed Year

H owever it might turn out, 1995
was going to be a significant year
in my life. I had three major concerns, all
very serious ones. The first was our marriage.

A year ago it had been close to collapse. We hadn't saved it yet,
but our relationship had improved a lot, and David was no longer
talking about separation. Could we continue to progress, given
my intensive birding plans? Second, my last melanoma recurrence had been late summer of 1990. Since the "big one" in 1981,
I hadn't yet gone five years without a recurrence and the attendant fear, possibility of illness, necessary surgery and scans, and
consequent time loss. What would happen in *this* fifth year? My
third worry was the race for 8,000, which I wanted very badly to
win—but so did my competitors. My yearly gain since I broke
7,000 had been somewhat higher than I anticipated, averaging
270 lifers per year. I only needed about 230 more this year to
reach my goal, but I'd have to stay healthy and keep traveling
steadily to do it. Also, I was going to have to squeeze in some productive private trips somewhere just to have a chance at this
many species. Returns were diminishing for me everywhere in
the world.

I was off to a promising start. I'd had a private trip to
Venezuela with two friends and Jeff Kingery of WINGS in the
planning stages for some time, and January was to be the month.

Since my original planning with Jeff, I'd been back to Venezuela on a VENT (Victor Emanuel Nature Tours) trip with Steve Hilty just this past summer, where we'd connected with some great birds—so I was now definitely down to the hard ones. Jeff's wizardry came through, however, and we saw wonderful creatures like Tawny-tufted Toucanet, Blue-backed Tanager, Roraiman Barbtail, Black-throated Antshrike, Yellow-crowned Manakin [Yellow-crested Manakin], as well as a number of Tachira and Maracaibo Basin specialties like my last screamer (Northern). It was grand good fun for all and quite an experience for my two neotropical neophyte friends.

Next was a return to the Philippines on Ben King's trip, which I'd done first in 1986, but which had had significant itinerary alterations since then. I'd conservatively predicted maybe fifteen lifers from his recent trip reports—and saw about twice that number! We had quite extraordinary good fortune, connecting with many rarely seen species, but missed the big eagle this time.

David actually accompanied me on the next trip, a cruise from Tahiti through the Tuamotus and Marquesas. There was simply mind-boggling snorkeling; there were also birds like Tuamotu Sandpiper, Blue-gray Noddy [Blue Noddy], *Pterodromas* and storm-petrels I hadn't yet seen, and a few special pigeons, parrots, and passerines. All these things were enjoyed on board a luxury cruise ship with all possible amenities, the foremost being excellent food.

Terry Stevenson's trips consistently provided great fun and equally great birding experiences, so I'd signed on for Uganda, even though I'd by now eaten away at the lifer possibilities here from all sides. Nonetheless, it would be wonderful to see a Shoebill again, and there were another ten or so reasonably possible lifers, such as Dwarf Kingfisher and Dusky Long-tailed Cuckoo. It all worked out very much as anticipated, and at long last I saw the Mountains of the Moon, a wondrously evocative name resonating from somewhere in my childhood.

Certainly one of the major bonuses of this incredible year was my initial venture into Colombia in June. I'd long been regretting that I hadn't gone on Steve Hilty's last comprehensive trip there in 1984, considering that the whole country quickly thereafter became an ill-advised location for birders. Anyhow, three of us arranged an excursion with Paul Coopmans, a leading expert on South American birds, to the Santa Marta Mountains, a relatively safe endemic stronghold. From there we would go on to Bogotá as circumstances allowed and simply play it by ear as to what we might be able to do.

The major snag in this promising plan was my oldest daughter Penny's sudden and totally unanticipated announcement that she and her long-time house-mate and fiancé had decided to get married on their only possible weekend of the summer, when I would be in Colombia. The notice was too short to change dates for Colombia, and Penny and Harlan couldn't change either. For a mother who had always dreaded putting on a wedding and hence encouraged the idea of elopement, I was surprisingly (to both Penny and myself) upset about missing my first daughter's wedding. But miss it I did, although the family in general attended in good numbers—and (as with the Ross's Gull I missed in St. Louis), I saw all the pictures and re-lived the event vicariously.

In any case, Colombia was a truly excellent trip. We saw nearly all the Santa Marta endemics and were able to do much more near Bogotá than I had dared hope, even getting as far as some great spots in the central Andes. The year was half over when I returned, and I was only about seventy birds short of my big target. I was ahead of schedule, with some important plans still to come. And I was also getting very close to five cancer-free years. So far so good!

In August, I was off to Gabon (a second time), but this time we were also going to São Tomé and Príncipe, islands which hold about twenty endemics that are relatively easy to see (and three or four that aren't). The island birding was generally successful and all quite straightforward—except that we narrowly missed being caught in a military coup, and our plane's engine caught fire just before take-off!

Mainland Gabon presented its usual logistical problems, as well as some unusual ones in the form of a major riot at the Libreville airport due to numerous previous flight cancellations to the interior village of Makokou. There was a great seething backlog of very angry passengers waiting to board the same plane as we were, destined for Makokou, with some damage resulting to both the plane and its pilot from this uncontrolled mob. The flight was abruptly cancelled, whereupon the baggage was then held hostage by the mob until well into the night. We spent a good bit more time than we wished at the airport and a worrisome night in Libreville, until we were finally re-united with our liberated baggage and had in the meantime managed to arrange our own charter flight to Makokou the next day.

The timing was not all bad, however, because our day-late arrival coincided with that of a migrant flock of African River Martins (in its own subfamily), which were perched along wires at the main bridge in town. The ways of Orni, the birder's contrived goddess of ornithology, are truly inscrutable!

Our stay in Makokou gave us some extraordinary forest birding at the M'Passa Reserve (where I'd contracted malaria on my
first trip in 1987) and also the opportunity to visit the rockfowl
cave several hours down the road and up a trail near the village
of Bokaboka. These extraordinary and exceptionally wary Red-
headed Rockfowl [Gray-necked Rockfowl] (*Picathartes*) gave us
several repeated but mostly fast-moving views, and it's a bird I
want to see under better circumstances some day. It was my last
family in Clements' list, however, so I was pleased to have had
any kind of exposure to it.

We went to a couple of areas in Gabon this time that were new
to me: Lekoni in the southeast, with interesting birds like Congo
Moorchat, Black-collared Bulbul (a monotypic genus that I'd actually already seen in northwest Zambia in 1988), and an amazingly elusive but vocal and beautiful Perrin's Bushshrike [Four-
colored Bushshrike]; and Ekwata Lodge across the estuary from
Libreville, which quite unexpectedly produced my last bee-eater
(Black-headed). The end of this trip left me a mere 23 birds short
of my target and now also past my five-year mark on the
melanoma. I was a shoo-in for being the first to 8,000, and I was
brimming with confidence.

In designing my 1995 plans toward late 1994, I had had no realistic expectations of being this far along at this time. Best play
it safe and build in some back up, I figured. Remember the tor-
toise and the hare! *Anything* could go wrong at any point in the
year, and I could be standing still just short of the finish line,
watching my competitors sail past. Thoughts like this one led me
to set up a private trip to Mexico with Steve Howell in September.
His excellent new field guide had come out, and it, along with
everything I'd heard about him, certainly impressed me. We

would make several trips from Mexico City, one long one by car and the rest by plane in several different directions, with carefully planned target species in mind for each location. The total possible target species for this three-week itinerary came to 24, with a couple of newly-split hummingbirds also possible. It was quite impossible to find 23 out of 24, I was certain (and so was Steve), but then I'd certainly finish up the game in October, when I was going back to Costa Rica with Paul Coopmans.

One by one, the birds fell into place. Despite a hurricane which moved through Baja the day we were en route there and blew our itinerary literally to the winds, we patched it all back together again on a day-by-day basis, and in the long run gained a critical bit of extra time. We found some extraordinarily unlikely birds, like White-fronted Swift and Bearded Wood-Partridge, as well as those we expected or that seemed reasonably possible. We missed one; we worked very hard for Worthen's Sparrow in the area where wintering flocks had been seen, but to no avail. After connecting successfully with the Baja birds and Purplish-backed Jay near Mazatlan, we were in San Blas and down to our final day—with my list standing absolutely amazingly at 7,999.

We'd taken a boat through the mangroves the evening before, looking for Rufous-necked Wood-Rail, but water was high (the whole town was flooded), and conditions weren't optimal. Anyhow, we'd seen none. The last morning we went up into nearby forest to look for the Mexican Woodnymph and Mexican Hermit [Western Long-tailed Hermit], both splits, one acknowledged and one pending. We heard a singing woodnymph, but even Steve couldn't locate it. He saw a hermit fly down the trail, but his young eyes are very quick, and I missed it—so my tally for the morning was zero. I guessed the big one would happen the first day or so in Costa Rica.

On returning to our hotel later in the afternoon, we got a message from our boatman of the previous evening. He had phoned to say he'd just seen three Rufous-necked Wood-Rails in his flooded boatyard at mid-day. We clearly had nothing to lose, though a few hours had elapsed since his sighting. We drove back to the boatyard and began to walk around in the flooded woods along the edge. There was a raised dike, densely wooded and with flooded mangroves on either side. The gods (Orni??) seemed to be smiling once again, and I had that nice anticipatory feeling that something good was about to happen. There was a walkable path along the top of the dike, so Steve, the boatman, and I started along it. It wasn't long before I glimpsed a furtive movement. The movement stopped, but I clamped my binoculars on where I'd seen the motion, and there it was, with its red head and neck, green bill, red eye, and red legs standing frozen in the tangled undergrowth: a Rufous-necked Wood-Rail. 8,000! It was all over now, and I'd won the game. Now we could really enjoy these rails (at least one adult plus a juvenile) and also gloat a bit in our success at having found every major target save one in the last weeks. I drank a lot of Bloody Marys on the flight home.

I'd done it with three months to spare, which was beyond my most optimistic dreams. My British rivals had just been with Paul Coopmans in Ecuador, so I knew exactly where they stood when I saw that wood-rail, and it was over 200 behind me. It had been a comfortable lead after all, and they really hadn't been able to narrow the gap in several years.

All three categories of my life that had been so worrisome in January seemed now smooth and under control. I was feeling really mellow. Costa Rica with Paul Coopmans was sheer pleasure, from the Slaty-breasted Tinamou to the Snowcap, and I didn't want to think about numbers at all anymore. Once I submitted my final "official" year-end list to the ABA and the *Guinness Book of World Records*, I'd be free to follow my own taxonomy and keep my own total simply as a percentage of what I consider the base world list to be. With as much taxonomic disagreement as there currently is, a raw number total just doesn't seem to make much sense anymore.

I squeezed in a quick trip to the Bahamas in November, before my final planned fling of the year, a return clean up of Ethiopia. There are a few charismatic endemics there, like Harwood's Francolin, Prince Ruspoli's Turaco, Stresemann's Bush-Crow, and White-tailed Swallow, that are significantly off the regular birding circuit and require a good bit of extra time, a sense of adventure, and a four-wheel-drive vehicle. So we did all that and more, missing only Ankober Serin (not for want of effort!). My official ABA total at year end was 8,040.

My health and marriage had held together. Most of our family got together for Christmas at a fairy-tale lodge in the Catskills, where David and I tried cross-country skiing for the first time, under ideal conditions and under the tutelage of our expert children. It had been one magnificent year—or maybe more like *thirty* magnificent years since that first Blackburnian Warbler!

~19~
The Next Era

My winding-down obviously could not begin overnight. The necessities in this international game include long-range planning and setting up a time and place for a trip with today's busy tour leaders: these things often have to be done two or more years in advance. In 1992 or 1993 it was impossible to foresee when (or even if) I might reach my final numerical goal, so I needed to build in some back-up security with trips to some offbeat locations.

Both David Bishop and Terry Stevenson were planning to take me and friends to some interesting spots in early 1996. Just because I'd actually now seen over 8,000 species wasn't going to change anything. David's long trip was to some little-known islands in the southern Moluccas: Tanimbar, Kai, Ambon, Seram, and Buru. Logistics and unpredictable flights were complicating factors, but David is very good at arranging travel details, and we began our major birding on Tanimbar. It was really just brilliant birding, with many interesting endemics in good forest and an incredibly lucky Lesser Masked-Owl to top it off. We also added quite a number of species to the island list, so much fun was had by all.

Airline schedules in remote Indonesia can't be predicted with confidence even from day to day, so we had to bypass the Kai Islands (temporarily, we hoped) and go on to Seram (by ferry, fortunately) from our Ambon base and airline hub. Here we were planning a major hiking expedition into the mountains, with camping gear, porters, etc., in order to have a chance at the higher-altitude endemics. Initially, though, we learned of a good new road across the island at medium elevation, so we planned to spend a day or so birding this easily accessible region.

Our first evening brought about an unforeseen change of plans. David had dropped us at the hotel and gone off with the driver and vehicle to check out some nearby sites in preparation for an early start the next day. On their return to town during a violent late afternoon rainstorm, there was a sudden, explosive tire blow-out, and the car skidded, turned, and rolled over a few times into an empty field. Fortunately, they'd been driving very slowly, so there were no immediately apparent injuries, but the car seemed badly damaged, cosmetically at least, and of course David and the driver were badly shaken, physically and emotionally. Seat belts or safety devices in general are not a standard feature in this part of the world.

Clearly, a revision of our plan was in order. David took the driver to the local hospital to be checked out but preferred not to go this route himself, claiming he was really okay, just traumatized. His suggestion was to go birding the next morning along the new road, if the hotel could find us another vehicle and driver. They did, and so we did. The birding was good, and we saw a number of the endemics, including our first views of the stunning Salmon-crested Cockatoo. We returned to the hotel in the afternoon to deal with the driver, who seemed okay, and the car, which didn't, and to give David some recuperation time.

We had with us all the gear for our hiking expedition, which we had purchased in Ambon, and David wanted to continue the plans by driving across the island the next day and arranging for a boat on the following day to take us across the bay to our jumping-off point. Fortunately, the hotel vehicle and driver seemed to be at our disposal. So we birded yet another morning on the cross-island road, with good views of a few more endemics and got to the village on the north coast, where we set up plans for a boat to take us and all our gear and food for several days to the designated drop-off. On the way back home to the hotel, it became obvious that David wasn't feeling well and was having some abdominal pain—a clear and definite signal immediately to abort all plans for our upcoming expedition. We still had about three weeks of our planned six-week trip left, but now the only thing to do was return to "civilization" in Ambon and proceed from there as seemed appropriate.

David saw a doctor in the Ambon hotel, phoned his wife and his own doctor in Australia, and made the sensible decision to return home for good medical attention to possible internal injuries. So our trip was over, and we left David in seeming good health and spirits in Bali. He was able to lead a Bhutan trip about three weeks later, so obviously he had no lasting physical problems.

Fortunately, we'd done by far the richest island (Tanimbar) first and had also found most of the Seram targets, with the exception of the higher altitude ones. On the way back to the Ambon ferry, we'd had further wonderful views of the cockatoo. We hadn't gotten to Kai or Buru as we'd planned, but that would just have to wait for another time, which might never come for me, since there are only about ten or twelve species I could possibly expect by returning, and none I can't live without. I'm having to confront that kind of choice in all my travel plans these days.

The eastern highlands of Tanzania in April with Terry Stevenson was next on my schedule. All went pretty much according to plan, and despite a washed-out road in the Ulugurus, we salvaged the situation by doing a many-mile steep hike and found the endemics we were seeking at the top, plus other interesting ones along the way. We saw three newly-discovered and then still undescribed and unnamed species in the Kilombero marshes (two cisticolas and a weaver), the recently discovered Rufous-winged Sunbird on the Udzungwa escarpment, the seldom-seen Iringa Akalat and other very special birds in the Iringa highlands, and most of the endemics in the Usambaras. Terry had arranged camping facilities for us with Abercrombie & Kent Ltd., a travel and safari company, in some of the remote locations, so we were well taken care of, and the whole adventure was most successful.

Several months before, I'd been told by a friend of a trip that Barry Walker was organizing to northern Peru and the Marañon Valley, which seemed to correspond closely to an adventure Jim Clements and his brother Bob had undertaken in the spring of 1995. They had seen some really great birds, including White-winged Guan and that most unbelievable of hummingbirds, the Marvelous Spatuletail. Barry is a birder and runs Expediciones Manu based in Cuzco, so he is the perfect person to arrange the formidable logistics and necessary camping involved in an undertaking like this one. How could I resist? I didn't even think twice.

We went in May, four British men plus Barry and me. It was tremendous fun and extraordinarily successful. I was heady with the excitement of seeing some of those marvelously special birds that Ted Parker had told me about years ago and that I had thought would be forever unavailable to me due to the rampant terrorist problems that developed in northern Peru and the generally formidable logistical snags of birding that remote area. But now, quite miraculously it seemed, I was here, and we found a very high percentage of our target species, including the much-wanted guan and spatuletail, my last plantcutter, Tumbes Tyrant, Bar-winged Wood-Wren, and three Inca-finches (a new genus for me).

While we were in Bogotá the previous summer, we had met Paul Salaman, the researcher and birder who had discovered the new-to-science Choco Vireo at his Río Nambi base in southwest Colombia. It sounded like an area well worth birding, and it was easy enough to get to by road from Quito, so we began to work on plans to do just that in June of 1996.

Now June of 1996 was here, and I was birding in Colombia again. In the region of the Río Nambi Reserve, which is at mid-altitudes, there is a higher elevation location with excellent birds and trails to get to them (La Planada) and also a lower elevation location (Pueblo Nuevo Trail). I found the latter one of the worst trails I've ever been on—recalling nightmares of Irian Jaya! Its saving virtues are that it is absolutely flat and that it's worth doing despite all hazards because of the birds one can find there. These three sites of significantly different altitudes gave us a wealth of birds, some of my favorites being Black Solitaire, Velvet-purple Coronet, Scarlet-and-white, Glistening-green, Moss-backed, Golden-chested, Purplish-mantled, and Blue-whiskered Tanagers, White-eyed Trogon, Five-colored Barbet, Star-chested Treerunner [Fulvous-dotted Treerunner], and one we picked up back in Ecuador, Scarlet-breasted Dacnis. We also found Paul Salaman's extremely interesting Choco Vireo.

Many of the birds in this southwestern choco region are also found farther north, as far as Central America. Consequently, a large number of species that weren't actually lifers, because I'd seen them in Panama, were at least new South American birds for me. I passed 2,500 for South America on this trip.

Immediately after we returned to Quito, I flew on to Lima to join a Field Guides tour to the Peruvian High Andes. We worked the mountains east of Lima, finding Peruvian Sheartail and Great Inca-Finch in the dry foothills, and then much higher up, Diademed Sandpiper-Plover, once again at the beautiful Marcapomacocha site where I'd found it in 1982, and this time White-bellied Cinclodes and Black-breasted Hillstar as well. Our main birding was in an area new to me, and one that had not been visited for some years due to Shining Path guerilla activity: Huascaran National Park, in the central Peruvian Cordillera Blanca. It was worth going for the magnificent mountain scenery alone, but in addition to that we saw Black Metaltail (*Metallura phoebe*, which I've always wanted to see for obvious nomenclatural reasons), Stripe-headed Antpitta (the only antpitta I've ever seen without hearing it first!), some highly localized and endangered species like White-cheeked Cotinga and Ash-breasted Tit-Tyrant, as well as my fifth and final Inca-finch (Rufous-backed). The spring and summer had provided a big South American bonanza for me, and I was planning to return to Ecuador one more time in October.

In July, my husband and I took a short trip to Kauai to visit our son. He was running a study project on the Puaiohi or Small Kauai Thrush, reduced now to a remnant of its former population. Tom's team had a base camp deep in the steep, wet, and muddy Alakai Swamp, so this trip was a perfect opportunity for me to attempt to see the Puaiohi. It's always a pleasure to bird with the local expert on a given species, and especially so when he is your own son! We went down (and up) some pretty incredible slopes, through some boot-sucking bogs, and found an adult and spotted juvenile, after which we spent the night at Tom's base camp. All of these experiences gave me a first-hand picture of the rigors of doing fieldwork in this kind of terrain.

White-water rafting is something my daughter Carol and especially her partner Nancy were experienced in. The rest of the family seemed willing to try it, and the Salmon River in Idaho in the late summer sounded like a reasonable river to run. We'd received our permit, and it was going to be a total family get-together, again with various and assorted friends. We all gathered at Carol and Nancy's home in Missoula, drove to the put-in with all our boats and camping gear, and took off for five exciting days on a beautiful and at times downright frightening river. Mostly, we all came through upright, with only one major spill in a class IV rapid. Carol said it was tame compared to doing the Grand Canyon or the Gulf of Alaska in a kayak—so once again I learned something about my own limitations.

My private Ecuador trip in October with Paul Coopmans got me some long-wanted species like Crescent-faced Antpitta (on the fourth try), Barred Antthrush, Chestnut-crowned Gnateater, Bicolored Antvireo, and finally a long overdue Pale-eyed Thrush. A long-planned trip to Yemen would complete my birding travels this first "relaxed" year of my alleged retirement from competitive birding. As with Ethiopia, it was a trip I'd always intended to take—some day. I kept putting it off, and then the serious civil war between the former North and South Yemen broke out, and it looked like that destination would be out for some time. Not as long as I'd feared, however, so I signed up immediately when

Puaiohi

Birdquest advertised a trip for November of 1996. Not only were there at least a dozen (depending on your taxonomy) likely endemics restricted to the Arabian Peninsula, but there were also a great many birds here that I'd seen before only in Africa. Despite its proximity to that continent, Yemen is of course in Asia, so I could add quite a lot of species to my Asia list. I hadn't done much traveling in Arab countries, and it's certainly not my favorite culture (a common enough viewpoint among emancipated western women), but both geographically and ornithologically I found it fascinating. We did beautifully with the birding. In addition to all the endemics, we had splendid views of Nubian Nightjar one evening, lots of Jouanin's Petrels on our boat trip, good views of Dunn's Lark in crossing the Empty Quarter with our Bedouin guide, and as a grand finale, I spotted a stunning Hypocolius (a male this time) on our last morning, for one of the very few Yemen records.

From mid-November through December, David's and my next challenge was to be learning to scuba dive. We'd both done a lot of snorkeling over some incredibly beautiful coral reefs in various parts of the world, and I'd always found it utterly enchanting and enticing. It is the only activity I've ever done that has made me wonder (almost seriously) why I was "wasting" all this time and energy watching birds! Snorkeling is certainly magical—but the lure of going deeper and staying longer was becoming irresistible. No, I *really* wasn't going to set out to see the fish of the world; I just wanted to try scuba to see how I felt about it. I had a number of friends and companions (birders, mostly) who encouraged me, and David seemed willing, though he was probably not as sold on the prospect as I was.

We signed up for classroom and pool instruction here at

home, and swam regularly at the YMCA for a few weeks prior to the class. There was no problem with this first part. For our open-water training, we'd decided to go to the Florida Keys, which sounded easy and was about the closest place to find tropical water in December. Unfortunately, our stay coincided with the coldest spell in the Keys in recorded history, and the water was unpleasantly turbulent on top and murky below—all very intimidating to novices. The advantage was that no one else was there (small wonder!), so we had a private instructor who was patient and kind, and helped us struggle through the necessary skills. It was more trauma than fun, but we were certified, and it could only get better. We both knew that the only place we really want to scuba is in the same kind of calm, clear, warm waters over tropical coral reefs where the snorkeling is great as well—maybe Bonaire or the Caymans (where the Vitelline Warbler also resides!). Two of our children are divers, and the others snorkel, so maybe some Christmas?

See? I *was* thinking about things other than birds!

~20~
1997

I didn't submit a 1996 year-end list to the ABA for the first time in many years, so that takes me "officially" out of numerical competition. It was meaningless now to me to continue counting birds in accordance with Clements' taxonomy, and after reaching my last numerical goal, I wanted to de-emphasize that aspect of world birding in my own life. I worked on my own taxonomic interpretation of Sibley's *Birds of the World* 2.0 (1996) computer program and decided to express my total life list as a percentage of that overall base list, as I've already discussed at some length in my chapter on "The New Taxonomy".

Additionally, I learned recently of the surprising and saddening death from cancer of Sandra Fisher, who along with husband Michael Lambarth, were my closest numerical competitors. Somehow, this event seemed yet another signal for an end to the competitive aspect of birding in my own life. The race is over for her, and for me as well, but I can happily go on birding on my own terms while others close in and eventually overtake my record. I hope I live to see my role model Peter Kaestner pass the 8,000 threshold one day.

I was still planning lots of travel, of course. I started 1997 with a Cameroon clean up on Terry Stevenson's trip, finally getting to the Bamenda highlands for those endemics, including a splendid close view of Bannerman's Turaco. I think I got there in the nick of time, as the pathetic remnants of habitat are being cut and burned more each year. In general, we observed many excellent birds this time around, and my want list for that country is now nicely diminished and about at the point where a return seems unlikely.

I made a quick trip to Ireland after Cameroon to connect, finally, with an adult of the nominate race of Iceland Gull (*Larus glaucoides glaucoides*), my last major gull-form on earth. From there, I joined a tour to Bulgaria, mainly to see the wintering spectacle along the Black Sea coast of thousands of the world's most beautiful goose—Red-breasted. Our luck held, and thanks to the leader's persistence, at the eleventh hour we also managed a fine view of one highly endangered Lesser White-fronted Goose amid thousands of Greaters.

Namibia was next. It was my second visit there, so I had only a handful of endemics to look for, and we connected with all but the ever-elusive Cinderella Waxbill. It was a different picture of Namibia this time around, however. Unprecedented rains had turned this usually parched, desert country into a green and blooming land. Birds were in full song (Monotonous Lark, for example—otherwise easily overlooked) and stunning breeding plumage (notably the extraordinary male Shaft-tailed Whydahs).

A year or two before, I'd arranged some private birding in Thailand with Uthai Treesucon, a local expert, for the month of April. There were some high-priority species here that I still desperately wanted to see, like Coral-billed Ground-Cuckoo, Blue-winged Pitta, Siamese Fireback, Giant Nuthatch, Brown Hornbill, and Red-faced Liocichla. We achieved truly spectacular views of all these and many others, leaving very little behind. Uthai was good fun, the Thai food wonderful as always, and the birding extraordinarily successful; it was one of those rare and nearly perfect trips. On the way home I stopped in Honolulu for a couple of days to look for the Oahu Elepaio, a virtually certain split, and undoubtedly my last findable Hawaiian land bird. Tom had given me information on a couple of sites, and after finding it quite easily at the first spot, I took a holiday and went snorkeling.

When I visited the Canary Islands in 1994, I birded with the resident expert, Tony Clarke. During our few days together, we discussed a lot of birding spots in the world, especially Australia. It was very obvious that Tony had had a lot of experience here, and I still hadn't really figured out how I was going to go about seeing the widely scattered forty or so species still remaining for me on that continent. Pretty quickly, the answer became apparent: have Tony set up the logistics and be my guide. We decided to concentrate on the North, since we could do a comprehensive trip all across it in the Aussie winter (our summer)—the best time for the hot tropics and the northern deserts. Even doing just the north, it was still going to take nearly six weeks.

This plan came to pass in July and August of 1997. Our comprehensive itinerary (which included a spontaneous couple of days near Sydney en route home) held chances for 29 species, plus a number of distinctive, disjunct races (always potential splits). Arranging the flight schedule, rental cars, etc. was something of a nightmare for Tony, because the flights never seemed to go where or when we wanted them to, and when he did get something established, then they would change. In the end, we came up with a workable if not ideal plan and met in Cairns to start the adventure.

Here we experienced our only miss of the entire trip—Lesser Sooty-Owl—but certainly not for lack of time and effort expended. Granted, time of year was not good for calling or response, but the birds are *common* in the various areas we worked. We did hear one, even fairly close, but the jinx persisted. As the weeks wore on, this miss became ever more frustrating, as we hit target after target on the truly rare or difficult birds.

We truly *did* northern Australia, from east to west: Cairns and Atherton Tablelands, Cape York Peninsula, Mackay and Eungella, Mount Isa, Alice Springs, Tennant Creek and the Barkly Tablelands, Borroloola, Katherine, Kakadu, Darwin, Kununurra, the Kimberleys, Halls Creek and the Canning Stock Route (certainly the biggest adventure of all), Derby, Wyndham, and finally the Blue Mountains and Glen Davis Road near Sydney! It was a massive undertaking, but incredibly, it all worked as planned—nearly.

Probably the biggest surprises were a beautiful perched Red Goshawk in the Kimberleys and a wonderful close fly-by Gray Falcon along the Canning Stock Route, not to mention flushing a Buff-breasted Buttonquail twice in the first few moments of our first attempt, an event we never repeated even after hours of working the best habitat with the local resident expert. A few target species acted almost as expected, like Rufous Owl, Golden-shouldered and Hooded Parrots, Regent, White-streaked, and Eungella Honeyeaters. Others, like Chestnut-quilled Rock-Pigeon, Black Grasswren, Yellow Chat, and Origma [Rock Warbler] made us really struggle.

The Canning Stock Route excursion was almost an afterthought. Tony had gotten somewhat belated information that it really was not as life-threatening as recent accounts had made it sound, and that Princess Parrots [Alexandra's Parrots] seemed to be reliable in July, if you got as far as about 400 kilometers south. So we tacked it onto the itinerary, knowing in advance that we'd need a four-wheel-drive vehicle, camping and basic survival equipment, food, lots of jerry cans of water and fuel, and probably an extra man to help dig us out of the sand dunes if necessary. We (i.e., Tony) had to drive over literally many hundreds of sand dunes, some minor, some impressively major. He quickly learned the best techniques, and we never did get seriously dug-in, which had been a prime concern, at least to me. By late afternoon of our second day, we were in the right area and were keeping all eyes and ears open for the alleged "noisy, conspicuous flocks" of Princess Parrots—which did not materialize. The entire next day we scoured both sides of the dry bed of Lake Tobin. We split up to cover more ground. I saw a small flock of our target species but in bad light and only as a quick fly-by, David Andrew (our third companion) saw two birds briefly perched—but Tony saw nothing, so he was close to suicidal by the end of that day. The trip was definitely not working out as planned. As a strategy, we felt it was probably best to stay in the same area the next day, since we knew at least that there were some parrots around—though certainly not as many as advertised from the past few years.

The next morning found Tony and me standing on a high dune near where David had seen his perched birds; we'd been there for a couple of hours, watching flocks of Budgerigars and not much else. About 8 a.m., whatever deities are in charge of all these wonderful and miserable experiences we birders have, decided to relent. Tony's anguish was apparently just too much for any gods (or humans) to bear. A pair and then three more unmistakable Princess Parrots made a long flight past us at less than 100 yards, in perfect light, showing their softly-colored tapered bodies, bright golden-green wingcoverts, incredibly long slim tails—and maybe even, with a little imagination, some pinkish showing on the sides of the throat. The relief for all was distinctly palpable. We'd come precariously close to missing what was clearly everyone's most-wanted species for the entire trip, and certainly the one that had cost us the most in terms of logistics, equipment, time, trouble, and potential risk. Now all we had to do was drive for two days back out of there and over all those dunes once more. No problem: virtually anything is possible when you've seen your bird!

The Sydney-area birds were a distinct bonus. Tony had just been to Glen Davis Road before meeting me in Cairns, so had told me there were lots of Regent Honeyeaters, several Plum-headed Finches, and a pair of Glossy Black-Cockatoos with Spotted Quail-thrushes and Origma not far away. Obviously, I couldn't resist and changed my flight home. All except the Origma cooperated nicely, and even that last holdout came through in the end. Statistically, with 28 out of 29 target species seen, it was certainly one of my most successful trips ever.

Two more trips would finish out the year. I was returning to Amazonian Brazil in September–October and then ending the year with my husband on a five-week cruise from South Africa down through the Indian Ocean subantarctic islands to the Antarctic continent and Emperor Penguin colonies and then back to western Australia. Meanwhile, I had some time at home and continued to work long but fascinating hours on my annotation and revision of Sibley's *Birds of the World* 2.0.

It was quite obvious by now that this would be an on-going project, one that I could continually update as new taxonomic studies were published. Not only would I add a few birds to my life list as I saw them on my travels, but I would also periodically be changing (mostly adding to) my base or master list. I had broken the list into eight major sections, and with Sibley's good, detailed table of contents along with Monroe's 1993 checklist and my own by now quite complete familiarity with the family sequence, I found I could easily go to the species in question, either on my hard copy or my computer. As it stood when I first finished the project in September 1997, I'd seen 8,383 out of 10,024 species, or 83.6 percent.

Amazonian Brazil, with its three major destinations of Manaus, São Gabriel da Cachoeira, and Alta Floresta, most of which I'd been to before, still netted me about 12 new species, with some good surprises, as well as some disappointing misses. We saw an incredibly close and totally unperturbed recently-fledged Harpy Eagle (my third encounter with this species), some new island specialties that had been discovered since my last visit to Manaus, and some new and exciting species at São Gabriel (where I'd never been), and also at Alta Floresta. Birds in the by-now-familiar category of "hoped-for but missed" included White-winged Potoo at Manaus and Rufous-necked Puffbird at Alta Floresta.

The latter was truly a serious disappointment. This species had been seen well by both groups in two different locations the previous year, and I'd spent every siesta-time at the Rio Cristalino Lodge scouring the forest on my own, on trails where this enticing puffbird had been seen in the past, but with no success at all. Ironically, one was seen very briefly by a lucky few at the head of a long line of 16 people, literally at the last minute, on our way out of the area—when I was near the end of the line. It was spotted close, flushed, and not seen again. Bret Whitney reported the only consoling factor to me: Ted Parker had never seen this species either, despite many attempts in numerous locations. I was in the best of company, at least!

By contrast, the limited new species to be encountered on the long cruise to the "far side" of Antarctica (only about nine) almost all appeared relatively easily, and in satisfying—or even overwhelming—numbers. The Emperor Penguins were simply unbelievable, in settings as good or better than any January or February calendar shots you've ever seen. We were extremely lucky with weather and ice conditions where it counted, and spent many long and extraordinarily comfortable, windless hours at several totally overwhelming Emperor colonies. In the end, it was worth *not* having seen a molting juvenile on an ice floe on my first Antarctic trip, because I now fully realized that *this* was by far the best way to see an Emperor! It was the best possible ending to a busy and productive year.

Phoebe observing Emperor Penguins in Antarctica, c. 1997

1998

S ome years start with a bang and others, like this one, with a whimper. I'd indeed taken a considerable chance in signing on for a repeat northeast Brazil trip, since we'd done very well in 1993, and I couldn't realistically hope for more than about five new species. Among them, however, were some major priorities that it seemed we had a serious chance for: the single wild Spix's Macaw, which Bret Whitney had gotten his previous group in to see, Buff-fronted Owl, very little-known and almost never seen, which was also found and seen beautifully that previous trip, and Pink-legged Graveteiro, the newly-described monotypic genus and species from southeast Bahia, which (you guessed it!) was *also* seen on that previous trip. In short, I went for three species, missed two entirely, and had such a brief view of the owl that it really wasn't at all satisfying.

The sad tale of the disappearance of the Spix's Macaw has already been told, in connection with discussion of some recent and totally unexpected avian discoveries in Brazil. So that was one hope forever dashed. We did manage to find a totally unexpected and excitingly beautiful new species, discovered only a few months before, an *Antilophia* manakin [Araripe Manakin], obviously related to Helmeted Manakin—but with an entirely white body, black only on the wings and tail, and with the dramatic blood-red crest of its congener. It was staggeringly beautiful, certainly, and quite easy to see, but unfortunately we spent way too much time here, and consequently lost our prime dusk hour for the Buff-fronted Owl. By the time of our arrival around 8 p.m., there seemed to be no response, until our co-leader heard a faint branch-shaking sound, shone his light, and for about two seconds the owl was perched and visible. Unfortunately, the light was behind people, illuminating them as well, and there was considerable commotion since we were all caught totally by surprise (there had been no vocal response at all). The owl turned and flew immediately, never to be seen again.

I clung to my final hope: *surely* we'll find this graveteiro on the final day, and at least I'll pull one new genus out of this trip. In the meantime, we were finding virtually all other targets, 99 percent of which I had seen on my previous trip, but one truly exciting bonus was the ultra-rare Alagoas Foliage-gleaner, seen very well with a mixed flock in the remnant bit of forest near Murici.

The final day came, and we spent many agonizing, unsuccessful hours playing the graveteiro tape and scrutinizing flocks, but really in areas peripheral to the species' stronghold, which was ironically only a few hours' drive south of where we had started our day. Only about noon did we head south and, for a variety of reasons, never really got far enough to optimize our chances. The whole frustrating day seemed to be a study in how *not* to find this species, and the trip had ended on a sour note for everyone, but especially for me.

Fortunately for the sake of morale, there was an extension. We were going to spend about three days in the eastern Amazonian forests at Caxiuanã—a logistically difficult site to reach, involving a flight on a small plane from Belém to Breves and then a boat trip of nine hours upriver.

The research station where we stayed proved to be a totally amazing place, unlike any tropical station I've ever visited. It seemed more like a college campus, built of steel and stone, with paved roads and streetlights, rooms with private bathrooms, closet space, and ceiling fans—a godsend, even though they went off with the generator. There was a tower for canopy observation, with 24 platforms each spaced six feet apart—so it went *way* up there! With the whole station seemingly built like the Rock of Gibraltar, it was something of a shock to find the tower platforms made of plywood and rotting away. Nevertheless, the rest of the structure was sturdy and rock-stable, so we just had to be careful to put our weight on the stairs or steel supports rather than on the plywood. With any luck at all, they'll have replaced the rotting platforms with metal grids before the next group gets there.

I'd pretty much put the agonizingly disappointing northeast experience behind me by the time we got there, so my morale, as well as my birding, had improved vastly. The first morning we had fabulous views from the tower of Golden Parakeets, a marvelously distinctive and unusual parrot, which would probably better be called a "macawlet". So there, finally, was my new genus (*Guarouba*) for the trip.

The next important event was the appearance, at last, of the Rufous-necked Puffbird I'd so narrowly missed seeing at Alta Floresta a few months before. This one responded to tape, gave marvelous views from all angles, and in general behaved as sluggish puffbirds so often do. It also destroyed my theory of "they're never seen twice in the same place", since this spot was precisely where Bret Whitney had seen one on his scouting trip months before. It all seemed so easy this time. I did wish, of course, that we could have shared those soul-satisfying moments with Ted Parker.

Nearly everyone on the trip badly wanted to see Dark-winged Trumpeters—and I wanted to see them better. Our single encounter with a group of these birds was simply mind-boggling, with incredible, close detail down to the purplish iridescence on the breast. There were also good views of amazing creatures like Vulturine Parrot, Chestnut-belted Gnateater, Blue-backed Tanager, Spotted Puffbird, and Crimson Topaz—not lifers, but beautiful and seldom-seen, at least by me. All in all, things ended well.

After my return home, a definite change of pace seemed in order after all the mixed emotions of this last trip. David and I decided to spend a week on Grand Cayman, mainly to improve our minimal scuba-diving skills and experience. We gained a good bit of confidence this time around, began to feel a lot more comfortable with equipment and techniques, and saw some wonderful fish—about fifty that I could identify and lots that I couldn't. Our day off for birding went well also. Vitelline Warblers (my only lifer here) were vocal and easy, and I found nearly all the other dozen endemic subspecies of this island, including a marvelous, close "singing" Caribbean Dove.

My plans were to leave for Colombia in early April, but I learned from many sources that two birders I know, along with two others, were being held hostage by guerrillas southeast of Bogotá. Colombians were taken also, at a major roadblock during the night on the major Bogotá-Villavicencio highway, but they were apparently released unharmed. With elections coming up in May, the guerrillas were increasing their violent protest activities. There were several fatalities at this last scene, when government forces attempted to remove the roadblock.

The area where the birders were unwisely traveling at night is a known guerrilla stronghold and, unfortunately, also the area

Dark-winged Trumpeter

that holds the newly-described Cundinamarca Antpitta (*Grallaria kaestneri*). This bird has been essentially off-limits to birders since its discovery by Peter Kaestner in the early nineties (described in 1992). Along with serious concern for my friends and other hostages, the inevitable question arose: "Did they see the antpitta before they were captured?!"

In any case, our group decided not to go there. We had been rudely shaken into acute awareness of potentially serious problems, even though our leader intended to remain in daily contact about the security situations on our proposed itinerary. Fortunately, it was a British trip, though most of the eight clients were American this time. In view of the U.S. State Department's upgraded advisory, any American company would simply have had to cancel the trip. *Déjà vu!* My first attempt to get to Darien, Panama was unfortunately timed as the Noriega crisis was building to major proportions, and then when the official advisory was issued only a few days before we were to leave, the trip was canceled. It was a few years before that trip was done again.

Quite frankly, I would tell the State Department that this trip is "essential". Okay, they've warned me about what happened, and the U.S. Embassy in Bogotá is not going to do anything in any case. You can't get much more "essential" to a birder than the chance at some of the species (and genera) that we might find in perfectly safe areas on this trip. We had a number of built-in safety factors, and we promised to be careful and to use good judgment about where and when to travel, setting no patterns of repeated visits to remote areas (probably our major mistake in PNG in 1986). My mountaineer daughter Carol told me my rationalizations sound exactly like those of mountain-climbers who persist in the face of serious avalanches, injuries, and even deaths of their companions just because "they want that peak!" Of course. Emotion and personal desire really do reign in all passionate endeavors, not objectivity and reason. And sometimes we're just plain lucky enough to get away with it.

My husband even asked serious questions concerning what I might want to do about ransom payments. Before our first Colombian trip (a private one to the Santa Martas and Bogotá area in 1995), we had even investigated the possibility of "ransom insurance"—which does exist, but turned out to be so outrageously expensive (especially for Colombia) and difficult to acquire that we quickly abandoned the idea. Anyhow, my answer was "no ransom".

During this first trip, we encountered some guerrillas on a military exercise in the Magdalena Valley near Honda. We were totally outnumbered, as well as helpless and vulnerable with a flat tire at the time, but they were very friendly, helped changed the tire, and looked at our bird books with evident interest. Then during the course of our visit to southwestern Colombia in 1996, we were fortunate enough to miss a major daytime highway roadblock cum robbery in the Patia Valley by about half an hour, thanks to the seemingly insurmountable difficulty of changing some money at a bank in Pasto. There were indeed human hazards in this country—but not to go there at all because of the possibility of encountering them? Unthinkable! It has become ever more clear to me that if I had spent my life avoiding any and all potential risks, I would have missed doing most of the things that have comprised the best years of my life.

As all of this background was going through my mind, and as various friends and relatives were expressing concern and advising caution, a good friend sent me a quote from Helen Keller: "Security is mostly a superstition. It does not exist in nature nor do the children of men as a whole experience it. Avoiding danger is no safer in the long run than outright exposure. Life is a daring adventure or nothing." My friend's addendum to this was: "We do have to remember that there is a fine line between adventure and stupidity!" And on that note I went!

We all had a fabulous trip, entirely trouble-free and highly productive. I saw about twenty new species, including three new genera, which was really excellent, considering this was my third trip to Colombia in the past few years. Many of our spectacular successes were birds that really epitomize Colombia for me: Tanager Finch, Multicolored Tanager, White-capped Tanager, Black-billed Mountain-Toucan, Wattled Guan, Saffron-headed Parrot, Brown-banded and Bicolored Antpittas, and all the accessible Santa Marta specialties.

One of the birder-hostages escaped while his captors slept, just about the time of our arrival, increasing our concern for the others. They were subsequently released unharmed, however, just as we got back home, so that scenario ended as happily as possible—except that no, they hadn't seen the Cundinamarca Antpitta.

One of the two main drawbacks was a lot of rain and fog in the mountains (which was most of the trip). The prolonged drought of El Niño ended with a vengeance in Colombia this April, and it did cut into our birding time and opportunities. The second problem (for me, at least) was constant, serious sleep-deprivation. I can offset the insomnia to some extent by skipping dinners, especially when good early breakfasts are available, which they miraculously were. Anyhow, I'm finding that a grueling pace for three straight weeks gets ever harder as I get older.

In this light, I was somewhat appalled to realize that I had signed up to go across the Tibetan Plateau in search of endemics with Ben King in the summer—a trip which would doubtless surpass nearly everything in my experience for miserable and grueling conditions (with, I hope, the exception of Irian Jaya!). There are those who think I'm a masochist—and they may be right!

In May I did a short and easy jaunt to Poland with a British group. Two of my three major targets—Corn Crake (another new genus) and Aquatic Warbler—cooperated well, with the Corn Crake experience nicely laying to rest the myth still persisting among many Europeans that these highly vocal creatures are "unseeable". They are difficult, yes, but it really is largely a matter of finding a calling one in appropriate habitat and employing an effective technique. The hoped-for Eurasian Pygmy-Owl, however, remained ever-elusive, like its cousin, the Northern Pygmy-Owl of North America. I hadn't found the secret to these two yet, but there surely must be one.

Lots of taxonomically interesting publications had appeared since I'd finished my master list the previous fall, the most outstanding being *Studies in Neotropical Ornithology Honoring Ted Parker* (Ornithological Monographs No. 48) published by the American Ornithologists' Union (AOU). There were also some European papers, an Ecuador checklist reflecting the Ridgely and Greenfield taxonomy to be used in their upcoming field guide, some *Wilson Bulletin* papers, a BirdLife International publication on *Endemic Bird Areas of the World*, a new field guide to West Indian birds (Raffaele et al.), and Ben King's *Checklist of the Birds of Eurasia*, as well as various other isolated publications. And then, of course, there was the new *Antilophia* manakin we'd seen in northeast Brazil! All in all, strong cases were presented for many new "species", so my master list by mid-year had leapt forward to 10,159, and my life list to 8,512, or 83.8 percent, nearly where I was on first completing this project the previous fall! Progress

Corn Crake

comes slow and hard these days.

Northwest China and Tibet did indeed live up to all dire expectations. I certainly got to the "roof of the world" and back, but as is so often the case, it sounds a good bit more glamorous than the reality of day-to-day surviving and birding there. Living conditions were by and large miserable, activities strenuous to impossible, drives agonizing, seemingly endless and overly-cramped. Fun? Well, sometimes. Successful? Certainly! We connected nicely with Biddulph's Ground-Jay [Xinjiang Ground-Jay] in Xinjiang, and I at least saw well all available Tibetan endemics, including such little-known and seldom-seen birds as Roborowski's Rosefinch [Tibetan Rosefinch], Koslov's Bunting [Tibetan Bunting], Buff-throated Monal-Partridge [Szecheny's Partridge] , and Ala Shan Redstart. It's easy enough to summarize the successes, but it must be remembered that all of them took nearly six weeks of *extremely* hard work at lung-searing altitudes. One especially gratifying reward for a long and strenuous climb was finding a downy chick Tibetan Sandgrouse, attended by two superb adults at 17,000 feet in a flower-strewn meadow surrounded by incredible snow-capped peaks. This is truly the ultimate sandgrouse, and a strong element of luck is always needed to find it—not that many have done so.

Our drive through the Tien Shan mountains was staggeringly beautiful, getting across the near-impasse of a major avalanche exciting, most of the climbs on foot were breathtaking (visually and physically), and overall the several initial birding frustrations led to success and relief in the end. The final effort—a severely taxing one—was an arduous climb at the end of the day up a mountain back of Reting Gompa, a monastery well north of Lhasa. The target here was our last endemic, Tibetan Eared-

Pheasant [White Eared-Pheasant], a new bird for all, including the leaders. Day was waning, we were exhausted, and the pheasants were calling sporadically from ever higher on the steep slopes. It got to be turn-around time—after all, we had to get back down a long, serious slope with enough light to see. Jon Krakauer's tale of the tragedy on Everest (*Into Thin Air*) was definitely in my mind. "There they are!" Ben's words transfixed us, and we (the few of us who had struggled up this far) quickly latched onto the huge and surprisingly dark *blue* (we had all expected *white*) pheasants. There were six adults with small chicks. We lingered for a full half hour of waning light, savoring the views, enjoying the details of their red facial skin and dramatic white plumes, and watching their leisurely behavior. And now I was on my way home, with no more mountains to climb, with only a tricky descent on shaky knees, a clammy night in a monastery, a long drive to Lhasa, and some very long flights between me and home—and, of course, the next adventure!

...which was back to Amazonian Brazil on a private trip with Andrew Whittaker (a neotropical ornithologist with expertise in Brazilian birds) and a good friend, starting with a *very* much out-of-the-way effort to find the graveteiro, our frustratingly disappointing miss at the end of the northeast Brazil trip in February. Success in this endeavor would seem to be dependent upon being in the heart of the species' range and probably at a better time of year (pre-breeding) than February. In any case, success we had, with wonderful studies of adults and immature, singing spontaneously and very responsive to tape playback. The same general area also gave us Little Wood-Rail and Plain-bellied Emerald, so the side trip had definitely paid off.

Local flights in Amazonian Brazil are typically middle-of-the-night "milk-runs", and we certainly experienced our share of these on our itinerary. Boa Vista gave us some highly localized birds found otherwise only in Guyana, like Rio Branco Antbird and Hoary-throated Spinetail. My second visit to São Gabriel da Cachoeira held nice rewards in the form of a marvelous pair of Chestnut-crested Antbirds, a wispy male Black-bellied Thorntail, and two most interesting experiences with Cinnamon Tyrant-Manakin [Cinnamon Tyrant] (of varying taxonomic position), a near look-alike for Ruddy-tailed Flycatcher. Yet another new genus in the form of White-naped Seedeater (much more interesting than it sounds) appeared on cue north of Manaus. Three new genera for this short trip, as well as some other high quality species, made it well worthwhile.

An idea for a special "Parker Memorial Expedition" to northern Peru had been brewing for over a year in the minds of a few of the participants on Barry Walker's 1997 Marañon trip, and by September 1998 we finally had it put together. Our main targets were two: *Herpsilochmus parkeri*, Ash-throated Antwren, the first bird named in honor of Ted Parker, and one which he never got to see in the wild, and *Wetmorethraupis sterrhopteron*, Orange-throated Tanager. The latter represents a monotypic genus and has an interesting story behind the generic name. In the early 1960s, the well-known ornithologist Alexander Wetmore stated unequivocally that all the birds of the world had been discovered, aside perhaps from some slightly different forms that might show up in museum trays. Not long afterwards, a Louisiana State University (LSU) expedition to a previously unvisited area in northern Peru discovered this strikingly different tanager. It was described in 1964 and named after the man who had discounted the possibility of anything "truly new" ever being found anywhere.

Less than forty years later, biologists have become quite accustomed to the reality that amazing new creatures (not just birds) are turning up all over the world, in the precious and precarious pockets of native habitats left on this planet. What an absolutely amazing and exciting time this is to be a birder-at-large!

So there we were in Tarapoto, Peru—a handful of Brits and Canadians, two American women, and Barry Walker. Tarapoto happens to be near the type locality for Huallaga Slaty-Antshrike [Northern Slaty-Antshrike], a potential split from the other "Eastern" Slaty-Antshrikes, and a form which had not been seen since it was collected many years before. Obviously, we had to look for this one. And looking hard, in several likely-looking spots, we found a cooperative pair and got the first-ever voice recordings.

Tarapoto is also a good base for birding the road to Yurimaguas, which rises on one side of the mountains, goes through a tunnel at the crest and down the other side, giving easy access to a number of different elevations and habitats. A splendid day spent birding this road produced an astonishing surprise—a pair of Plumbeous Euphonias, a first for Peru, and totally out of range, being otherwise a bird of lowland Guianas, southern Venezuela, and northern Brazil. Needless to say, we were all in a fine frame of mind to start the "real" part of the expedition.

From Jerillo we rode horses, with an attendant caravan of pack mules carrying our camping equipment, food, and personal duffles, for several hours uphill to the environs of Jesús del Monte, a mountain village that hadn't seen the likes of us since the LSU expedition there that initially found our target antwren. Thanks to Barry's logistical arrangements and his skilled camp staff, we lived in comfort on a high grassy knoll for several days, with good access to a long forest trail through a range of habitats and with a marvelously pro-

ductive fruiting tree just ten minutes from camp. Almost anticli-
mactically, we heard the *Herpsilochmus* singing while we had our
first lunch, before we'd even set up camp, and had splendid views
(as well as photos and videos) of a male shortly thereafter. Our first
real target achieved, we could now just have fun birding for a few
days, and indeed we did. Bar-winged Wood-Wren is common here,
but we struggled for good views. Milky-rumped Manakin [Blue-
rumped Manakin], Rufous-vented Whitetip, Napo Sabrewing, and
a gorgeous pair of Fiery-throated Fruiteaters in that fruiting tree
added zest to the following days, which also gave further excellent
views of a pair of "Parker's Antwrens" [Ash-throated Antwren]—
our real reason for being here.

The road to our *Wetmorethraupis* destination was going to be a
very long one indeed, with nights of camping and even a hotel or
two, but we were also going through habitat for some great birding (over Abra Patricia, through Florida and on to Bagua, then
north). Some well-chosen select stops yielded lifers for nearly
everyone, the ultimate being a male Marvelous Spatuletail, waving
its unbelievable tail wires low and close in roadside flowers, which
made us all forget the rain we'd been standing in for an hour.

Vehicle problems in northern Peru are almost to be expected,
and this trip was no exception. Barry's logistical finesse was put to
the test in Bagua, where our bus finally collapsed (thank God it was
here, and not in a remote spot en route!), and alternate transport
had to be acquired for the trip north to Imazita. Here again, Barry
had to find vehicles that could get us up the mountain road and
through some serious-looking quagmires to the proper elevation
and forest before we could even begin our *Wetmorethraupis* quest.

With surprisingly little trauma, we got to a site dubbed "Peña
Blanca" by the locals and set up camp, or rather Barry's staff set

up camp while we birded the road. Barry had had the foresight to bring with us a young man from Imazita who claimed familiarity with our target species and its voice. We had an afternoon, a full day, and another morning to work the area, which our guide said certainly held our tanagers—though he acknowledged that they do move around. We had interesting birding that first afternoon, with quite a different avifauna than we'd encountered on the trip so far. In one mixed flock of rapidly moving birds, I had a split-second view of a tanager-sized bird with a throat that glowed like a Blackburnian Warbler. It got away as quickly as it had come, and I was left with the awful certainty that I had glimpsed our target, but really inadequately. We had to do better than this, especially since no one else had seen it at all.

The next morning at first light, our guide Marco shot out of his tent, excitedly saying he heard the tanagers calling. A very tall isolated tree, with its top intermittently disappearing in the early morning mist, held a few birds, but even scopes could barely reveal any features on the dark shapes. The sharp diagnostic voices were coming from here, however, and as the light improved and the mist momentarily cleared, we all got an admittedly distant and mediocre but definitive view of one very chunky tanager with a dark head and back and an orange throat. It was good enough for a tick, but we hoped to do better. The birds flew from what was evidently their roosting tree as soon as we'd gotten onto the first one, so after breakfast we were birding off down the road once again—with Marco carefully in tow. The morning progressed, and we had some false alarms with voices but no sightings and then another false alarm with chunky, orange-throated birds—which proved on inspection to be Black-spotted Barbets.

Our moment finally came, as it so often does when you simply spend enough time in the field. We could hear the tanagers calling, close this time, and lo and behold, here was a close bird, perched on a branch, singing its choppy *too-wee-choo* song and letting us study it in the scope. That fiery orange throat with the black surrounding head was certainly what I'd briefly glimpsed the day before, and now I was seeing it as I really yearned to—all features, including the iridescent, dark-blue shoulder. It was simply marvelous, and now the quest was over, the pressure was off, and we could have more fun birding for our remaining time here, which yielded a few nice surprises for everyone, including a Vermiculated Screech-Owl and some Ecuadorian Caciques.

Somehow, however, after surviving quite nicely the rigors of some really arduous climbing in Tibet a couple of months before, I managed to injure my knee on our easy and gentle downhill stroll for *Wetmorethraupis*. Fortunately, it was after I'd seen all the birds I wanted to, because it was painful and quite incapacitating for a full month afterward—most of which was spent at home, since (fortunately, once again) I had no more travels planned until early November.

So I fussed and fumed, felt geriatric and miserable, went to an orthopedic specialist and did a course of physical therapy, and generally railed against my aging body and its increasing vulnerability and slowness in healing. I acquired a good knee brace and an effective topical analgesic, got together my geriatric supplies, such as folding cane and stool, loaded up on painkillers and arthritic ointment, and set off in early November for a month in Malawi and South Africa.

I'd birded Zambia quite extensively ten years before, so there weren't a lot of new species for me in Malawi, but there were a few very special ones. The itinerary was well-designed to cover all major avifaunal areas, and we found nearly everything I could reasonably hope for. Even though I'd seen it well in Botswana, wonderful daytime views of Pel's Fishing-Owl were a major highlight. Livingstone's Flycatcher and Lilian's Lovebird are specialties of the south, and we had many fine views of both. A chance at the virtually endemic Cholo Alethe demanded a stiff, steep climb, for which I wore my very best knee brace and did fine both up and down. We were rewarded by an almost immediate fly-in of a very tape-responsive bird, which nonetheless managed to stay mostly out of sight, yielding brief and adequate but never great views. We came precariously close to missing the stunning White-winged Apalis, but our leader finally pulled out a marvelous pair at the eleventh hour. One really has to learn to keep hope alive until the absolute bitter end, because so often the miraculous appearance does actually happen in those final moments, when many have given up.

I'd been to the Nyika Plateau on my Zambia trip in 1988, and we had done very well with the forest birds, but had missed Scarlet-tufted Malachite Sunbird [Red-tufted Sunbird]. Since my daughter Carol had become familiar with this bird when she was leading mountain climbs on Mt. Kenya, it would be a "family catch-up" species for me, and I knew this trip was really my only chance. I was never going to be able to climb to the habitat on Mt. Kenya (above the dreaded "vertical bog")—especially with a bad knee. Once we finally found the right spot (blooming proteas in the ravine behind the Zambia Rest House), the birds seemed reasonably regular, and we had good views of a couple of turquoise-blue males.

My most-wanted species on the trip was White-winged Babbling-Starling [Babbling Starling], primarily because it is a monotypic genus, and my chief numerical goal these days is to whittle the remaining genera down to 100 living ones (out of nearly

2,100) remaining for me to see. We had fine studies of this unique bird in its miombo habitat, and that left me with 11 genera to go to get down to 100 (which would probably require two more years of birding). This bird seems to look, sound, and act like a babbler rather than a starling, so it would make an interesting case for a DNA study.

The Lilongwe area rounded out our Malawi birding, with an unexpected flock of Locustfinches and some more miombo specialties like Stierling's Woodpecker, Pale-billed Hornbill, Anchieta's Sunbird, and Whyte's Barbet. Shelley's Sunbird never came through for me, but that was the only miss of an expected species, and I do think it's one I may be able to live without.

This question is one I confront on every trip now: is this particular missed bird one that's important enough to pursue again during my increasingly limited life span, or am I willing to let it go? As experience mounts, it becomes ever clearer precisely which species fall into that category of the approximately 15 percent that I will never see. This prediction is based on my current position of having now seen 84 percent, hopes of having a few more years left to play this game, and realistic expectation that there will be a lot more splitting during those years, making it ever harder to increase an already high percentage.

I'd made plans to go on from Malawi for a South African clean up of a handful of species we'd missed on my two previous trips there. It was still too early in the season to be prime time for my missing South African flufftails, but there were a few other birds to work on: Cape Parrot [Brown-necked Parrot] (the southern form, due to be split), Knysna Woodpecker, Spotted Ground-Thrush, Lemon-breasted Canary [Lemon-breasted Seedeater], and I wanted a good view, finally, of Swee Waxbill. We found them all, and had wonderfully satisfying views, but the icing on the cake was a "beyond-my-wildest-dreams" experience with a beautiful male Buff-spotted Flufftail that paraded back and forth in a perfect location in a gloomy patch of forest, searching for the female calling from our tape recorder. Never mind that we got locked into this Durban park in the late afternoon and had to escape by climbing over a fence topped with barbed and razor wire; my guide and flufftail expert was a policeman, after all.

It was the end of the birding year—unless I could find a Northern Pygmy-Owl in Idaho. I planned to take a tape and a flashlight to our family holiday reunion; after all, some of my kids wanted this one too.

The Snetsinger family in Montana, June 5, 1998. Clockwise from the top are: David, Susan, Phoebe, Carol, Penny, and Tom.

~24~
1999 ⊹ Beginning of the End

Fortunately, our family Christmas reunion was a huge success, because the owl search certainly was not. The jinx persisted.

The new year began with a visit to Tiputini, a new and remote lodge in Amazonian Ecuador. I had a very short list of targets and managed to connect with three (Salvin's Curassow, Reddish-winged Bare-eye, a lovely male at an antswarm, and the Amazonian form of Striped Manakin, sure to be split from the form I'd seen in Bahia, Brazil). As so often happens, I was with the wrong group on the day that a White-bellied Dacnis was beautifully seen from the canopy tower. My prime quest (new genus) was Black Bushbird, seen easily and well there by the leader on the scouting trip, but as luck had it this time, we didn't even hear one.

I'd learned to my considerable dismay the previous fall that an eagerly anticipated trip to the Ivory Coast (including a stay in the Tai Forest with good chance for Yellow-headed Rockfowl [White-necked Rockfowl] or *Picathartes*) had to be canceled due to lack of clients. I'd done this trip a few years before (1993–1994), agonizingly missing a chance encounter with this species, but that was before the stakeout area at Tai had become known and logistically feasible. Now it looked like another miss was looming, but for quite a different reason. After a considerable flurry of communications (thank goodness for email), I managed to get the leader, Nik Borrow, to take me privately for a week just to Tai for this one major target species.

I already had a frequent flyer ticket to London and back, with dates easily changed, so from there we flew to Abidjan and with hired car and driver, drove west across the whole country and then north on some pretty awful dirt roads to a basic tourist "lodge" at the edge of the Tai Forest. Violet-backed Hyliota surrendered itself here late that afternoon, providing an auspicious omen. The next step was a ten-kilometer hike the next day through beautiful forest to a considerably more basic forest camp (with mosquito nets on high platforms, accessed by ladders). This spot would be "home" for four nights.

Step by step, four days after leaving home, I was at least getting closer to looking for my quarry in a likely area. Early the next morning, we set off with our local guide for an hour's hike and scramble to his rockfowl site, a beautiful forested slope with huge mossy boulders and sheer rock faces, on one of which was located a single mud-cup nest, used in a previous rainy-season nesting. We picked some semi-secluded perches nearby and settled down for a long wait. Little happened for about an hour, when suddenly a harsh call revealed the presence of a startled rockfowl. It had come around the corner of the rocky outcropping and been shocked by the close presence of humans. It flew to a vine, perched briefly, then flew to an open branch at a safer distance, where I had an exquisite view of this astonishing creature. From there, it leapt to the ground and bounded silently into deeper forest and out of my view. Instant, total success! Now we could just have fun birding, which we did for the rest of that day and the next, finding a few more treasures like Red-chested Owlet and

Forest Scrub-Robin.

Since this was almost certainly a once-in-a-lifetime experience, I wanted to savor it as much as possible by returning to the Yellow-headed Rockfowl site on our final morning. We took our same seats, waited the same length of time or less, and then suddenly the rockfowl simply materialized and perched in classic pose on a boulder below me, on the opposite side from where it had appeared before. Another superb view was had by both Nik and me, and we walked away feeling very mellow. On the way back to camp, we encountered a swarm of driver ants and paused to check the bird activity. Our guide excitedly exclaimed "*Picathartes!*"; he'd spotted a rockfowl perched inconspicuously on a rock at some distance upslope. The bird sat still and preened, allowing us prolonged views, until we noticed another one on a log just nearby. It was totally oblivious to our presence and occupied in examining and occasionally picking off the insects disturbed by the ants around it. We must have enjoyed the whole scenario for half an hour, totally unprecedented even in Nik's considerable experience. The idea to go back for a second time had more than proved its worth; it had given me a morning I will remember forever, with the gnawing void of past frustration now replaced with that wonderful, warm feeling of total fulfillment that all birders know so well.

It was now time to come to grips with that ever-elusive Northern Pygmy-Owl. My daughter Carol in Missoula, Montana had contact with the local owl expert, Denver Holt. Early February was an appropriate time, it seemed, so I flew out to visit and spend a couple of days in the quest. There were no stakeouts this year, but Denver did know some territories where the owls often were. Rain alternated with heavy snow our first day, and Denver's whistling went unanswered everywhere we looked. When we returned home that afternoon, we learned that Carol's neighbor had seen one just up the road, sitting on a telephone wire! But there was no sign of it when we arrived an hour later, or the next morning when I went back there with Denver. The weather was vastly improved, however, so we returned to one of his "best" locations—where we had failed the previous day. He made it seem easy this time. An owl answered his whistles; we tracked it down, and came upon a pair, copulating and even entering a nest hole, providing glorious entertainment for over an hour.

Officially, the AOU (and hence the ABA) still lumps this form with the one in the southwestern U.S. and northern Mexico (which differs vocally). This northern one is actually probably more closely related to the Eurasian Pygmy-Owl (which I haven't seen either). Considering the present taxonomic explosion of pygmy-owl splits in the New World, it will doubtless be formally declared a full species one day soon, but until then it's one "in the bank".

Bonaire was our diving destination this year. There were no new birds for me here; I was after such wonders as seahorses, frogfish, scrawled filefish, and spotted drum. I missed the frogfish and spotted drum, but I planned to return. One of my better finds was a diver and birder who runs a fish ID course at one of the dive resorts. The problem was finding a time to sandwich this course in between birding trips.

My last visit to French Polynesia (1995) had been mainly ship-based, and we'd done very well with seabirds and the special target of Tuamotu Sandpiper, but the land birding had left a lot to be desired. So I signed on to return with WildWings, a British com-

Northern Pygmy-Owl

pany, starting in the Cook Islands, a new destination for me. Rarotonga was a stunning success, with a handful of special and rare local endemics. We island-hopped to Atiu for two more, and with an unexpected day to spare some of us hopped once again to Aitutaki to encounter the stunning Blue Lorikeet. We couldn't work in Mangaia with its endemic kingfisher and reed-warbler this time, but both it and Rarotonga are good diving and snorkeling destinations, so there's an additional good reason to return to these relaxed islands.

The four Tahiti endemics had totally eluded me in 1995, so I wanted to do it right this time—and we did. The monarch [Tahiti Monarch] is the rarest and most difficult, but with the right local contact we ended up with marvelous views of one of the rarest of the world's birds. A cross-island trip the next day produced the reed-warbler [Tahiti Reed-Warbler], swiftlet [Polynesian Swiftlet], and at the last gasp, the kingfisher [Tahiti Kingfisher].

We then went onto the cargo/passenger ship *Aranui*, which was to take us through the Tuamotus, stopping at Tahanea atoll for the sandpiper, and ending in the Marquesas, with a flight back to Tahiti and home. Logistics were difficult overall, but tour leader David Rosair handled them masterfully. The atoll for the sandpiper is hardly a regular stop on this cargo/tour route, and even the captain had not been here before. Local information about how to get inside this huge atoll to the necessary islets for the sandpiper had failed to take the tides into account, and we ended up taking a circuitous and time-consuming route around the edge to the major entrance into the lagoon. We still had a ride in a small whaleboat for an hour to get to the first islet—where we *didn't* find the sandpiper. Having seen this special bird very well in 1995, I should have been relaxed about the whole undertaking, but I found myself every bit as nervous about the outcome as the rest of my nail-biting companions. So we climbed back into the whaleboat for another crossing to our second and last-chance islet, where it was late morning on arrival—but this time we hit it big. We found about twelve birds overall, clambering about in bushes like rails, and feeding in the rubble on the tide-line. They were tame and close, providing excellent photo opportunities. Bristle-thighed Curlew on its wintering grounds was a nice addition. This islet, which we had time to enjoy thoroughly before our more than two-hour whaleboat journey back to the *Aranui*, was a magical and unspoiled place. The Tuamotu Sandpiper was the prime target bird for everyone on the trip, and the feeling of joy and relief in all was palpable. My second experience with it had been every bit as exciting as the first.

We made two stops in the Marquesas, our last one being Nuku Hiva, home of the highly endangered Nuku Hiva Pigeon [Marquesas Imperial-Pigeon]—which some had had very distant views of on our 1995 trip, but I'd missed entirely. Our one chance for this species was in the mountains on the drive across the island taking us to the airport for departure, and it was my final landbird target for the trip. Our drivers knew the prime area, and we made an appropriate stop after someone in the first vehicle had glimpsed one in flight. As we were standing around and hoping, one flew out of the trees close by and right toward us, then swerved away, providing a great view for all of a very distinctive pigeon. We'd really done the whole thing right, from start to finish. It's not often these days that I see all my targets and a bonus (Blue Lorikeet) besides!

April was to hold my final return to the Philippines on a Birdquest expedition to some of the seldom-visited outer islands and remote spots for special endemics not usually encountered on the more standard excursions. A promising start on Mindoro, where we were camped at the penal colony, produced the endemic hornbill [Mindoro Hornbill], flowerpecker [Scarlet-collared Flowerpecker], most interesting hawk-owl [Philippine Hawk-Owl], and after a long, hard, and dangerous climb up a rocky ravine, Steere's Coucal [Black-hooded Coucal]. Our descent of this ravine was in the rain, so I was holding an umbrella and trying to negotiate carefully the tricky and in places very slip-

Tuamotu Sandpiper

pery footholds. I misjudged one, making an unfortunate jump—
and missed. I fell to the side, but not far, and put my right hand
out to break the fall. I heard a distinct snap as I landed and immediately knew I'd done something awful to my wrist, though
the pain seemed only moderate. It dangled at an odd angle and
though I could still wiggle my fingers, it was useless, with all
strength suddenly gone. The umbrella was in a similar condition
but seemed less of a problem somehow. The wrist swelled immediately, so the distortion became less perceptible. I wrapped it
tight in a bandana and got back to camp with assistance, where I
soaked it in the ice cooling the beers—and had a couple of those
to wash down the painkillers.

There were no doctors on this trip, or anyone very knowledgeable to consult, so I was pretty much left to my own conclu-
sions and decisions. I'd never broken a bone before and had always assumed that the pain would be unbearable, so based on
that and a lot of wishful thinking, I concluded I'd probably just
sprained it badly. I put the "snap" I'd heard when I landed in the
back of my consciousness somewhere.

There was nothing I could do about it until we got to Manila
anyhow, and we were going to Panay first—for another very
long and seriously dangerous rocky gorge climb. Foolishly, I did
most of it (one-handed, but I'm not quite sure how) and saw the
White-throated Jungle Flycatcher [Negros Jungle-Flycatcher]
for my efforts. We all failed on our big target, Rufous-headed
Hornbill [Writhe-billed Hornbill]. On return to camp, my companions all assured me I could not possibly have done what I
did with a broken wrist, so it must just be sprained. I agreed; I
was taking painkillers nonstop. They did the job, and I could
get by during the day and even sleep at night, with sleeping

pills. I could hold and focus binoculars without a problem, but I'd put my scope away right after the accident, not to be used again for months. Awkward to impossible situations arose in all those innumerable circumstances where I was used to using my right hand or needed both hands—like stuffing a sleeping bag, zipping a duffle, wringing out a pair of wet socks, cutting food, or even zipping my pants. My formerly dominant hand was simply unusable, and the simplest things had became extraordinarily inconvenient. The trip was turning into a survival experience, but I was there, I felt I could do most of what was left, and we had a chance at some very good birds that I'd come a long, hard way to see. It was now or never for me with these particular species.

We passed through Manila, but I'd already made the decision to stay on and do what I could. Getting the wrist x-rayed and treated would have meant aborting the trip and returning home, more painful to me than sticking it out. We went on to the Zamboanga Peninsula and to Cebu, missing important targets in both locations, and then to Negros. Here things picked up, with Negros Striped-Babbler and one of my favorites of the entire trip— the gorgeous Flame-templed Babbler. I called my husband from the hotel after this sighting to tell him what had happened, that I'd decided to carry on to the end, and to get me an immediate appointment on my return with an orthopedic specialist!

The next stop was Bohol, an island I had birded before. I had only one major target here, the newly split form of Wattled Broadbill [Visayan Broadbill], and we missed it. At least we were now staying in hotels, which was easier on my wrist than camping, and the trails were all non-life-threatening. This would be true in eastern Mindanao as well, with the final tough camping bit at the end in northern Luzon. I preferred not to think about the difficulties just yet; one step at a time.

Our main target in eastern Mindanao was the newly-described Lina's Sunbird on Mt. Pasian. Finding this species was an all-day undertaking, a long drive up the mountain on a road that degenerated into impassible mud, leaving us with a long uphill walk at the end. The day we chose was a holy horror—fog, nonstop rain, and a howling wind—not exactly ideal for finding sunbirds. Needless to say, we failed. Re-evaluating our original (and probably over-optimistic) itinerary given the current aberrant (La Niña) weather patterns, we decided to stay at this site, do a day of lowland birding and then try the mountain one more time. The lowland birding proved brilliant, and I even saw a lifer, Little Slaty Flycatcher. On our next attempt at Mt. Pasian the weather and bird gods were smiling, and we saw several beautiful Lina's Sunbirds.

Then, it was back to Manila to prepare for the final tough days of hiking and camping in the Sierra Madre Mountains of northern Luzon. My wrist seemed to be improving a little. I could even use my right hand to lift a beer mug, but as the swelling went down, it had become apparent that the wrist had a definite kink to it. Fine motions were a problem; I could write only with difficulty and somewhat illegibly. I'd been keeping my notes to a minimum during the whole trip because of the writing problem.

There were several major targets for me in this last portion of the trip, Koch's Pitta [Whiskered Pitta] being the prime one for everyone. The first step was a long three-to-four-hour hike in open sun on a hot afternoon through birdless cultivation to our first camp. There were horses available, and I chose to ride one, which was a tremendous energy saver. I knew I would have to do a much longer and tougher hike the next day to our final camp (Hamut Camp) for a chance at the pitta and everything else and knew if I arrived exhausted at the first camp that I simply would be unable to do what was required the following day. This did indeed happen to at least one other person, so thank goodness for that horse.

The next full day's hike was indeed long, arduous, and miserable, involving seeming miles of "tunnels" through arm-slashing saw-grass. It was enlivened by a number of good birds, though— Furtive Flycatcher (near our first camp), Green Racquet-tail, Golden-crowned Babbler, Luzon Striped-Babbler, and "Sierra Madre" Crow (a subspecies of Slender-billed Crow endemic to the Sierra Madre Mountains of northern Luzon). We heard a Koch's Pitta and tried for it with no luck, but did have a quite amazing encounter with Rabor's Wren-Babbler [Luzon Wren-Babbler], and actually saw this elusive bird in our binoculars. Final access to Hamut Camp was difficult, down a steep, muddy, and awkward trail, but the tents were a welcome sight at the end of a very long day.

The next full day was our best chance at the pitta and most of the other species to be found along the ridge trail. It was a great day, which included stunning views of Marche's Fruit-Dove [Flame-breasted Fruit-Dove] and a male Blue-breasted Flycatcher, though I narrowly missed a Merrill's Fruit-Dove [Cream-breasted Fruit-Dove]. We heard the pitta calling way down a long steep ravine and simply went down, down, down after it. It had stopped calling after we started the descent, but a little later, after we were *way* down, it began to call again, excitingly close. With adrenalin surging, we all scanned low in the forest, and Tim Fisher located it briefly through his binoculars. Gone again, as pittas so often are, its disappearance led to more scanning for this supposedly terrestrial bird. Then one of our prime spotters located it way up in a tree, hopping along the slanting trunk, and soon we all had it perched 20 meters high and singing. All features were duly noted and commented on, from the intense glowing red of the underparts to the pale pinkish whisker. It proved incredibly tape responsive, and we had several other soul-satisfying views in trees, tangles, and on the ground, as it hopped past us, pausing on an occasional rock or stump. It was truly beyond our wildest imaginings. The climb back up the ravine was a mere nothing, and it was a bunch of happy campers that returned to Hamut Camp that evening.

The next day I went up the ridge again early in the morning, with Tim Fisher, hoping to find the Merrill's Fruit-Dove I'd missed the day before. We didn't have any luck, so we met the group at the pass at the former site of Rand's Flycatcher [Ash-breasted Flycatcher] and started the long descent. Before we left the good forest, we heard a Merrill's Fruit-Dove calling, Pete Morris played his tape, and unbelievably, it flew in (as they so rarely do) and perched in full view for us. So it was back through the awful saw-grass tunnels with a happy heart, down past the turn-off to our first camp, and ultimately all the way to the village. I had hoped to meet up with my horse again, but they had substituted another one farther along, which proved an intractable beast with a saddle from a torture chamber. I rode it about 100 meters and then decided to walk, whereupon the guide mounted the horse and rode it back to the village. Pete Morris, scanning the trail back from the village, where he and the other speedy hikers were waiting, noted something amiss about who was on the horse. Never mind—we'd seen the pitta and a lot else besides.

One disheartening bit of news was that those who had elected to stay at the first camp, instead of making the long hard trek to Hamut Camp, reported that loggers had moved in while they were there, chain-sawing, burning, and destroying the forest literally right around them. Such destruction is an ever-present factor in the Philippines, but seldom do birders witness it in such an immediate fashion.

It was all over now, except for a more than five-hour drive (with bridge construction delays) from Manila to Subic Bay. We birded the Naval Magazine area, which had been off-limits when I'd been there years before and which produced good views of Spotted Buttonquail, Hooded Pitta, and Green Racquet-tail and an impressive all-time record number of over 1,000 Philippine Ducks in Subic Bay. My saga of survival in the Philippines had ended happily, and I returned home with my hurt wrist to get a professional verdict on the damage.

"Do you know what you've done to your wrist?" the orthopedist growled at me. X-rays showed a clean break across the radius and minor fractures in two other places. After consultation with a hand surgeon, they decided just to put it in a cast and let it finish healing. Yes, it was a bit out of alignment (quite obvious, actually), but re-setting would require surgical re-breaking and starting the healing process all over again, whereas it was already three weeks healed and mostly pain-free on my return. The opinion was that with intensive therapy I could adjust to any handicaps created by the new kink.

Four months later, after much therapy and reasonably diligent exercise on my continuing travels, strength slowly returned, and I'd basically learned to cope with the handicaps—primarily handwriting. I lost some feeling in the thumb and fingertips and found I had to hold my pen in a new and rather awkward way—but I could manage the essentials, like using binoculars, scope, and computer without a problem.

So life, travel, and birding continued, but I found ever more limitations as age began to close in. My horizons were still broad, but I sensed them gradually narrowing. No more major expeditions, for instance; the peril-to-bird ratio was simply getting too high! I've had chronic backaches and knee problems for nearly a year, which represented distinct changes in my life, though aside from the broken wrist there was nothing too seriously incapacitating. Still, I had felt less willing and able to undertake the really tough excursions than I ever have before, and I think that was a distinct sign of aging.

Fortunately, I had a spell of time at home for wrist recuperation and therapy. Two weeks in a cast made me know I could not have continued the trip if I'd had a cast put on in Manila. In the long run, I think I would make the same choice again—but I hope I never have to. In any case, I can live with present results, and there is that nice, replete feeling of having seen Flame-templed Babbler, Lina's Sunbird, and especially Koch's Pitta [Whiskered Pitta].

The next trip was a short and easy jaunt to the Mediterranean for a few endemics: primarily the warbler [Cyprus Warbler] and wheatear [Cyprus Wheatear] on Cyprus, and Marmora's Warbler, the nuthatch [Corsican Nuthatch], and Citril Finch (to be split) on Corsica. We had a good visit and great birding with Hugh Buck on Cyprus and exchanged broken wrist stories. He'd had a similar but worse event happen in Micronesia a couple of years ago, but at least he got his set straight.

The birds (with many other endemic races) fell nicely into place, leaving me with Scandinavia as my last European source for about three new birds (Siberian Tit [Gray-headed Chickadee], Siberian Jay, Eurasian Pygmy-Owl). My daughter Carol returned from a kayak trip on the Noatak River in Alaska and reported having seen Siberian Tits and a white-morph Gyrfalcon. Family grip-offs are never-ending!

The next big challenge was an ambitious and lengthy (five-week) visit to Peru. There would be high altitudes to deal with and camping at nearly 12,000 feet at Bosque Unchog, but I felt I could do it, if I'd managed what I had in the Philippines with a freshly broken wrist. I took and used my scope for the first time since my accident and found I could manage quite well. It would indeed be a painful parting, if I had to give up using a scope entirely.

We started with just two of us on a privately-arranged quick jaunt from Lima up to Lake Junin at 14,000 feet, and a boat trip onto the lake to see the flightless Junin Grebe. It may sound simple, but the logistics involving the boat and motor were a nightmare. So many factors had to fall together properly at the same place and time for us even to attempt this trip—but they miraculously did, and we had close, stunning views of the grebes and a wonderful comparison with their look-alike congeners, Silvery Grebes. I'd had a very frustrating experience here three years before, so this time the outcome was doubly satisfying.

Back in Lima, we joined the Field Guides group trip for Carpish Pass, the Paty Trail, and Bosque Unchog. I'd been to Huanuco and the Carpish Mountains with Ted Parker on my first Peru trip way back in 1982, so my targets here were primarily the difficult skulkers and recent splits—antpittas and tapaculos. We did astonishingly well and saw nearly everything I was looking for. Bosque Unchog was a major adventure back in 1982, involving a long horseback ride and pack animals to carry camping gear, so it was not a part of standard Peru trips at that time. Not a lot has changed, but the access has definitely been improved, with a road of sorts up to within walking distance of the wet meadow camping area. Most of the birding is farther on, down the east slope from camp. At that altitude, the return up-hill to camp is a long, tough struggle on foot, but the horses that had carried our gear to the camp were also available to carry us back up at the end of our long days here—a wonderful and welcome energy-saver.

Our targets here were a few very special, restricted-range birds, encountered on the average of once in a few days. Tapes were of little use except for tapaculos; it was mostly old-fashioned birding by sight, with luck and time in the field as the factors determining success or lack of it. We spent four days up there and needed every one of them, finding our final target, the stunning, glowing Golden-backed Mountain-Tanagers only on the last morning before the fog rolled in. There were two new genera here for me, the relatively common Pardusco (*Nephelornis*) and Bay-vented Cotinga (*Doliornis*). The latter was my 2,000th genus, leaving me with only nine to go to get down to the final 100 genera (out of the slightly over 2,100 still existing on earth).

When I had signed up for the Bosque Unchog trip nearly a year before (after the successful 1998 excursion there), I'd noticed that there were two short trips immediately following, both to areas in southeast Peru, where I had not been since 1982—the lowland Amazonian Tambopata region and montane Abra Malaga and Machu Picchu. Might as well include them both, I figured, as long as I had the time and was going to be in Peru anyhow. Even the legendary Ted Parker had been unable to produce everything in that immensely rich region on one trip, but I feel it's a major tribute to him that on returning with experienced guides 17 years later, I saw only four new species (one of them, Diademed Tapaculo, first described in 1994) in three weeks. There were some good ones, though: Rufous-headed Woodpecker at long last, and Semicollared Puffbird, to which I devoted many solo hours, connecting gratifyingly well in the end.

Next was a short trip to a remote new lodge in southeast Ecuador near the Peruvian border—Kapawi Lodge, on a tributary of the Pastaza River. Remote it is, by anyone's standards, requiring good enough weather to fly from Quito over the Andes in a small plane and land on a dirt airstrip near an Indian village. Then one takes a canoe for several hours (at least it can take that long when you're birding en route) along a wonderfully wild (the forests on either side, not the river itself) river to the lodge. And here, miraculously, superior management has created a base as comfortable as a good hotel. It includes excellent food and service, delivered cheerfully at birders' hours (meaning 5 a.m. hot breakfasts), private bathrooms with hot showers (solar-heated water bags provided each afternoon), plenty of treated drinking water provided in all rooms daily, rooms made up daily with clean towels when you want them, and a convenient veranda for hanging clothes to dry. The 24-hour electricity is all solar-powered, with no noisy generator, a trade-off being *very* dim light in the bedrooms but good light in the bathrooms. Overall, it struck me as being the most comfortable base for a long-term visit in the whole Amazon Basin.

Almost all of the birding is done along forest trails reached initially by either short or long canoe rides, with only one trail accessible on foot from behind the lodge. Like most Amazonian trails, there are a few crossings requiring balancing on logs, but nothing that can't also somehow be done another way, providing one always wears wellies. These log-balancing acts and areas with insecure footing have become increasingly difficult for me and others of my age-group, I find, and it's something for tour leaders and local guides to stay conscious of as they lead increasing numbers of geriatrics through the forests.

We had a reasonably small group of nine, and with skillful management of the clients and birds by our brilliant leader, Paul Coopmans, a very high success rate of sightings (including many secretive species) was achieved by all. Black Bushbird was my prime target here, since we'd missed it at Tiputini in January. I had been told Kapawi was an excellent location for this species, but there was a good bit of suspense involved, since several days passed without our hearing any. It wasn't until our final (eighth) morning that our local guides finally took us to a stakeout site, where we did indeed find a most cooperative pair of what was a new genus and species for me—and everyone else except Paul. Additionally, we encountered the newly described Ancient Antwren, a long list of seldom-seen species (e.g., Buckley's Forest-Falcon, Chestnut-headed Crake, Pearly Antshrike, Lunulated Antbird, White-lored Antpitta, White-chested Puffbird, Pheasant Cuckoo, Reddish-winged Bare-eye, Pavonine Quetzal, and Ecuadorian Cacique), and were very lucky with a male White-bellied Dacnis and Slender-billed Xenops, despite the lack of a canopy tower.

A few additional post-trip days on both slopes of the Andes from Quito netted me some other fine species, like Paramo

Tapaculo, Black-chested Fruiteater, Blue-rumped Manakin, and the newly-split Dagua Thrush [White-throated Thrush]. Our final afternoon on the west slope gave me an unexpected and enticingly close auditory encounter with the elusive Moustached Antpitta, recently found on both slopes in Ecuador. I managed to stalk a continuously calling bird to within a very few meters of its hidden song perch, but never even glimpsed it. Nonetheless, it was challenging, exciting, fun, and surprisingly lacking in frustration, to be so close to a great rarity, even if the final sighting and consequent tick totally eluded me. Now that adding numbers or ticking new species is no longer such a prime focus for me, maybe appreciating the challenges of the pursuit, whether successful or not, has become more enjoyable. It certainly was in this case, and my own laid-back reaction caught me a bit by surprise.

Partially because this one-cohesive-group Kapawi trip run by a British company followed so closely upon my experiences in Peru and the January Tiputini trip run American-style (i.e., with up to 16 clients divided into two groups with two leaders, each group going daily or often twice daily to different destinations), the differences struck me as apparent and significant. I do feel that group psychology is a major consideration, and tour companies need to accept human nature for what it is, rather than dictate what it should or could be.

The two-group system simply re-creates constantly (once or twice daily) the situation that birders dislike most, i.e., missing something their trip companions have seen. The justification is that the experiences mostly even out over a period of days, and that everyone in a group of eight on narrow forest trails with difficult birds has a better experience than they would in a group of

16. The reality is that potential for frustration abounds. The greatest experiences are rarely repeatable for the second group, and too often a bird of prime importance to someone is missed simply because they are in the wrong group. Birders and humans in general are a perverse lot, often obsessing more about birds missed than relishing the ones seen—but it would seem wise for tour companies to acknowledge this tendency and to try to reduce rather than to increase potential for frustration.

I personally would rather be in a single group of nine or ten and at least have a chance at what is being seen by the leader or someone else at the given time. In the first case, the situation is at least somewhat under your control and subject to your own skills. The miss, if it happens then, is not nearly so painful and fraught with "if onlys" as hearing later about what the other group saw. In my experience, the two-group system also confuses and complicates the nightly checklist session, as well as leading to a superficially misleading final trip report. By now, I've repeatedly seen one group of nine or ten birders (either with a single leader, or with two co-leaders) under difficult forest conditions handled so well, and with such tremendous psychological advantage over the two-group system, that I'm finding myself increasingly uncomfortable in a very large split group.

ں: ∞ ں

I was headed next for an attempted clean up of Australia, to complete what Tony Clarke and I had done mainly across the north in June and July of 1997, but this time my targets were in the east and south. There were 14 all told, and we had reasonable and even repeat chances for most of them—but they were some of the most difficult and remote birds of Australia.

I'd had tickable but not exactly lingering or enjoyable views of Red-necked Crake in 1997, so the first undertaking was to clean up that one. We stayed in the northeast (Cairns area) at Cassowary House, which provided some wonderful close-up experiences with some of the great birds of those rainforests: yes, a gorgeous female cassowary, brush-turkeys everywhere, scrubfowl, a tree full of Macleay's Honeyeaters, Spotted Catbirds wolfing down chunks of papaya, and Victoria's Riflebirds almost close enough to touch. It was all very nice but not what I was after. Toward dusk, a lovely Red-necked Crake appeared in the shrubbery and came out to the edge, nearly to my boot tips, for a handout of cheese, providing amazing views, of course. It repeated the act in the early morning (when I had no cheese to offer it), then quickly disappeared in the bushes to sulk.

We had been trying without success for some weeks to reach John Young of Ingham, several hours' drive south of Cairns. He is widely known in Australia for his superb photography of owls, his amazing knowledge of their whereabouts, nests, and habits, and his ability to produce them for birders on night excursions. Tony and I just weren't doing very well by ourselves with Lesser Sooty-Owl or masked-owl. We had appropriate tapes, some promising sites, and a good spotlight, but were just getting no response. It was definitely beginning to look as though our single miss and jinx bird of 1997 (Lesser Sooty-Owl) was going to do it to us again.

We'd driven down to the Paluma Range, just south of Ingahm, to try again for both species, on the basis of promising reports and site information. We had our typical failure with both—neither was even heard. On our final day in the area, we stayed at a motel in Ingahm, where Tony had located a possible back-up contact who might help us. Tony tried John Young once again, and miraculously, he was home, with a project canceled for that evening, so he was free to take us owling. That was the best possible news, and we were thrilled. John made no promises, but said, "We'll just see what we can see." Good enough; the man knows owls in depth and practically lives with them. (Owls don't usually have phone lines, which is why we'd been unable to reach him!)

We started at dusk at the edge of a patch of native grass and shrub habitat, an island in a sea of sugar cane fields. At the magic hour, an amazing eruption of about eight Australasian Grass-Owls occurred. They flew in close to investigate John's squeaking, and we had marvelous views of both sexes—a new Australian species for me. Good start! After a bit of driving around the dirt roads, checking favorite perches, we came upon a lovely white male masked-owl, perched high in a tree. The disproportionally large head and feet give it quite a different appearance from Barn Owl, which we then saw soon afterward. A visit to a corner of a nearby forest patch paid off handsomely. A pair of Lesser Sooty-Owls had nested here the year before, so we played a tape. A fairly distant screeching response put us on alert, then some softer calls let us know that there was a pair, and close—but we didn't know exactly where they were in the darkness of the forest edge, and John didn't want to spook them by shining the light around. Another soft bit of tape, and one of the pair flew over us to an obvious perch on a sloping bare trunk, giving superb views, with its huge dark eyes glowing red as coals in the light beam. That was four *Tytos* within a couple of hours! I don't think there's another spot on the planet where that can be done. I was pretty impressed and certainly pleased at having two more difficult target species, including that jinx Lesser Sooty-Owl, under my belt. It was still early, so we drove up into the higher-elevation forests forming the southern end of the Atherton Tablelands. Here we found the "Rainforest" Boobook, which will certainly one day be split from the widespread Southern Boobook, and then topped it off with a Tawny Frogmouth and a Barking Owl on the way back to Ingahm. We were back at the motel by 10 p.m. and had seen six owl species, two of them lifers for me. I've never had an owling experience to equal that anywhere in the world.

The following day, we were off to Brisbane, having achieved everything we'd come for in northeast Queensland. Here we met Terry Reis, a birder friend of Tony's who is also an expert herpetologist and who was to come with us for most of the rest of our plans. Terry had a stakeout for Greater Sooty-Owl near his home on Mt. Glorious and had heard the bird quite recently. Our evening to try for it was simply abominable—windy and raining heavily—so of course we had no success at all and gave it up pretty quickly. The following 4 a.m. was no better, so we didn't even get out of bed. This was the beginning of rain that was to plague us for much of the rest of the trip, and in some most unlikely places.

We then drove north to Cooloola National Park, where we found a nearby motel as a base for our Ground Parrot quest. This target, being a monotypic genus (or perhaps in a genus also including the impossible and virtually unknown Night Parrot), represented in any case a genus new for me, so it was a highly important one. It was necessary to walk through a wet heathland, with the hopes of flushing a bird. Our best site was vast— and there were only three of us, and not many Ground Parrots. We walked long enough to begin to feel this could be a very

time- and energy-consuming undertaking, when we happened
on a narrow sandy track through the heathland, making the
walking a lot easier—at least for me, since I kept to the track
while my two companions fanned out on either side. I almost
stepped on my lifer Ground Parrot, which was in the grass on
the edge of the track. It took off from under me, making a long
low flight in beautiful afternoon light, gliding and twisting,
showing its green and yellow coloration and long pointed tail to
good advantage. Done! We wouldn't need to come back to try
again the next morning.

Next on the list was Black-breasted Buttonquail, and Yarraman
State Forest, a few hours inland, was the place to try. Because it is
so localized and endangered, the bird is famous in the nearby
town; everyone from the motel manager to the barman at the pub
knew what we were looking for.

It all started out looking very promising. There were indeed a
lot of "platelets" or round scrapes in the dry ground made by
these buttonquail, sometimes with droppings in the center, often
very fresh ones. Obviously, the birds were there, and we were
quite close to them at times. We spread out within sight distance
of each other in the forest, and walked slowly and as silently as
we could, listening for scratching or rustling in the leaf litter, and
carefully scanning the ground ahead, passing many platelets and
just *knowing* the birds were near. Someone even made that fatal
statement, "It's just a matter of time!"—which now causes me to
shudder, because it's been said so often in situations when in the
end time has simply run out on me. We did a sweep again in another spot, and again—and yet again. Hours passed and dusk
came. My companions talked of having seen the birds very readily on past attempts, and of other birders, some of whom spent

hours and failed, some of whom saw the birds almost immediately. Well, we'd been unlucky that day, but we'd be back in the morning for a try in a small vine-scrub patch that was absolutely riddled with platelets.

The next morning, we failed miserably in that hot spot, as well as in the other prime sites we tried. By noon we all needed a change of scene. Tony suggested we drive to the Bunya Mountains to check a site where sometimes a Greater Sooty-Owl had a day-roost inside a hollow fig tree. John Young had told us the site was still used but not every day. It was worth a try, and we were all tired of buttonquailing. They'd changed the trails at the Dandabah area in the Bunya Mountains National Park, and for some time we couldn't even find the all-important fig tree. During our search for the tree, however, we came upon a nice Russet-tailed Thrush, which posed very cooperatively for examination and which, as the crake had been, was another of my targets for clean up views. As it turned out, we never had really good views of that species again. In the end, we did find the tree, stepped in, and looked up—and found nothing. The owl wasn't using that roost on that particular day.

We returned to Yarraman in the late afternoon and to our promising hot spot, but now without much enthusiasm or optimism. But—there was some furtive movement at the base of a vine tangle—and I stuck with it. It was a buttonquail, and it couldn't escape, because I was in the forest, and it was on the very edge, and my two companions were closing in from either side. Eventually, it moved into the open enough to see the pale eye and the patterning of a male Black-breasted, as it moved from one secluded spot to another. Finally, apparently feeling just too threatened, it exploded vertically into the air like a rocket and flew over the treetops and out of view. Females of buttonquail are prettier, of course—but that male would certainly do very nicely as a lifer. It had taken about twelve hours of serious searching to achieve—and never was really easy. Whew! We were still at 100 percent of targets achieved.

We made the rather spontaneous decision to drive back to the Bunya Mountains for the evening and try at night with tape and light for the Greater Sooty-Owl, which was probably around there somewhere. At least now we knew how to find the fig tree! We gave it a serious try, and it didn't work, a situation that seemed somehow familiar to me. I'd had failures with this species before, and maybe this *Tyto* was to be our jinx for this trip. The next day we had to drive back to Brisbane, but we would be in Greater Sooty-Owl habitat at Lamington for three nights, so all was not lost. However, since our motel was in Kingaroy, back up the road toward Yarraman, we would have to drive through the Bunya Mountains again the next morning enroute to Brisbane. So of course we stopped at Dandabah and the fig tree once again, I stepped inside the dark tree and looked up with the light—and incredibly, there it was, perched in full view on a cross branch in the hollow fig, looking down at me with its enormous dark eyes. It very quickly went back to sleeping or dozing, with eyes half-closed, and allowed us all simply stunning views. We left it sleeping peacefully and returned to Terry's home at Mt. Glorious on the outskirts of Brisbane, where the weather was once again simply awful. But we were overjoyed at having seen the Greater Sooty-Owl so well, and especially at *not* having to go owling again, either here or at Lamington!

Lamington National Park was next, and now that I'd seen Greater Sooty-Owl and Russet-tailed Thrush, the only target here was the very difficult Rufous Scrub-bird. We had plenty of time, since we'd planned to spend three nights, and this was the season (October—the austral spring) when they tend to be most vocal, at least letting you know (sort of) where they are. The weather didn't look good but was predicted to improve. We'd gotten there early, so had much of the first day for our initial attempt. We had been told of a scrub-bird site quite near O'Reilly's Guest House, and of course tried that first. No singing, no response to the tape. We knew the birds were located various places along the six-kilometer-long Bithongabel Track, so we walked an hour or so, then suddenly heard one call on a relatively open slope, close to the track.

At this point, just when we thought we might actually see the thing, it began to rain heavily, and the falling drops made it impossible to pick out any subtle bird-motion—because *everything* was moving with raindrops. A few minutes later, something scuttled across the path and disappeared. I sort of glimpsed it, but Tony had actually been looking down the path and said it was two scrub-birds crossing, almost together. There was no sign on the other side, which had denser undergrowth, no further calling, and no response to the tape. I continued to watch the track for want of something better to do, and suddenly a rufous-brown bird with a semi-cocked tail scuttled rodent-like back across the track to the original slope. Quick, but adequate; it *was* a Rufous Scrub-bird. After no more events in this location, we moved on, hoping at least to hear more, but without luck. It continued to rain, and we ate our lunch in a downpour at the Bithongabel overlook. We slogged the long trail back, hearing another scrub-bird in beautiful moss-covered *Nothofagus* forest, but seeing nothing, despite spending some time

Rufous Scrub-bird

there, among fallen logs and branches, playing the tape, squeaking, and pishing.

The sky looked brighter when we emerged from the forest in the late afternoon, and I had high hopes for the next day, which began as we entered the forest before first light. We had been told of a site for the bird between two ravines with a distinctive type of plant growth, only about an hour's walk along the main track. We simply stopped, listened, and waited, finally hearing a scrub-bird sing down slope, but not too far away. I eased myself gently and slowly down toward the voice, while my companions waited on the trail, occasionally playing a bit of tape. The bird had stopped its loud staccato, choppy song, but I had come to a promising-looking pile of dead branches and was hearing the high-pitched "squeaky wheel" song near there. Before long, this rufous-brown mouse-like bird was scuttling under and through the branches, then over a mossy log and around the corner of a tree stump, and up toward the trail, where Tony glimpsed it as well. Good enough—not brilliant views, but an unmistakable species—besides which, at that point it started to rain again in earnest, so there was no point in continuing.

I'd seen the bird, heard its song, and gotten a distinct feeling for its behavior. I'd seen Noisy Scrub-bird in the southwest at Two People's Bay very well, years before, so I figured I'd now completed the family. And there was still another day to go, with maybe better views to be achieved. The relentless rain continued, however, and we woke the next morning to driving wind and heavy rain, decided good enough was enough, and bailed out of there, returning to Mt. Glorious—and quite astonishingly, glorious weather. Weather in Sydney, where we were flying the next day, looked bad. We thus canceled plans to visit Gloucester

Tops, another site for Rufous Scrub-bird, but one which hasn't
proven too reliable lately, and just took a rest day or two in Sydney, visiting Royal National Park and finding my second-only
Origma [Rock Warbler] in classic habitat, among sandstone
rocks near a stream.

The outback part of our itinerary was now beginning. We
flew to Adelaide, where we met Terry Reis again, who had flown
in from Brisbane and pre-arranged our four-wheel-drive vehicle.
The notorious, easy-to-get-lost-in mallee habitat of Pooginook
and the new Gluepot Reserves, accessible from the town of
Waikerie, were our destinations for Red-lored Whistler and
Black-eared Miner. Prior information proved misleading. We
connected with the miners (fitting all field characteristics, but
of course still possibly genetic hybrids) at Pooginook and finally
had an excellent study of a female Red-lored Whistler (along
with Gilbert's females for direct comparison) at Gluepot—
which reversed what we'd been told about likelihood. In any
case, we'd learned how to use our newly-acquired Global Positioning System (GPS), so we didn't get lost—and we were still
at 100 percent of our targets.

The important one(s) to come were primarily Scarlet-chested
Parrot and Nullarbor Quail-thrush [Cinnamon Quail-thrush]
(still officially lumped as a subspecies). There was a chance for
the parrots at Yumbarra Reserve out of Ceduna, but a fruitless afternoon and the next early morning here convinced us we'd better go into the heart of the range, i.e., across part of the Nullarbor
Plain and then north into the Great Victoria Desert.

It was for this excursion, which would mean camping for at
least three days in the desert, that we'd brought our camping gear,
food and water for five days (if necessary, as it sometimes is), spe-

cial jacks, extra parts and tires for the vehicle, jerry cans of diesel, etc. The deserts of Australia are not to be trifled with, as many have learned the hard way.

So we drove west across the Nullarbor Plain to the last fuel and overnight spot before heading north and into aboriginal lands and the Great Victoria Desert for the Scarlet-chested Parrot. The Nullarbor Quail-thrush we found relatively easily by driving along a sandy track near the roadhouse in the late afternoon. A lovely male, elusive and trying to stay hidden, was nonetheless interested enough in the tape we were playing from the car to come out between the saltbushes to investigate.

Early the next morning, we headed north to Cook, a former railway community, now virtually deserted, and then north across the barren Nullarbor and into scattered trees again, with grasses and shrubs, but also the beginnings of the sand dunes. We saw camels, dingos, and a few typical desert-edge birds. The weather looked ominous. Instead of the expected bright blue skies and brilliant desert sun, it was totally overcast, darker toward the north (where we were headed) and actually drizzling most of the time. About noon, with still several hours of cross-desert driving to go to get to Volkes Hill Corner, the heart of the range of Scarlet-chested Parrot and where we planned to camp, a larger parrot flew past us and back down the track. Terry got out to check it, assuming it was probably a Mulga Parrot (which it indeed was)—but on returning to the car, he glanced up at a bare tree along the track and saw a male Scarlet-chested Parrot perched close—an unmistakable, mind-blowing, full-front facing view! He yelled out to Tony and me, still in the car, and turned back to find the parrot had disappeared. Getting out of the fully-packed vehicle was a bit of a comedy for Tony and me, our efforts verging on the frantic, and once we'd done so there was nothing evident—until we looked a bit farther away and saw another bare tree with six to eight perched male Scarlet-chesteds in it, again facing us with the unbelievable chest color and blue faces glowing at us. It was a Christmas tree, lighting up the landscape and my life! They sat for scope studies, simply unbelievable as we approached closer.

We never got any farther north, and technically, even though we'd crossed some dunes, I think we never actually got into the Great Victoria Desert. A pity—I really wanted to see that thorny devil (lizard) that Terry was so keen on. We also never found any female Scarlet-chesteds and wondered whether they were all sitting on eggs. But as for those males—WOW!! After we'd had absolutely incredible, repeated all-feature views of several males (and who wants more, really?), it began to rain quite seriously. The north looked even worse, and having been warned about these sandy roads with their clay content, and what happens when they get really wet (Gluepot Reserve, for instance, gets its name from what it's like after heavy rains!), we turned around and headed south again, back across the Nullarbor Plain to Cook, and then south to the paved east-west highway.

The last long stretch from Cook south, which that morning had seemed like such a good hard road, was indeed turning to slippery glue with the increasing rain. There was a heavy downpour that night, and the Cook road was closed the next day, so we couldn't have even started on our northbound adventure then. If we'd continued north after seeing the parrots, we'd have almost certainly been seriously mired at some point, and even if we'd reached our destination (Volkes Hill Corner), we couldn't have gotten back out when we'd hoped to, but would have had to wait for the track to dry out. That's of course why we had the extra food and water supplies, a GPS, and a radio for emergency contact—but it definitely would have interfered with the rest of our itinerary. All in all, this Scarlet-chested Parrot day may have been one of the luckiest days of my life. We got in, found it, and got out—quickly—and I never even used my tent.

That was the big one for all of us, and we were still at 100 percent! We drove back to Adelaide, spent a really interesting time with John Cox, said a final goodbye to Terry, who was returning home, and then Tony and I continued on to Melbourne. Yellingbo Reserve, east of Melbourne, which holds the much-studied, localized, and endangered "Helmeted Honeyeater", which is currently lumped as a subspecies of the more widespread Yellow-tufted Honeyeater. It is, however, a striking form with a bushy golden frontal crest, genetically quite distant from Yellow-tufted, and certainly a good candidate for a split. Good information led us to an appropriate site, and we found a stunning male after only a couple of hours.

I'd been to Tasmania in 1990 and seen the endemics, but little or nothing was known then about Tasmanian Masked-Owl [Australian Masked-Owl], which may or may not be a good species. Now there is a stakeout site near the Hobart airport, but in reality it turns out that the directions and information are quite confusing. We never could find the particular tree with the distinctive hole referred to by others, and we spent a fruitless evening from dusk onwards in a serious attempt for this owl, which was my fourteenth and final target for this trip.

After a lot of experience, I've become a believer (along with

Ben King) in early morning, pre-dawn hours for finding owls. By then, they've fed and often seem vocal, territorial, and tape-responsive. It is also quiet, with little or no human activity and insect noise. It's do or die within an hour or so, and dawn simply ends the quest. You don't completely exhaust your physical resources by staying out all night on a fruitless endeavor. Yes, it's hard to get a group up and going at 4 a.m., but for a dedicated individual or two, I really feel it's the best approach.

So we returned to the general area at 4:30 a.m., drove the roads a bit with no result, and ended just pre-dawn at the stakeout site. We heard a *Tyto* give the typical rasping screech, walked toward the sound, played a bit of the tape softly, and Tony saw it fly in. We zapped it in the spotlight and had excellent views of a surprisingly white male, definitely a masked-owl. It must be the darker female that has earned the name *castanops*. That was the game—14 out of 14—100 percent, even at the end. That left me with only Night Parrot (which was impossible—there were no valid recent sightings) and Western Corella (a recent split that I care very little about) yet to see in Australia. And that's actually better than I've done on my home turf of the U.S.A., where I still have a few to find—mostly recent splits.

Of course, as my husband points out, this game never *really* ends. It's simply a matter of perspective; as I see it, one of the wonderful aspects of birding is that it *is* endless. There's always, as long as one lives, some new place to go, some exciting new thing to find. No one knowledgeable will ever say, "I've done it all—now what?"

So it didn't quite end with my fourteenth and last target species, and my fourth new *Tyto*, in Tasmania that early morning. We made a quick flight change, got back to Sydney, and drove south to Wollongong. We'd been in touch with Tony Palliser, who had reported almost unbelievable sightings of Amsterdam Island Albatross (either that or a totally new species) off Sydney and Wollongong in the previous couple of weeks. It's virtually my last albatross, even with the recent proposed splits, and I'd about written it off, figuring I just would never get to Amsterdam Island (in the northern Indian Ocean). But we could arrange a boat trip, it seemed, with some notable albatross researcher like Lindsay Smith. The lure was irresistible, of course. We went to sea, learned a lot from the albatross specialists, found a lot of Wandering-types, including a probable Tristan Albatross (*D. [exulans] dabbenena*)—but nothing remotely resembling the Amsterdam-types they'd been seeing. Oh well, win a lot, lose some! I went home happy.

Phoebe at home, 1999

Epilogue

By Thomas Snetsinger

Phoebe's year was to close with a November–December trip to Madagascar. Terry Stevenson, one of Phoebe's
longtime favorite guides, and John Coons
were leading the trip (her fourth) to this "different planet" for
Field Guides. It was to be a typical clean-up trip for Phoebe, as
the brevity of her want list clearly demonstrated. This list enu-
merated a mere 23 species, by definition all lifers, many of them
endangered and some of them potentially extinct. Five of these
species represented new genera, important in Phoebe's eyes, as
her most recent numerical goal was to reduce her number of un-

seen, extant genera to fewer than 100.

Phoebe flew from St. Louis to Antananarivo (Tana), Madagascar via Paris, where she joined the majority of the group traveling on the pre-tour extension to the Masoala Peninsula in northeast Madagascar. A midnight arrival was followed the next day by a charter flight to Maroantsetra. Some coastal birding turned up a new Madagascar species for Phoebe in the form of 25 Lesser Crested Terns. The next day the group took a two-and-a-half-hour boat trip to a beach campsite at Ambanizana on the Masoala Peninsula. The group hiked up into the forest and enjoyed a mixed vanga flock with White-headed, Blue, Red-tailed, and Rufous Vangas along with a marvelous red-ruffed lemur. Phoebe misstepped while descending the steep trail back to camp and sprained her ankle. She was as upset with herself and as embarrassed at her clumsiness as she was bothered by her ankle. The injury seriously slowed her down, and back at camp, a physician examined her foot and wrapped it. He felt confident that it was just sprained, and while hobbled by the injury, Phoebe felt grateful that it was not more serious.

The next two days were spent birding along the trails from The Peregrine Fund's camp, Andranobe. The day before Terry had gotten permission to bird the area and learned about stake-out nests for Bernier's and Helmet Vangas, both new genera for Phoebe. The trail to the Helmet Vanga nest was difficult to traverse with her bad foot, as it required several crossings of a rather large creek. Phoebe couldn't easily step across the rocks, but with help she was able to make the crossings and climb the trail to the nest. As she and John arrived at the stakeout, they observed this fantastic bird brooding young just 30 feet away.

The female remained on the nest for a few minutes before flying off and then returned to feed two small chicks with that improbable, huge, arched blue bill—every detail visible from the dark tip to the purplish gape line, the staring yellow iris around the large dark pupil. This bird was a new species and genus for everyone, including Phoebe and Terry.

The excitement of seeing the Helmet Vanga was tempered by two pieces of information that The Peregrine Fund researcher, Russell Thorstrom, shared with the group. The first bit of news, that the male of the pair had been accidentally killed ten days earlier by a visiting researcher taking blood samples for his vanga research, was ameliorated slightly by the fact that the female was apparently raising the chicks on her own. The second piece of information was that the stakeout Bernier's Vanga nest

**Phoebe on route to locate Helmet Vanga on
Masoala Peninsula, Madagascar, 11/15/99**

had fledged the previous afternoon. The nest was not far from camp, but it was on a slope in dense forest, so that roaming around the area with a group to look for the adults and young would be nearly impossible. While still a possibility, the species that had seemed a virtual certainty a few hours earlier now appeared decidedly much less likely.

While the group worked the trails in the vicinity of the vacated nest, waiting and hoping for a chance encounter with one of the Bernier's Vangas, a bird began singing a series of short *boop* notes back up the trail. These were not the notes of the vanga, but it was the song of another new genus for Phoebe, the Short-legged Ground-Roller. Two birds cooperated nicely, and soon everyone had excellent views of a perched pair of these huge and most difficult to find of the ground-rollers. They showed off their long dropping buff whiskers, the characteristic white-spotted cheek, neck, broad white necklace, and long rufous tail. Both Phoebe and John remarked how this bird resembled a *Malacoptila* puffbird of the Neotropics. This bird represented Phoebe's second new genera, and lifer, in one day and was a nice compensation for the missed Bernier's Vanga.

Back at Andranobe for the second day of birding, the group hiked a kilometer and a half from the camp, playing tapes for Madagascar Serpent-Eagle and birding the forest trails. Russell had found the serpent-eagle along this track recently, so spirits—and hopes for a sighting—were high. The hiking, however, was taking its toll on Phoebe's ankle, so she stopped here to rest. The others continued up the trail, working the forest and playing tapes. Eventually, Terry found a Dusky Greenbul, and while trying to relocate it for the group, he also discovered a Scaly Ground-Roller hopping along the ground. Both these birds were high on Phoebe's list of target species, so while others stayed on the ground-roller and tried to relocate the greenbul, Terry raced back down the trail and brought Phoebe up. Phoebe immediately got on the bird, her last ground-roller and her third lifer of the trip. She had excellent views of all of the intricate details of this *Zoothera*-like species as it hopped about on the ground: the finely scaled crown, two dark face lines, and the rufous nape. While current taxonomic thought considers this bird to belong to the same genus as the Short-legged Ground-Roller, Phoebe noted the very different appearance and behavior and suggested in her notes that it should probably be re-classified under its own genus. The group had no luck with the serpent-eagle; nor did the greenbul cooperate with a reappearance. A few people went back to the site of the Bernier's Vanga nest that afternoon but didn't find their target, nor much else of interest, and Phoebe felt glad that she had made the decision to remain at camp in order to let her ankle rest for the latter part of the day.

The next two days were spent traveling. The pre-tour contingent shuttled back from the Masoala Peninsula to meet up with the rest of the group for the start of the regular tour in Tana. They all then flew south to Fort Dauphin and drove to the private Berenty Preserve for two nights and a full day of birding the alien spiny forest of this area. They had nice views of a Banded Kestrel and a Sakalava Weaver colony on the commute to Berenty. Neither was new for Phoebe, so the highlight for her was probably the dramatic improvement in her ankle.

The two days of travel had allowed her ankle to heal, and by their first morning in Berenty it was nearly back to normal. An early-morning walk yielded a surprising lifer for Phoebe, as she was not expecting anything new here: a pair of copulating Madagascar Sparrowhawks near their nest in huge, spreading legume. The entire group had diagnostic scope studies of these birds, and Phoebe took extensive notes: the sexes were alike, but the female was much larger than the male; they had bright yellow eyes, long legs, and spindly toes; their plumage showed fine "whisker-like" throat striations; the dark slate-gray plumage above was offset by crisp, fine blackish barring on white underparts, and the diagnostic, immaculate white under-tail coverts were the clinching field mark. The birds put on a complete and eminently satisfying show, including a series of calls, which Terry was able to record.

The next two days the group birded en route as they moved from Berenty to Tulear on Madagascar's west coast. They birded the spiny forest east of Berenty, worked back to Fort Dauphin, and were treated to nice studies of Subdesert Brush-Warbler [Madagascar Brush-Warbler], Running and Olive-capped Couas [Red-capped Couas], as well as a singing, creamy-eyed Arch-bold's Newtonia, and a warty chameleon. The following day the group flew to Tulear, arriving in the heat of the afternoon. They visited an area of Euphorbia scrub east of the airport, hoping for an encounter with the recently described Red-shouldered Vanga. There was no response to the tape, but eventually the tour spotted a distant Verreaux's Coua, which cooperated for an excellent scope study.

They birded the spiny forest to the north the next day, obtain-ing nice views of an orange-mandibled Common Jery and Madagascar Munias, as well as amazingly close views of a breed-ing pair of Long-tailed Ground-Rollers near their nest hole. On the return to Tulear, a Crab Plover along the coast proved to be a new Madagascar species for Phoebe.

November 23rd started early. The group birded the Euphorbia scrub south of Tulear on the road to St. Augustin for another try at the Red-shouldered Vanga. They heard one singing in the dense scrub forest, and eventually John was able to record its ringing, repeated *tui-pheeeee* phrases. The male flew in for close repeated study in tape response. The robust shape, long bill with hooked tip, black face-pattern and bib were like those of the Red-tailed Vanga. The prominent pale brow, gleaming yellow eye, and extensive rufous on the wing coverts confirmed the identity of this bird as its red-shouldered cousin, first described in 1997.

Feeling elated from the experience with this lifer, they began to bird their way back towards Tulear and on towards Zombitsy and Isalo Massif with hopes of finding Appert's Greenbul, another of Phoebe's targets, there. A flat tire delayed their departure and allowed Phoebe some time to update her checklist as well as to write up her field notes on the vanga. She noted sighting several Sooty Falcons during a roadside break—then silence, a stark, thick slab of empty pages in her field notebook.

Phoebe was tired. The 4 a.m. wake-up had taken its toll, and she wanted to be prepared for any effort required for the greenbul search later in the day. She lay down in one of the middle seats of the bus and napped.

When the bus crashed, Phoebe, binoculars in hand, was killed instantly. Undoubtedly, she was dreaming of the Red-shouldered Vanga or the hoped-for Appert's Greenbul. A few others on the bus sustained injuries (a broken wrist, a broken arm, and assorted bruises, cuts, and abrasions), but none were life-threatening. Phoebe had simply been in the wrong place at the wrong time.

Phoebe recognized that there always was some possibility of her dying while on one of her trips. She had made it known to her family and to the tour companies she used that if she should die on a trip, she wished to be cremated in that country. She also had asked her family to gather together and spread her ashes in some mountainous area that she enjoyed, suggesting that they do some hiking and birding while there. Her husband and children birded, hiked, and spread her ashes in one of her favorite areas, the beautiful Tetons of Wyoming, in August of 2000.

Phoebe's death was precisely what she termed "the best that one could possibly ask for": a successful trip including five lifers, representing two new genera; excellent views of some of world's most amazing and difficult-to-find birds (Helmet Vanga and Short-legged and Scaly Ground-Rollers); a sudden, unsuspected, and according to her traveling companions, painless death. She went out, as she had always hoped, at the very top of her game, in the middle of doing what she most loved to do.

After the blistering pace of international travel, which she had set in her race to become the first person ever to see 8,000 species, she had had time to slow down and to reconnect with her deep passion for the real fun and challenge in birding: puzzling out a difficult identification, working patiently to tease a skulking lifer into view, or just being awed by the diversity, beauty, and gaudy spectacle that makes the world of birds what it is. She relished this opportunity to rediscover these aspects of her obsession. Her index cards and field notes describing her sightings morphed from short bullets describing the salient features of a particular species and the quality of the sighting to essays about a marvelous encounter with a lifer. Her delight in the entire experience of birding comes through clearly in many of these later notes.

While Phoebe maintained that she was cutting back on international travel and her time away from home, this reconnection with the source of her love for birding, among other reasons, kept her post-8,000th-species schedule full. Her anticipated itinerary for 2000 scheduled an international birding trip in every month except February: January to Panama for *Xenornis* and *Sapayoa*, two of her unseen genera; February to Bonaire, a family vacation and an opportunity for some more scuba experience; March to the Cape Verde Islands; April to Bhutan; May to northeast Venezuela; June to Amazonian Brazil; June 24th to Oregon for Tom and Christina's wedding; July to Iquitos, Peru; August–September to Papua New Guinea; October–November to southeast Brazil; November–December to New Zealand followed by a subantarctic cruise. And that was "cutting back"!

Nevertheless, the schedule that Phoebe maintained had changed over time. As she had added experience throughout all corners of the globe, her preparation time and the days spent writing up trip notes diminished, as the intensive work done in preparation for and writing up results from previous trips paid its dues. Further, the types of trips she took had also begun to change. In her last few years, Phoebe had felt her body and stamina failing to hold up to the rigors of some of the more difficult trips. Chronic knee pain, several troublesome sprains, and a broken wrist sustained on recent trips all made it clear that she needed to realistically evaluate her abilities in planning any prospective trip. Due to these considerations, she had begun to select easier itineraries in which long hikes on steep terrain or technically difficult trails were kept to a minimum. However she planned (or thought about planning) for trips in the abstract, I suspect that if she were confronted with a good opportunity to find a highly-desired species, she would have given her best effort to surmount any obstacle in order to see it.

Phoebe's legacy in the world of birding is larger than life. She possessed a hard-earned, near encyclopedic knowledge of the world's birds. Her drive to observe, and observe well, as much of the world's avifauna as possible, with a special emphasis on its diversity, is well-known, clear from her writing, and, in some circles, the stuff of legends. Those who shared her passion and had the opportunity to bird with her are effusive in their praise of her integrity, abilities and knowledge, and her open, warm, and sharing personality. There is no need to exaggerate the difficulties she faced over the course of her life and in pursuit of her passion: a shipwreck, the brutal rape and attack in New Guinea, earthquakes, political upheaval, and a diagnosis of terminal cancer and subsequent recurrences. All of these factors combined to form the reality of her seemingly mythical life.

However impressive her reputation, this larger-than-life figure inhabited a very human form—mother, wife, sister, daughter, and friend. From my point of view she was a quirky, eccentric, chocolate-loving woman who was perpetually en route to or from some foreign country. These quirks were largely rooted in her obsessive behavior. Phoebe was a master of focusing her intense energy on whatever chore was at hand, be it studying, writing up notes, birding, or even resting. She had a system for each of these tasks, as well as many others. In order to not waste her waking hours on plane flights, a sleeping pill, an eye-mask, and earplugs closed out the world and did wonders for her powers of avoiding jetlag. Undoubtedly, this is precisely what she was doing on the bus ride to Zombitsy: resting and conserving energy for the next demand on her reserves. She was not going to miss the Appert's Greenbul because she needed a nap!

Like her technique for minimizing jetlag or her index card system for recording her sightings, if Phoebe found an effective technique for dealing with some chronic difficulty, she added it to her long list of practical field techniques for the outdoor enthusiast. If she found something that she liked, she bought a lifetime supply. She had too often found that the "new and improved" versions of products were not as effective as their predecessors or that the product itself was just taken off the shelves (e.g., her typewriter ribbons). My mother's field craft served as lessons that peppered our childhood education in the basics of life. My sisters and I learned early on how to sort clothes for the laundry and how to prepare a meal, but we also learned to tuck our pants into our socks to avoid chiggers around the ankles, to tie the "Snetsinger-knot" (a simple, no-mess shoe-tying technique that simply does not unravel, in which you double wrap the rabbit's ear), and to use Swiss Army knife scissors to neatly snip leeches in half, causing the offending head merely to fall off. My sisters also learned that a small umbrella fits securely under the bra, between the breasts, freeing the hands and keeping the rain off binoculars.

Phoebe brought together several seemingly mutually exclusive traits. She was an unpresuming woman in stature and personality, preferring in most aspects of her life to live quietly in the background rather than to be at center stage. While she was birding, other facets of her personality came to the fore. On the deck of a ship or scoping shorebirds, this typically retiring woman would open up and readily share her vast knowledge, experience, and birding expertise with others, helping them locate sought-after species. The quiet and retiring sides of her personality were juxtaposed with the determined, strong, competitive, and forthright qualities that gave her a seemingly unlimited drive. These latter traits surfaced in her goal-oriented pursuit of birds, as well as in the way she voiced her fiercely held opinions. She did not shy away from sharing these convictions, and she openly battled the ABA on their position of counting heard birds, her position being that to be truly appreciated (and counted) a life bird must be seen.

This was no mere philosophical point for her—Phoebe lived by it. In 1992, shortly after I moved to Hawaii, my then 60-year-old mother came to visit and bird Maui and the Big Island. This was my first serious experience as an adult birding with her. We spent a few days on the Big Island and managed to get excellent views of the three endemic endangered Hawaiian honeycreepers and then traveled to Maui.

The Maui endemics would be new for me as well, so I was as excited about the visit as my mother. We got permission to hike into The Nature Conservancy's Waikamoi Preserve, primarily to search for the endangered Akohekohe, or Crested Honeycreeper, and Maui Parrotbill, but with dreams of Nukupuu and Bishop's Oo (each reported only a handful of times from the 1970s through the 1990s). We drove up Haleakala in the predawn and then hiked the pleasant trail through Hosmer Grove into the preserve as the sun was rising. Along the hike the endemic Maui Alauahio gave us a great show along with the more widespread Iiwi, Apapane, and Hawaii Amakihi, the alauahio being a life bird for both of us. We began working the upper area before descending into the forest. Almost immediately we both caught a flash of a chunky green-yellow honeycreeper fly into a dense bush, accompanied by a non-descript contact call. I observed the bright flash of a broad and bright yellow supercillium—a Maui Parrotbill. It was a poor look for me, poorer yet for my mother—she wouldn't count it. We worked the shrub thoroughly, but the bird had simply vanished.

We spent the remainder of the morning working the upper portions of the boardwalk, finding several immature Akohekohe trap-lining a cluster of ohia trees festooned with their striking, red pom-pom blossoms. By mid-afternoon, I was tiring and beginning to lose hope of finding a cooperative parrotbill. Though nearly thirty years my senior, my mother's hope, persistence, and sheer stamina for looking at every single bird never flagged. She needed to see this species adequately—better yet, well.

We birded farther down the boardwalk to another area that reputedly held a Maui Parrotbill territory. We worked the area hard into mid-afternoon without even a hint of success. I was tired and lackadaisically watching the moss grow. I looked over and saw my mother actively scanning and putting her binoculars on anything that moved. She wasn't just giving a cursory glance to identify the species. She watched the Iiwi and amakihi nectar-robbing a *Clermontia* and paused to jot down a few notes on their plumage and behavior. She turned her gaze to a bird hitching up the trunk of an ohia and exclaimed, "There's a parrotbill!" Just then an unusual song broke out, a short series of descending *chewey-chewey-chewey* phrases. I quickly located the bird, and we watched it work the area for ten minutes before it moved off. We high-fived in mutual celebration and began climbing the trail out. We got to the gate at dusk. She had earned her Maui Parrotbill.

Phoebe was a driven and highly-intelligent woman. This combination of characteristics, combined with a substantial financial inheritance from her father, and all of the resources (e.g., knowledge and expertise, reference materials, access to remote locations, ease of communications) that this Golden Age of birding brought together for the avid birder, alone may not have been enough to push her to pursue her ultimate achievements in the world of birding. I have little doubt that the sword of Damocles hanging over her head, in the form of her diagnosis of malignant melanoma, helped push her to pursue birding with the zeal and ferocious energy that she did—packing as much as humanly possible into each day, month, and year. Phoebe's passionate pursuit of birds in the 1960s and 1970s transformed into a drive and dedication to birding that were all-consuming through the decades of the 1980s and 1990s. Was she running from a death sentence, as she sometimes stated, or was she embracing an aspect of life that offered her immense fulfillment? Perhaps, it was both.

Phoebe's spirit continues to live through the memories of those that knew her, as well as those who only knew of her through stories that were shared. The one thing that stands out most clearly from all of these tales is that she embraced life and seized every opportunity to live it to its fullest. White-water rafting with our family down the Salmon River, learning to scuba dive at sixty-five, and even cross-country skiing for several days (before a sprained thumb sidelined her) all make it clear that this zest for life was not restricted to bird-related adventure. If Phoebe had a motto by which she lived her life, it was: *carpe diem.* Her advice to all of us—family, friends, and all of those whose lives she touched—would be the same: embrace life and live it to the fullest. *Carpe diem!*

Appendix I

Milestone Birds

Remarkably, Phoebe did not see her first genuine "lifer" until the age of 34. Three decades later, she had become the first person to see 8,000 world birds. Space limitations prohibit listing all the species Phoebe saw during her extraordinary run from belated novice to world's top lister, but the following table does itemize the major "milestone" birds that she saw along the way.

SPECIES	IMPORTANCE	DATE	LOCATION
BLACKBURNIAN WARBLER (*Dendroica fusca*)	"First" species observed	1965	New Brighton, MN
SHORT-TAILED HAWK (*Buteo brachyurus*)	600th ABA species	1/28/80	Everglades
BLACK-BREASTED PUFFBIRD (*Notharchus pectoralis*)	2,000th world bird	2/14/81	Achiote Rd., Panama
DIADEMED SANDPIPER-PLOVER (*Phegornis mitchellii*)	3,000th world bird	7/1/82	In bog at 14,000' + near Lima, Peru
BLACK-BREASTED WEAVER [Bengal Weaver] (*Ploceus benghalensis*)	4,000th world bird	2/2/84	Bharatpur, India
PHILIPPINE BULLFINCH [White-cheeked Bullfinch] (*Pyrrhula leucogenis*)	5,000th world bird	3/8/86	N. Luzon, Philippines
XANTUS'S MURRELET (*Endomychura hypoleuca scrippsi*)	700th ABA species	4/27/86	Offshore waters of Santa Cruz Is, CA

SPECIES	IMPORTANCE	DATE	LOCATION
OLIVE-CHESTED FLYCATCHER *(Myiophobus cryptoxanthus)*	6,000th world bird	2/3/89	Loreto Rd., N. Ecuador
CEYLON FROGMOUTH *(Batrachostomus moniliger)*	7,000th world bird	1/29/92	Kitulgala, Sri Lanka
RED-HEADED ROCKFOWL [Gray-Necked Rockfowl] *(Picathartes oreas)*	Last of Clements' families	8/18/95	Bokaboka, Gabon
RUFOUS-NECKED WOOD-RAIL *(Aramides axillaris)*	8,000th world bird	9/26/95	San Blas, W. Mexico
BAY-VENTED COTINGA *(Doliornis sclateri)*	2,000th genus	6/30/99	Bosque Unchog. Peru
RED-SHOULDERED VANGA *(Calicalicus rufocarpalis)*	Last new species observed	11/23/99	South of Tulear on road to St. Augustin, Madagascar

Appendix II

---- ❧ ----

Sample Index Cards

In order to detail her "whole experience with a species", Phoebe faithfully kept, for more than twenty years, elaborate notes about behavior, field marks, and vocalizations on 3x5 index cards. Color-coded names in the upper right-hand corner indicate all the places where she had seen the species. When Sibley and Monroe's Distribution and Taxonomy of Birds of the World was published in 1990, adding approximately 500 new species to the list of world birds, Phoebe's notes allowed her to ascertain that she had gained close to 150 lifers, giving her an edge over other competitive world listers who did not keep such detailed records. The cards reprinted here contain her notes on Pintail Snipe.

Pintail Snipe   SL   I
         ~~And.~~   NA
   Gallinago stenura   Th·Bu·HK
                     Y   Ph
                        J

2/18/84 NE India. Jaldaparra -
Several flushed. Buffy on upper
wingcoverts - marked contrast w.
remiges. <u>No</u> white trailing edge to
secondaries. Feet protrude beyond
short tail. Barred breast, belly pale.
Direct flight - no zig-zag.
Soft 'zap' call on take-off.

May 25-26 '84 Attu. 1st N Am. record!
Soft call on take-off- 'zap'- repeated
2-3x. Dark underwing contrasting
w. white belly (white underwing on
race of Common Snipe present). Strong
rufous wash on breast. Towering,
hovering flight. Pale panel on
upperwing cov. In dry grass each
time - flushed 4-5x. Rel. short bill.
<u>No</u> white trailing edge to second.
Jan-Feb. 85 Thail-Burma-Hong Kong.
Soft call + no white trailing sec. edge
(Poorly-def. narrow paler brown trail. edge)

Not accepted by ABA

Feb. 86 Philippines (Luz, Pal.)
Apr. 86 Hong Kong
Mar. 90 Japan - Ishigaki. 1 flushed
w. many Commons. Dark underwing
+ white belly (cf. to white underwing
+ underbody of Common) Slender;
no white trailing sec. edge.
Feb. 91 Andamans.
Mar. 91 Thailand
(Nov 91 - see accepted record of Attu

Pintail Snipe- AB Fall 91 p. 485 SA. 1984
bird seen + heard at least as well- ∴ OK!
Feb. 92 - Sri Lanka. On ground-
Long tail extending substantially
past tertials, but def. Pintail
when flushed (∴ wing/tail config.
in Shorebirds not valid).
Feb. 95 Phil. Luzon. Candaba marsh.
Oct. 96 N. Yemen. Taizz lagoon. Exc.
long flight views w. Common. On
ground - diff. subtle. Smaller, plainer,
grayer than Common. Tail shorter.

Index

Birds

Kagu

Index

Names

Phoebe with Doris Brann

Index

Places

Phoebe in Ecuador